R & D STRATEGY AND ORGANISATION

Series on Technology Management

SERIES ON TECHNOLOGY MANAGEMENT – VOL. 5

R&D STRATEGY AND ORGANISATION

MANAGING TECHNICAL CHANGE IN DYNAMIC CONTEXTS

VITTORIO CHIESA

Università degli Studi di Milano–Bicocca, Milan, Italy

ICP

Imperial College Press

Published by

Imperial College Press
57 Shelton Street
Covent Garden
London WC2H 9HE

Distributed by

World Scientific Publishing Co. Pte. Ltd.
P O Box 128, Farrer Road, Singapore 912805
USA office: Suite 1B, 1060 Main Street, River Edge, NJ 07661
UK office: 57 Shelton Street, Covent Garden, London WC2H 9HE

British Library Cataloguing-in-Publication Data
A catalogue record for this book is available from the British Library.

R&D STRATEGY AND ORGANISATION
Managing Technical Change in Dynamic Contexts

ISBN   1-86094-261-X

Printed in Singapore by Uto-Print

Preface

This book treats key issues and trade-offs in R&D strategy and organisation, paying attention especially to dynamic competitive contexts where technology plays a key role. These topics are treated assuming the perspective of the decision taker, i.e. the manager who makes decisions in terms of R&D strategy and organisation. It addresses typical problems of large firms having a structured R&D and operating businesses where R&D is source of competitive advantages. Although it strongly focuses on R&D, it sees R&D as a part (although, a key part) of the process of technological innovation; therefore, as an activity to be strongly and appropriately integrated with other functions to make innovation successful.

This book is mostly conceived as an academic review of research topics. Therefore the primary audience is composed of scholars, researchers, Ph.D. students. However, in the author's opinion, it could be useful also for postgraduate students, attending MBA electives, or students attending courses dedicated to technology management. It seems also relevant to R&D managers and more generally people responsible for units having to do technological innovation.

Why a book on R&D strategy and organisation? For two reasons. First, it is important to review the role of R&D in a dynamic perspective, i.e. to study the effects of the acceleration of technical progress and the increasingly dynamic character of competition among firms on the strategy and organisation of a firm's technology-based innovative activities. In other words, it is important, in the author's opinion, to understand how the present competitive context (where, increasingly, what a firm is able to do now and in the future is strongly affected and even more depends on what it has done in the past) affects strategic and organisational decisions in R&D. Second, it looks appropriate to pay attention to strategy and organisation of R&D, which have been rather neglected in the last few years. Recent streams of thought (such as the process-based, resource-based, competence-based approaches) have strongly emphasised the role of managerial processes as key elements to make R&D effective. Therefore, great attention has been paid to R&D management processes. It is the author's opinion that, beside this, it is worth also to examine, in the domain of R&D, how the definition of the content of R&D activities (strategy) and the organisation of such activities are affected by the increasingly dynamic character of competition.

How this book treats these issues. As far as R&D strategy is concerned, it identifies the key decisions in R&D strategy, i.e. the selection, the timing of development and introduction, and the acquisition mode of new technologies, and examines how concepts like the competence based competition, the learning factors, the time-based competition affect the what, the when and the how of technology development and acquisition and the evaluation and selection of the R&D projects to be undertaken.

As far as R&D organisation is concerned, it recognises that the dynamics of competition brought to remarkable changes. In the past, R&D was usually seen as one function and the key decision concerned the criteria by which the function was structured. Nowadays, the structural dimensions of an R&D organisation are multiple: degree of centralisation versus decentralisation, degree of geographical dispersion of R&D units, degree of separation between R and D, use of external sources and organisation forms of technological collaborations. Each topic is here deeply analysed.

The empirical basis. The book relies upon the empirical basis and the results of an eight year research programme (1992-1999) led by the author on 'R&D strategy and organisation' (composed of three sub-projects: Internationalisation of R&D, Technology strategy development: methodo-logies and practices, Technological collaboration: organisation and management) at the Centre for Strategy and Strategic Management of Politecnico di Milano. Specific characteristics of the empirical survey and sample companies are described in the chapters. In general terms, the empirical works have been conducted through direct interviews to R&D managers and Chief Technology Officers, R&D people, technicians and engineers. Globally, about 90 firms were involved mostly from technology-intensive industries such as automotive, chemical, electronics, pharmaceutical, telecommunications. Cases and examples are mentioned and reported throughout the book.

The structure of the book. In the introductory section, the book briefly describes the technological innovation process and major characteristics of the innovative activities within firms. Then, major implications on a firm's technology strategy and

R&D organisation are discussed. Part I in depth studies the critical dimensions of a firm's technology strategy which are the technology selection (choices related to which technologies to develop or acquire), the timing of technology development and introduction, the technology acquisition mode (whether through internal development, external acquisition or collaborations). It faces the problem of strategic decisions at two levels: a first level concerns the definition of the technology policy (identification of the critical technologies, time horizon of technology development, acquisition policy, etc.); a second level concerns the process of definition, evaluation, selection of R&D projects and of resource allocation, providing an overview of major supporting techniques. Part II faces key issues in the organisation of the R&D activity within firms. It especially deals with four critical dimensions of the R&D organisation design: the organisational structure of R&D units, the balance between centralisation and decentralisation, the geographical dispersion of the activities (internationalisation of R&D), the organisational form of technological collaborations and external technology acquisition. It analyses pros and cons, and trade-offs of different approaches and solutions.

Finally, I would thank people who gave a contribution to this book in different forms. First of all, I am grateful to Umberto Bertelè, my Master Degree thesis supervisor and, since then, a constant adviser on my research work. I would also thank Francesco Jovane for his suggestions and ideas, during my ten years spent at CNR of Italy, and Chris Voss for his support and cooperation at London Business School. I am also in debt with Raffaella Manzini (co-author of Chapter 7) with whom I shared many ideas and works in the area of technology management. Finally, my thanks to Federico Tecilla and Silvia Galinta for their editorial support.

The author.

Vittorio Chiesa is Professor of Business Economics and Organisation at Università degli Studi Milano-Bicocca. He also teaches Business Economics and Organisation at Politecnico di Milano and Università di Castellanza. He obtained his Master Degree in Electronic Engineering at Politecnico di Milano. He was previously with Ciba-Geigy and Pirelli, and with the National Research Council of Italy as Senior Researcher. He was Visiting Researcher at London Business School at the Operations Management Department.

His main research areas are: technology strategy, international R&D, R&D organisation. He is author of many papers on international journals, books, conference proceedings.

CONTENTS

CHAPTER 3
FORMULATING TECHNOLOGY STRATEGY IN DYNAMIC CONTEXTS

CHAPTER 6
THE GEOGRAPHICAL DISPERSION OF R&D ACTIVITIES

CHAPTER 7
THE ORGANISATION OF THE EXTERNAL ACQUISITION OF
TECHNOLOGY *(with Raffaella Manzini)*

CHAPTER 1

INTRODUCTION

Firms outperforming competitors often derive their success from innovation and in many cases such innovation is technology based. Creating new products, processes and services is recognised as a major source of competitive advantage and technology is often the enabler of such innovations. This book attempts to contribute to our understanding of the relationship between technology and the creation of competitive advantage. In particular, it concentrates on the role of R&D and aims to identify the factors affecting major decisions in terms of R&D strategy and organisation.

This chapter aims to introduce some basic key concepts, provide the background of this book and introduce the main topics treated. Therefore, it first gives and discusses the definitions of 'technology' and 'technological innovation'; then, it examines the major characteristics of the technological change and the implications of such change on the process of technological innovation and the firms' innovative activities; finally, it focuses on R&D, giving definitions related to R&D and identifying the implications of major trends in innovation on R&D strategy and organisation. These concepts also provide the framework for the development of the content of this book.

1.1 KEY CONCEPTS AND DEFINITIONS

Technology

A comprehensive definition of technology is 'a body of knowledge, tools and techniques, derived from both science and practical experience, that is used in the development, design, production and application of products, processes, systems, and services' (Abetti, 1989).

This definition provides evidence of some key concepts related to technology and its role in competition:

(i)   technology is embodied into products and also into processes or methods used to generate new products or services;

(ii) technology is knowing how to apply scientific and engineering knowledge to achieve practical results, i.e. products, processes and services, or knowing how to achieve practical results on the basis of experience;

(iii) technology has to do with science and practical experience (technique). Often these terms are not used appropriately. To the end of clarity, definitions are here given and commented. Science is general knowledge, aimed to progress our knowledge about nature and society, accepted by the community on the basis of its consistency, and its ability to explain and foresee. Technology is general knowledge, aimed to identify general solutions to specific problems accepted on the basis of its operational applicability. Technique is specific knowledge aimed to solve specific problems, accepted case by case on the basis of its actual appropriateness independently from the knowledge of the underlying general principles. Science, technology and technique are therefore three forms of knowledge which can be distinguished on the basis of their level of generalisation, aims and acceptance. Science and technology are both forms of general knowledge as they lie upon the knowledge of the underlying working principles. Technique is a form of specific knowledge, as it is the skill to solve a problem with no knowledge of the underlying principle. As far as the aims are concerned, science is knowledge related to natural or social phenomena, whereas technology and technique both relate to know-how, i.e. practical results. The acceptance is also based on different criteria, as science is such when accepted by the scientific community, whereas technology and technique are recognised as such when they solve practical problems and achieve practical objectives. Firms are involved and interested in technology and technique, as these relate to practical results;

(iv) there are two distinctive processes of generation and development of technology. On the one hand, there is a process which starts from scientific knowledge and brings to applications. On the other hand, there is a process which starts with the accumulation of empirical knowledge and brings to technology through its generalisation;

(v) from a business perspective, technology is not good per se but when intrinsically related to innovative objectives;

(vi) technology, science and technique are all related to forms of explicit knowledge. Within firms there are also forms of tacit knowledge, i.e. knowledge embedded into people, technical systems, management systems, culture and values which is not explicit but is a key factor in solving problems and achieving results.

Technological Innovation

There are many definitions of technological innovation. We assume the definition given by Freeman (1976). Technological innovation is a process which includes the technical, design, manufacturing, management and commercial activities involved in the marketing of a new (or improved) product or the first use of a new (or improved) manufacturing process or equipment.

This definition looks comprehensive and suggests a number of common issues related to technological innovation.

Innovation vs. Invention

As Roberts (1988) emphasised, innovation is composed of two parts: (1) the generation of an idea or invention, and (2) the conversion of that invention into a business or other useful application. In other words, he says, innovation is invention + exploitation. The invention process covers all efforts aimed at creating new ideas and getting them to work. The exploitation process includes all stages of commercial development, application, and transfer, including the focusing of ideas or inventions towards specific objectives, the evaluating of those objectives, the downstream transfer of research and development results, and the eventual broad-based utilization, dissemination and diffusion of the technology-based outcomes. The overall management of technological innovation includes the organisation and direction of human and capital resources towards effectively fulfilling all these activities: (i) creating new knowledge, (ii) generating technical ideas aimed at new and enhanced products, manufacturing processes and services, (iii) developing those ideas into working prototypes, and (iv) transferring them into manufacturing, distribution and use.

Product vs. Process Innovation

Innovation concerns products, services and production processes. An innovation can not be defined as a product or process innovation in absolute terms. To define an innovation as a process or product innovation, it is necessary to assume the perspective of a specific firm. An innovation is a product innovation when it concerns the output of a firm's activity, whereas it is a process innovation when it concerns the production means used to produce the firm's product. Therefore, a product innovation for a firm is a process innovation for another one. A typical example is that of an innovative industrial machinery, which is a product innovation for the machinery manufacturer and a process innovation for the firm who buys the machinery and makes use of it.

Incremental vs. Radical

Innovation includes both major (radical) and minor (incremental) innovations. In other words, it can be a minor modification of an existing entity or an entirely new entity. Incremental innovations are usually the result of a continuous improvement process often based on the modifications carried out by the technical people of the manufacturer firm and on the suggestions of users. Radical innovations are discontinuous event, which are often the result of R&D activities carried out in industrial, academic or research centre labs.

The distinction between incremental and radical is usually given on the basis of the content of newness of the innovation, and, as a consequence, of the effort behind the innovation. This is not related with the economic impact of an innovation. An incremental innovation can result in high profits whereas a radical can fail on the market.

1.2   TECHNOLOGICAL INNOVATION

1.2.1   The Characteristics of Technological Innovation and Innovative Activities within Firms

It is common knowledge that the rate of change of the competitive context is rapidly changing and that technology is a major engine of such change. The rate of technological change is high and grows very quickly. The ability to produce new knowledge increases and the speed and ability to exchange knowledge increase too. As the result of the accelerated rate of technological change, technological innovation and, as a consequence, innovative activities within firms assume peculiar characteristics. Such key characteristics are here mentioned and commented.

Cumulativeness

The innovative activities are more and more cumulative in development over time. What a firm will be able to do in the future strongly and even more depends on what it has done in the past. As Pavitt (1991) states "actual and desirable performance characteristics of products and production processes are usually multidimensional and complex and cannot easily be reproduced from scratch". He also states that tacit knowledge, i.e. the knowledge obtained through experience and embedded into people and technical systems or procedures is of central importance.

Specialisation

Firms tend to focus on narrower range of activities. Given the cumulative nature of the innovative activity, firms need to concentrate their efforts on few technological disciplines. Therefore, a process of technological specialisation among firms is in place.

Geographical Division of Technological Labour

Given the cumulative nature and increasing specialisation of innovative activities, a division of labour in the process of creation of technological knowledge takes place. This favours the birth of pockets of advanced knowledge in geographically limited areas.

Uncertainty

Given that the technological progress accelerates, the uncertainty related to the innovative activities grows. The amount of unknown to be faced to effectively innovate grows and this increases the uncertainty of innovative activities.

Technology Integration

The accelerated progress of the whole range of technological disciplines gives space for new forms of innovation. Technological innovation is not only the result of breakthroughs in one specific field; often, it can be achieved putting together pieces of knowledge from different fields and integrating them in a new way. Therefore, there is a form of innovation which takes place by integration of different technologies rather than by deepening knowledge in one technology. Such form of innovation is called in a variety of ways: technology integration, technology fusion, systemic innovation. This form of innovation has sometimes generated totally new disciplines: optoelectronics is the integration of optical and electronic technologies, mechatronics is the integration of mechanical and electronic technologies. In relation to this concept, Gibbons et al. (1994) identified a Mode 2 of knowledge creation and innovation as compared to the more traditional Mode 1. His attention is on knowledge creation rather than on innovation; however, these key concepts are valuable and sound for innovation modes within firms. In Mode 1 problems are set and solved in a context governed by the interests of a specific community (mainly the scientific community), whereas in Mode 2 knowledge is developed in a context of application. Mode 1 is disciplinary while Mode 2 is trans-disciplinary. Mode 1 is characterised by homogeneity, whereas Mode 2 is characterised by the heterogeneity of the skills and experience involved in the process of knowledge production.

These intrinsic characteristics of the technological progress make the process of technological innovation change and call for new ways to conceive and shape it within firms. In the next section, models of the technological innovation process are briefly reviewed.

1.2.2   Models of the Technological Innovation Process

The increasing complexity of the technological change and of the innovative activities within firms has also stimulated thinking about how to model the process of technological innovation.

Traditionally, there were two ways to view the innovation process: the technology push approach and the market pull. The former views the process as simple linear and sequential. The emphasis is on R&D and the market is seen as a receptacle of the results of the R&D activity. The market pull approach views the innovation again as simple, linear and sequential; the emphasis is on marketing. The market is the source of ideas to direct R&D which plays a reactive role.

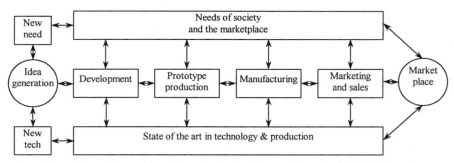

Figure 1.1. The coupling model of innovation (Source: Rothwell and Zegveld, 1985).

Later, a generally accepted view of the technological innovation process is the interactive or coupling model. Two different representations are given of it. They were put forward by Rothwell and Zegveld (1985) and Roberts (1988). They seem to agree that technological innovation comes from the coupling of market needs with technological opportunities. They essentially suggest that the innovation process is rarely the result of pure technology push or market pull forces and that it is the result of the matching and combination of the two. The process is still sequential but with feedback loops. R&D and marketing play a balanced role. The emphasis is given to the interface between the two, i.e. the integration of R&D and marketing, seen as the basis for combining technology opportunities and market satisfaction.

The simple linear model (either technology push or market-pull) prevailed during the 1960s and early 1970s, the more interactive and coupling model was dominant until mid 1980s. Rothwell (1992) identified two further generations of the innovation process.

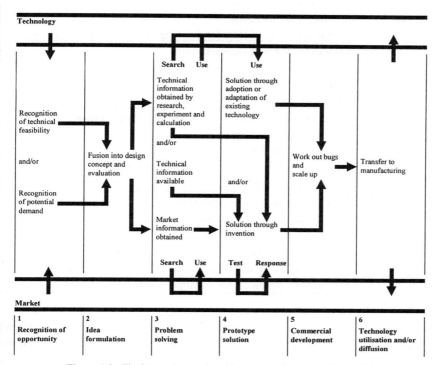

Figure 1.2. The interactive model of innovation (Source: Roberts, 1988).

The fourth generation marked a shift from the innovation process seen as predominantly sequential with the activities shifting function to function, to innovation as a parallel process involving simultaneously R&D and other functions (typically, prototype development, manufacturing, marketing). The innovation process is carried out by integrated teams. Emphasis is placed on the integration between R&D and manufacturing. There is also a strong involvement with both upstream suppliers and lead users or key customers downstream; horizontal collaborations take place too during the innovation process.

Table 1.1. The five generations of the innovation process (adapted from Rothwell, 1992).

First generation: *Technology push*	Simple linear sequential
	Emphasis on R&D
	Market is receptacle for the fruits of R&D
Second generation: *Market pull*	Simple linear sequential
	Emphasis on marketing
	Market is source of ideas for directing R&D. R&D has a reactive role
Third generation: *Coupling model*	Sequential but with feedback loops
	Combinations of push and pull
	Balance between R&D and marketing
	Emphasis on integration between R&D and marketing
Fourth generation: *Integrated model*	Parallel development with integrated development teams
	Strong supplier linkages
	Close coupling with leading edge customers
	Emphasis on integration between R&D and manufacturing
	Horizontal collaborations
Fifth generation: *Systems integration and networking*	Fully integrated parallel development
	Customer focus at the forefront of strategy
	Strategic integration with primary suppliers
	Horizontal linkages
	Emphasis on corporate flexibility and speed of development
	Increased focus on quality and other non-price factors

Finally, the fifth generation is identified which is the fully integrated parallel development. Linkages with suppliers and customers are very strong along with the whole innovation process (for example suppliers are involved in co-development of new products, and/or share the technical systems used for it). Horizontal linkages take place in a variety of forms (joint ventures, consortia, alliances, etc.). Emphasis is placed on organisational flexibility and speed of development.

The latter two generations emphasise that technological innovation is not sequential, is cross-functional by nature and often multi-firm. These concepts strongly challenge especially the organisation and management of the technological innovation process within firms.

Technological Innovation as a Business Process

The fourth and fifth generations (seen in the previous section) strongly emphasise the role of organisation and management in making the process of innovation effective. Several contributions have suggested that the process of technological innovation within firms is viewed as a business process. Rothwell (1992) states that "it is generally acknowledged that today's rates of technological change are high. What is less recognised is that the process by which technology is commercialised - the innovation process - is changing". This calls for a deeper understanding of such process. Tidd et al. (1997) identify the generic activities the innovation process involves: scanning the environment (internal and external), defining the responses to give to the signals identified, obtaining the resources to enable the response, implementing the innovation project to respond effectively. On the basis of a review of many literature contributions, Chiesa et al. (1996) view innovation as a set of processes. They identify four core processes:

- new product concept generation, the process which brings together technology and market needs to develop new product concepts;
- technology acquisition, the development and management of technology per se, i.e. the process of acquiring the technology necessary for product and process innovation through internal R&D and/or other means;
- product development, the process of bringing a new product concept through development and manufacturing to the market;
- production process innovation, the process of innovating and developing new production processes;

and the enabling support processes which are:

- leadership, providing the top management leadership and direction in the innovation strategy process, and setting and maintaining a climate for innovation;
- resourcing, the provision and deployment of human, organisational and financial resources;
- systems and tools, the provision and effective use of appropriate systems and tools to support the core processes of innovation.

Each of these in turn can be seen as a set of sub-process. Table 1.2 shows the sub-processes and the related references.

The process based approach to innovation suggests that to explain the innovation performance more profoundly, the related capabilities and processes have to be analysed. Great attention needs to be paid to how such processes are shaped and which are the practices in use, as these factors become the key to success in innovation. Therefore, this approach stresses the role of organisation and management in affecting the performance of the innovation process.

Table 1.2. The processes of innovation and the related sub-processes.

Product innovation
Generating new product concepts
– uncovering market needs and opportunities
– building long-term relationships with customers and especially lead users
– screening new product concept ideas
Product innovation planning
– linking the product innovation plan to the corporate plan
– prioritising product development projects
– integrating processes for generating new product concepts, planning product innovation and realising new products
Innovativeness and creativity
– eliciting and supporting new product ideas and initiatives
– structuring organisation for favouring creativity and inventiveness
– choosing the appropriate people for critical innovative roles
Exploiting innovation
– evaluating alternatives for developing new business opportunities
– assessing the relatedness of entrepreneurial initiatives
– using governmental funding mechanisms
Product development
Product development process
– managing product development projects from concept to launch, including phases, gates, reviews
– integrating all relevant functions in the product development process
– early involving the key internal functions and external organisations
– facilitating communication among the different groups involved in the development process
– problem solving
– reviewing project progress
Transfer to manufacturing and distribution
– linking manufacturing and engineering
– handling engineering chances
– taking products into manufacturing
Teamwork and Organisation
– use of cross-functional teams
– use of organisational integration mechanisms
Industrial design
– incorporation of industrial design into product
– use of inside or outside design consultancy teams

(follows)

Process innovation

Formulating a manufacturing strategy
   − evaluating the capabilities of existing production processes
   − matching process capabilities to the requirements of the marketplace
   − linking process innovation to product innovation
   − developing new process technologies
Implementation of new processes
   − matching technology complexity to the capability to adopt
   − managing the links with suppliers in the development and implementation
   − making the appropriate changes to the organisation
Continuous improvement
   − identifying opportunities for improvement in processes
   − integrating process improvement with quality control
   − benchmarking production process performance
   − involving manufacturing process developers in improvement after installation

Technology acquisition

Formulating a technology strategy
   − understanding trends in existing and future technologies
   − assessing competitors' technological capabilities
   − identifying emerging technologies
   − understanding core technologies and competencies of the firm
   − building the required core competencies based on the technological capabilities and market needs
   − relating technology to business objectives and strategies
Selection, generation and sourcing of technology
   − choosing sources of technologies (in-house R&D, licensing, partnering, external alliances)
   − selecting R&D projects
Management of intellectual property
   − protecting intellectual property rights (patenting, trade secrets)
   − exploiting intellectual property (licensing out)

Leadership

Goals for innovation
   − defining the firm mission in technology and innovation
   − building innovation strategies into corporate strategies and plans
   − identifying the core competencies
Process for innovation
   − evaluating processes for generating and implementing innovation
   − benchmarking processes for innovation against best practices
   − making innovation processes visible to top management
Climate for innovation
   − encouraging new idea development, risk taking and entrepreneurship
   − making innovation policies shared and understood in the organisation

Resourcing

Human resources
   − identifying resources needed for innovation
   − recruiting, developing, evaluating and rewarding human resources
Funding
   − funding R&D activities and technology acquisition
   − funding product and process development
   − sharing risks and reducing costs of innovation

(follows)

Systems and tools

Systems
     − information and product systems used to support the processes for product development
     − information systems enhancing communication in the innovation process
 Tools
     − use of tools for capturing customer needs
     − use of tools for designing new products
     − use of tools for promoting creativity
 Quality assurance
     − managing quality in the design process
     − methods used to analyse and improve the quality of innovation processes
     − integrating process improvement and product innovation with quality management

1.3   THE ROLE OF R&D WITHIN THE PROCESS OF TECHNOLOGICAL INNOVATION

R&D includes a variety of activities. A traditional classification of the activities included within R&D concerns the macro-phases which compose the R&D process: basic research, which is an activity aimed to generate knowledge related to the working principles of natural and social science without direct relation to industrial applications (products, services, production processes); applied research aimed to the production of knowledge required to define the means to fulfil a specific and explicit need; development, which consists of the systematic use of knowledge oriented to the development of materials, methods, tools, systems. The development is in turn composed of different phases: design, prototyping and testing (aimed to generate a prototype or a pilot plant), engineering (aimed to scale up the manufacturing process to produce the product or use the production process on an industrial scale), installation, maintenance and post-commercialisation service.

R&D clearly plays a major role in all the phases of the process of innovation. In parallel to the conception and development of the models of the innovation process (the five generations seen above), there have been identified generations of R&D and the corresponding different styles of management and organisation.

The first generation is that followed in the 1950s and 1960s. It can be summed up as 'Put few bright people in a dark room, pour in money, and hope'. R&D acted as an ivory tower where future technologies were decided with no interaction with the rest of the company. Therefore there was a lack of business/R&D integration and no explicit link to business strategy. R&D was seen as an overhead cost. R&D tended to be put under corporate control because of the absence of any kind of inter-relationship and communication with business. This style of management corresponds to the technology push view of the innovation process.

The second generation 'provides the beginnings of a strategic framework for R&D at the project level and seeks to enhance communications between business and R&D management by making business or the corporation as the external customer for R&D practicioners alongside - and equally as important as - the "internal customer", R&D management'. In other words, a strategic framework has been built to manage R&D projects and at the project level there are combined business/R&D insights. This view has forced companies to put R&D under control of business units rather than corporate. The imperative was to establish mechanisms ensuring that R&D and marketing communicate and strong links between business strategy and R&D projects. There is the introduction of the market pull view of the innovation process. There are two major drawbacks to this approach: on the one hand, a too strong market orientation which may prevent firms from investing in emerging winning technologies too far from business interests; on the other hand, it does not catch the advantages from cross-project and cross-business synergies.

The third generation addresses this further strategic dimension of R&D management: the interrelationships among projects within a business, across business, and for the corporation as a whole. It introduces the portfolio concept. The result is a strategically balanced portfolio of R&D projects that is formulated jointly by general managers and R&D managers. 'R&D seeks to respond to the needs of existing businesses and to the additional needs of the corporation while at the same time contributing to the identification and exploitation of technological opportunities in existing and new businesses'. There is an holistic strategic framework and R&D and business strategies result integrated corporatewide. R&D strategy formulation is paid attention by top management at both business and corporate level in order to achieve a balanced portfolio of R&D projects in terms of risk and temporal horizon of investments. Therefore, this style of management attempts to support a balanced combination of technology push and market pull views.

The recent models of the innovation process (Rothwell's fourth and fifth generation) emphasise the role of feed-backs and of the non-sequential character of the process. Moreover, the process-based approach stresses the point that innovation is by definition cross-functional. R&D is only one of the functions involved in such process. These recent modes of conceiving and designing the innovation process force changes in the organisation and management of R&D. Several contributions have emphasised that the key characteristics of R&D management and organisation have further changed. Miller (1995) puts forward the concept of the fourth generation, where there is a process of concurrent learning with customers. The accelerated pace, the global scope of change force firms to balance the increased risk with business factor opportunity. This means to experiment new ideas in strong integration with customers' R&D, emphasising the role of teams which from cross-functional and cross-disciplinary become cross-firms too. New ideas tend to be validated in demonstrated practice in closed-loop feedback process. In this process IT tools may play a central role.

Finally, a fifth generation can then be anticipated. This is based on the concept that management systems are collaborative and not competitive and focus on a total innovation system involving competitors, suppliers, customers, distributors, other partners and stakeholders. A sort of R&D enterprise is created, where knowledge flows and learning occurs cross-boundary.

Therefore, the latest generations emphasise that R&D is increasingly projected outside the boundaries of the firm, interacts directly with customers, and creates a network of collaborative activities around itself.

Table 1.3. The R&D generations.

First generation	R&D as ivory tower
	No interaction with the rest of the company
	No link with business strategy
	R&D under corporate control
Second generation	Business as the customer of R&D
	R&D under business control
	Link between strategy and R&D projects
	Strong market orientation
Third generation	Attention to cross-business and cross-project synergies
	Introduction of the project portfolio concept
	Both business and corporate control
	Link with both corporate and business strategy
Fourth generation	Integration with customers
	Concurrent learning with customers
	Cross-disciplinary teams
	Cross-firm teams
Fifth generation	Strong collaboration in R&D
	R&D as part of a total innovation system including competitors, suppliers, customers, distributors
	Cross-boundary knowledge flows and learning

1.4   IMPLICATIONS ON R&D STRATEGY AND ORGANISATION

The above introduction makes evidence that the process of technological innovation is changing and the nature of the technology-based innovative activities is also changing. This book deals with how R&D faces this challenge.

In particular, it focuses on strategy and organisation of the R&D activities. It attempts to respond to the following key questions:

(i)   how an R&D strategy should be conceived and designed in the context of dynamic competition? which are the main dimensions of an R&D strategy? and the main factors affecting a firm's technological choices?

(ii) how the organisation of R&D should be designed within firms? which are the main variables affecting the design of the organisational structure of the R&D activities?

Why do these aspects appear critical?

(i)   The accelerated rate of technological progress is a major engine of the dynamics of competition. The characteristics of technological innovation and, as a consequence, of the innovative activities within firms have changed. The cumulative nature of the technological competence, the increasing specialisation of a firm's technical activities, the uncertainty associated with technology development are all factors which strongly affect decisions related with technology and therefore strongly challenge technology decision takers. An R&D strategy, which is aimed to build and maintain the capability to technologically innovate in the long term, has to take into account these factors. Therefore, a first area of challenge for R&D managers seems to be grasping the variables affecting the technological choices to conceive an appropriate R&D strategy in dynamic environments.

(ii) The complexity of the process of technological innovation and its cross-functional nature strongly challenges the management and organisation of R&D. On the one hand, great emphasis has been placed on the integration between R&D and the other functions involved in the process of technological innovation. On the other hand, as the fifth generation of R&D management styles suggests, the structural design of the organisation is strongly challenged. The R&D activities are carried out in a variety of units and the R&D function no more coincides with one unit: the R&D activity is carried out in different parts of a firm's organisation. Moreover, R&D activities need to be organised to interact with the external context. Therefore, they may be needed to be geographically distributed and designed to cooperate with external actors. In summary, the organisation of the R&D activity needs to be shaped in such a way to face its projection towards the outside world.

The book is articulated into two parts. The first part deals with R&D strategy and deals with the key technology decisions and the factors affecting such choices. The second one deals with R&D organisation and the related structural dimensions.

Two comments need to be made helping clarify the scope and the objective of this book. The first is that the focus on R&D does not mean that it is more important than other functions in the process of technological innovation. The above introduction to the concepts of technology and technological innovation emphasises that R&D is a function playing a major role in technological innovation but innovation is a process which is by definition cross-functional, where R&D integrates with many other functions. Key issues and key inputs to the process of technological innovation comes from a variety of sources. Innovation is the result of the efforts of the firm as a whole. On the other hand, the emphasis on time based competition and speed of development also requires that there are specific *loci* within firms which ensure that there is a continuity in the accumulation of key competencies. R&D is by definition the locus where technological competence is accumulated and is charged of the responsibility for creating and maintaining such capabilities over time. Therefore, in technology intensive firms, R&D strategy and organisation are of central importance to conceive a long term strategy.

The second comment aims to clarify the scope and the domain this book wants to explore. The book focuses on R&D strategic decisions and on the organisational structure of R&D. It does not deal with the management of the R&D activities meant as the managerial processes in use. For example it does not deal with project management techniques or human resource management, or the practices in use to ensure that there is a strong integration between R&D and other functions. Sometimes reference is made to them, but they are not central to the book. Of course, these factors are at least as much important as the dimensions studied in this book. The decision to concentrate the book on these dimensions is related to the point that both R&D strategy and organisation (from a structural point of view) seem to have been rather neglected in the last few years.

REFERENCES AND FURTHER READINGS

Abetti, P.A., Technology: a key strategic resource, *Management Review*, 78, 2 (1989), 37-41.

Adler, P.S., McDonald, D.W. and McDonald, F., Strategic Management of Technical Functions, *Sloan Management Review*, Winter, 19 (1992).

Amidon Rogers, D.M., The Challenge of Fifth Generation R&D, *Research Technology Management*, July-August (1996), 33.

Burgelman, R.A., Kosnik, T.J. and van den Poel, M., Toward an Innovative Capabilities Audit Framework, in Burgelman, R.A. and Maidique, M. (Eds.), *Strategic Management of Technology and Innovation* (Irwin, 1988).

Chiesa, V., Coughlan, P. and Voss, C.A., Development of a Technical Innovation Audit, *International Journal of Product Innovation Management*, 13, 2 (1996), 105.

Coombs, R., Core Competencies and the Strategic Management of R&D, *R&D Management*, 26, 4 (1996), 345.

Freeman, C., *Economics of Industrial Innovation* (Pinter Publisher, London, 1976).

Gibbons, M. et al., *The new production of knowledge – The dynamics of Science and Research in Contemporary Societies* (Longman, 1994).

Gupta, A.K. and Wilemon, D., Changing Patterns in Industrial R&D Management, *Journal of Product Innovation Management*, 13 (1996), 497.

Hamel, G. and Prahalad, C.K., *Competing for the Future* (Harvard Business School Press, Harvard, 1994).

Miller, W.L., A Broader Mission for R&D, *Research Technology Management*, November-December (1995).

Pavitt, K., What we know about the Strategic management of Technology, *California Managmeent Review*, Spring, 32 (1990), 3-26.

Pavitt, K., Characteristics of the Large Innovative Firm, *British Journal of Management*, 2 (1991), 41.

Roberts, E.B., Managing invention and innovation, *Research Technology Management*, 31, 1 (1988), 13-29.

Rothwell, R. and Zegveld, W., *Reindustrialisation and Technology* (Longman, Harlow, 1985).

Rothwell, R., Successful Industrial Innovation: Critical Factors for the 1990s, *R&D Management*, 22, 3 (1992), 221.

Roussel, P., Saad, K. and Erickson, T., *Third Generation R&D* (HBS Press, Boston, 1991).

Tidd, J., Bessant, J. and Pavitt, K., *Managing Innovation - Integrating Technological, Market and Organisational Change* (J. Wiley, Chichester, 1997).

PART I

R&D STRATEGY

A firm's R&D strategy consists of 'the definition of the set of R&D projects required to achieve the fixed objectives in terms of technology acquisition defined within the overall strategic framework of the firm'. This definition addresses some key concepts which are worth to be further stressed:

(i)   the actual output of an R&D strategy is a set of R&D projects to be undertaken,
(ii) the objective of an R&D strategy is the acquisition of technology (where acquisition is meant as both internally developed and externally acquired, including the variety of collaborative forms),
(iii) the technology is not good per se but has to be useful to achieve the firm's overall objectives and therefore there needs to be consistency between the R&D strategy and the firm's overall strategy.

The above definition clearly identifies that there are two major conceptual steps or elements in an R&D strategy. A first step which fixes the objectives of the process of technology acquisition and, therefore, identifies the technologies to be acquired (this element is the formulation of the firm's technology strategy). A second step aimed to structure such strategy into projects and allocate the resources available among these projects (this element is the R&D project portfolio definition). These two steps have not to be considered sequentially related; actually, there are two-ways flows between the two. The strategy analysis can lead to identify the appropriate technologies to develop, drive the R&D project generation, definition and selection processes, and, ultimately, define the allocation of resources among R&D projects. On the other hand, the R&D activity helps identify new directions of the technological progress, discover new (potential) technological findings, and, ultimately, provide a roadmap for technology strategy formulation.

Traditionally, these two elements (technology strategy formulation and R&D project portfolio definition) have been the subject of different streams of contributions. A first stream is that related to the technology strategy formulation, which aims to develop methods to formulate a technology strategy within the overall strategic framework of the firm. A second stream concerns the allocation of resources in R&D which addresses areas like R&D project evaluation and selection, and the identification of the portfolio of R&D projects.

The part I of the book which concerns the R&D strategy is structured into three chapters. Chapter 2 treats the conceptual approaches to technology strategy, the relationship between technology and strategy and the major dimensions of a firm's technological choices. Chapter 3 deals with the formulation of a technology strategy (the first step of the R&D strategy) and attempts to identify the key variables influencing the technological choices. Chapter 4 deals with the allocation of resources in R&D and the process which leads to define the set of R&D projects to be undertaken (the second step of the R&D strategy).

CHAPTER 2

APPROACHES TO TECHNOLOGY STRATEGY

The early 80s witnessed the real acceptance of technology's strategic importance. Before, technology was absent in strategic management thinking and practice: "technological innovation traditionally had been portrayed largely as a subject separate from other management practices, including strategy"; "a strategy when related to technology was considered as belonging to the realm of R&D"; "technology was treated as an implementation issue: a firm determines its strategy and this drives how technology will be used" (Friar and Horwitch, 1986).

Since early 80s, many works dealt with technology as a strategic variable. They actually faced two key problems:
- how to link technology strategy and corporate/business strategy;
- the identification of the categories of decisions in technology strategy, i.e. the dimensions along which to make the strategic choices or trade-offs.

Most contributions have treated these aspects jointly. This chapter reviews major contributions on the relationship between technology and strategy, the process of technology strategy formulation, and the identification of the major categories of decision related to technology. The chapter is structured as a chronological excursus of the key contributions to our understanding of the problem.

2.1   THE POSITIONING APPROACH TO STRATEGY

2.1.1   Porter's Framework

In the late 70s and early 80s, several works dealt with how to treat technology as a strategic variable. They mostly contributed identify the categories of decision related to technology and the types of innovation strategies firms can follow. A comprehensive work which in the early 80s addressed the point of how to formulate a firm's technology strategy studying both the link with the business strategy and the key dimensions of technological choices is that of Michael Porter (1980) and (1985).

Actually, Porter's works *Competitive strategy* and *Competitive advantage* provide a first comprehensive framework to the formulation of a firm's technology strategy. The basic elements of the Porter's approach to strategy at the business level are the following:

- competition is searching for favourable competitive environments (selecting the appropriate business area), where favourable means that firms in that business area are likely to be profitable in the medium-long term;
- strategy is defining how to achieve a sustainable competitive advantage (positioning within the selected business area). He identifies four generic strategies: cost leadership, product differentiation, cost focus, differentiation focus.

Therefore, there are two key decisions: selecting the business area and positioning within this. He suggests two tools supporting the two key decisions: the five forces model and the value chain, respectively.

The business area is selected on the basis of the industry attractiveness. Determinants of the industry attractiveness are the following five forces: rivalry among established firms, substitute products, new entrants, relations with suppliers, relations with customers.

The position of the business against its major competitors is diagnosed through the value chain which is composed of the set of activities performed by the business unit: the primary activities (inbound logistics, operations, outbound logistics, marketing and sales, service), support activities (firm's infrastructure, human resources management, technology development, procurement). This diagnosis defines the foundations for actions meant to create and sustain competitive advantages; as already mentioned there are four generic competitive strategies: cost leadership, product differentiation, cost focus, differentiation focus.

Porter recognises that:

- technology is a determinant of the industry structure and therefore affects the profitability within the industry;
- technology affects a firm's potential to generate competitive advantages and can be at the basis of the firm's positioning within the business area.

He emphasises that technology can affect each of the five forces, and that the technological change can modify (either increasing or decreasing) the profitability of the industry (Table 2.1 shows examples of factors affected by technology which in turn affect the industry attractiveness).

Table 2.1. Technology influence over the five forces – Examples.

- *Rivalry among competitors*: modification of the cost structure, substitution costs, exit barriers
- *Potential new entrants*: economies of scale, learning curve, access to distribution channels
- *Substitute products*: substitution threats coming from completely different industries, modification of the relative price of products
- *Power of customers and suppliers*: change of switching costs, opportunity/obstacle to vertical integration, modification of the bargaining power (increasing/reducing the number of customers/suppliers)

On the other hand, technology affects each activity of the firm's value chain both primary and support (Figure 2.1). It can therefore support or be directly source of advantage in terms of cost or differentiation. Therefore, it can be at the basis of each of the four generic strategies: cost leadership, product differentiation, cost focus, differentiation focus. These strategies can be all the result of or affected by either product or process technological change (Table 2.2).

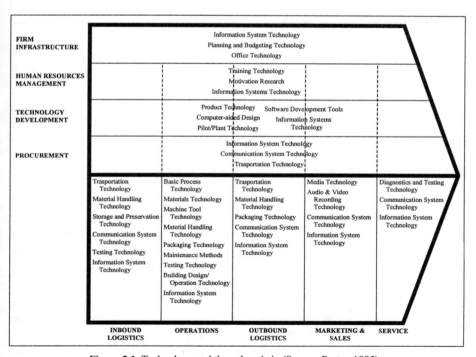

Figure 2.1. Technology and the value chain (Source: Porter, 1985).

Table 2.2. Generic strategies and examples of product and process technological change

	Cost leadership	Differentiation	Cost focus	Differentiation focus
Product technological change	Reducing the materials used Ease of manufacture Lean logistic systems	Improve product quality Enhance product functional performance Improve deliverability	Development of the product minimum features required	Development of the product key features for the market niche
Production process technological change	Learning curve Economies of scale	Quality control Scheduling reliability Response time Time to market	Cost minimisation	Development of process characteristics required to improve the key features for the market niche

Then, Porter in depth studies the elements of a firm's technology strategy. He suggests that technology strategies consist of three key elements, which correspond to three key decisions:
- the selection of the technologies to develop;
- whether to be leader or follower;
- whether to sell the technology or not.

Selection of technologies. The selection of the technologies to develop is based on two principles:
- the coherence of the technological choices with the firm's basic strategy (cost vs. differentiation, focus vs. broad range, which are the two dimensions of the matrix in Table 2.2). At the core of a technology strategy there is the type of competitive advantage a firm is trying to achieve and the basic question to answer is how technology can support this (the previous table shows examples of technological change consistent with the generic strategies);
- the test of whether the technological change is desirable for the firm. The technological change is desirable when the advantage generated is sustainable for the firm and when the changes in the industry structure is favourable. Porter emphasises that often firms do not pay attention to the changes

generated in the industry structure. This may prevent from realising that, although a technological change can generate advantage for the firm, such change may reduce the profitability of the whole industry and therefore decrease the profitability of the innovating firm too in the long term.

Leadership vs. followership. The choice whether to be leader or follower is based on three factors:
-   the sustainability of the technological leadership;
-   the advantages of being first mover;
-   the disadvantages of being first mover.
Each is in turn affected by a number of factors.

The sustainability of the technological leadership depends on four factors:
-   the source of the technological change. If the source of technology is within the industry, the technological leadership can be easier sustained, whereas, when technological source is external, other firms can access such source and the leadership is not sustainable;
-   advantages related to the activity of technology development. A firm which has advantages in the activity of technology development such as scale economies in R&D, higher R&D productivity, higher R&D efficiency, can sustain its leadership over the long term;
-   the relative technological competencies. If technological competencies are unique with respect to competitors, the leadership can be easier sustained;
-   the rate of diffusion of the leader technology. The diffusion of a firm's technology and the process of learning by competitors can take place in a variety of ways such as reverse engineering, technology transfer through suppliers and customers, technology transfer through consultants and press, personnel turnover, scientific publications. The leader can protect its technology through a variety of instruments: patenting, internal development of prototypes and production equipment, vertical integration of the production of key components, personnel management policies.

He also in depth studies the advantages and disadvantages of first movers. These are reported in Table 2.3. Each of these will be later commented in the section about timing of technology development and introduction (Chapter 3).

Table 2.3. First mover advantages and disadvantages.

First mover advantages	First mover disadvantages
- reputation	- pioneering costs
- positioning	- uncertainty of demand
- switching costs	- changing customers' needs
- selection of the distribution channels	- specific investments
- learning curve	- technological discontinuities
- access to input sources	- imitation at low cost
- standard definition	
- institutional barriers	
- initial profits	

Box 2.1 – Leadership vs. followership

Initial works on technology strategy considered whether to be leader or follower, or, more generally, the timing of new technology introduction as the central decision in technology strategy formulation. Early contributions (Freeman, 1976; Maidique and Patch, 1978) classified innovation strategies on the basis of the time of new technology introduction and emphasised their implications in terms of required capabilities. Freeman classified technological innovation strategies into six categories, especially making subtle distinctions on the forms of followership. The six categories are:

1) *offensive*, designed to achieve technical and market leadership by being ahead of competitors in the introduction of new products/processes;

2) *defensive*, aimed to be ready to put products on the market just behind the leader; this strategy can be as research intensive as the offensive policy;

3) *imitative*, aimed to follow way behind the leaders in established technologies, often a long way behind. Whereas defensive strategies aim to produce products which are an improved version of the product of the leaders, the imitative strategy is that of a firm which purely imitates the products of the innovating firm(s);

4) *dependent*, which is the strategy of a firm accepting to operate as a satellite or in a subordinate role of stronger firms. Innovation is the result of a specific request of its customers;

5) *traditional*, which corresponds to the strategy of firms operating in industries where the market does not demand a change and competition does not compel to do so;

6) *opportunist*, which corresponds to the niche strategy.

(follows)

Maidique and Patch (1978) identified categories of technology strategy and studied the implications on the functional capabilities of the firm required to support these strategies. They identified four sample strategies:

1) *early, first-to-market*, or leader strategy which aims to put the product on the market before competitors,

2) *second-to-market*, or fast follower strategy which involves early entry in the growth stage of the life cycle and quick imitations of innovations pioneered by a competitor,

3) *cost minimisation* or late to market, which aims to achieve cost advantages over competitors,

4) *market segmentation* or specialist, which focuses on serving small pockets of demand with special applications of the basic technologies.

Licensing a technology (whether to sell or not). The decision about technology licensing is related to the introduction of a new technology onto the market rather than its development. The decision to licence a technology should be taken when licensing out allows to:

- exploit the technology which otherwise would remain not exploited;
- access markets otherwise not available;
- introduce more rapidly a new standard;
- create 'good' competitors, who may play a role in stimulating the market demand, share pioneering costs, and raising entry barriers;
- have higher profits than those granted by the exploitation on the market.

Later, Twiss (1986) strongly emphasises that often firms neglect that there is a secondary business which is generating technologies of commercial value unrelated with the corporate objectives, and that a technology strategy should consider selling technologies as a real business.

Finally, Porter also suggests how the process of technology strategy formulation is structured:

- identification of the specific technologies and sub-technologies of the firm's value chain;
- identification of the relevant technologies available in other industrial sectors;
- definition of the probable patterns of technological change;
- identification of the technologies critical for the firm's competitive advantage and favourable for the industry structure;
- valuation of the firm's capabilities and the required investments for technology development;

- selection of a technology strategy able to reinforce the firm's competitive position (the technology strategy is composed of the elements given above, i.e. selection of the technologies on which to invest, decision whether to be leader or follower, decisions whether to license out technologies). A further decision concerns whether to acquire technologies from external sources.

2.1.2   Hax and Majluf's Contribution to Technology Strategy

A valuable contribution to our understanding of technology strategy has been given by Hax and Majluf (1984) and (1991). Their conceptual background relies upon Porter's framework. Their contribution especially clarified the major decision categories associated with technology strategy (Box 2.2).

Hax and Majluf (1991) and later Hax e No (1992) structure the above decisions in a process which brings to formulate a firm's technology strategy (see Figure 2.2).

The main elements of their framework are the following:
- the technology strategy is integrated in the overall strategy formulation process, as one of the functional strategies. The unit of analysis of the technology strategy process is the *Strategic Technical Unit* (STU). In their first work, STUs are defined as the technologies embodied in a certain product and in its production process. Later (Hax and No, 1992), STUs are defined as the skills and disciplines that are applied to the firm's products and processes in order to gain technological advantage. They also suggest to be broad enough to include technologies which show a high potential although not yet applied;
- the technology strategy process starts with the technology environmental scan and the technology internal scrutiny. The former is aimed at identifying technological opportunities and threats and assessing the attractiveness of each STU. This analysis includes both the potential for enhancing competitive advantage and long term value added, and the impact of the technology on the industry structure. Moreover, they suggest to identify the source of each technology (lead users, customers, suppliers, competitors, companies from other industries). The internal scrutiny aims to recognise strengths and weaknesses associated with each STU and determines the specific technological competencies to be built to gain competitive advantage;

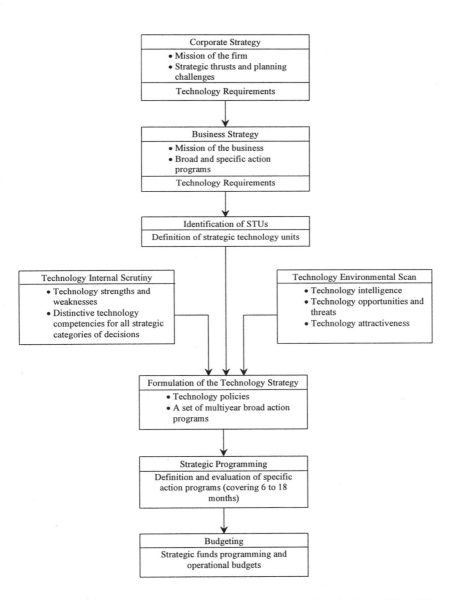

Figure 2.2. A framework for the development of technology strategy (Source: Hax and No, 1992).

Box 2.2 - Major Categories of Strategic Decision Linked to Technology

Technology intelligence

An effort oriented at gathering information concerning the current and future state of technology development. Some of the tasks associated with it are: identification of strategic technical units (STUs), evaluation of competitive technical strengths by STU, detection of the focus of innovation by key product areas (users, manufacturers, suppliers, others), collection and comparison of expenditures in technology by key competitive firms.

Technology selection

It addresses the issue of selecting the technologies in which the firm will specialise and the ways in which they will be embodied in the firm's products and processes. Some of the issues to be recognised are: selection of the technologies needed for product and process innovation, assuring the congruency of technology development with the business life cycle and with desired business strategy, and assigning the appropriate priorities to resulting technological efforts.

Timing of new technology introduction

It involves the decision as to whether to lead or lag behind competitors in process and product innovations. Issues to be addressed are: identifying the benefits and risks associated with a leadership or followership strategy, and assuring the congruency of the

selected technology strategy with the generic business strategy.

Modes of technology acquisition

The extent to which the firm will rely on its own internal efforts in developing internal capabilities, versus resorting to external sources. The options available for the modes of technology acquisition of products and processes are: internal development, acquisition, licensing, internal ventures, joint ventures and alliance, venture capital, and education acquisition.

Horizontal strategy of technology

It consists of identifying and exploiting technological interrelationships that exist across distinct but related businesses. It is a mechanism by which a diversified firm enhances the competitive advantage of its business units. Sources of technological interrelationships: common product technologies, common process technologies, common technologies in other value-added activities, one product incorporated into another, and interface among products.

Project selection, evaluation, resource allocation and control

The principal concern in this case is the appropriate allocation of resources to support the desired technological strategy. Issues to be addressed are:
(follows)

criteria for resource allocation, project oriented resources versus loosely controlled funds to support and plan projects, the degree of fluctuation in technology funding, and the magnitude in the profit gap filled by new products.

Technology organisation and managerial infrastructure
It is oriented toward the definition of the organisational structure of the technology function. It includes the identification of the horizontal coordinating mechanisms needed to exploit the technological interrelationships existing among the various business units and the activities of the value chain. Issues to be considered are: centralisation versus decentralisation of the technology function, development of career paths for scientists and technical professionals, use of project team, use of lateral mechanisms to facilitate sharing technological resources, design of motivational and reward systems for scientists and technical professionals, degree of involvement of top managers in technological decisions, decision-making process for resource allocation to technological projects, protection of technological know-how, patent policies, and publication policies.

Source: Hax and Majluf (1991)

- the formulation of a technology strategy follows and is articulated into three major decisions: selection of the technologies to develop, timing of new technology introduction, modes of acquisition. Such decisions lead to define multiyear action programs. All the above decisions have to be consistent with the overall business strategy and are essentially driven by the inputs from corporate and business levels;
- the strategic programming defines and evaluates specific action program (R&D projects) and budgeting fixes strategic fund programming and operational budgets on an yearly basis;
- the organisational and managerial dimension is a strategic decision related to technology.

2.1.3 Practitioners' Contributions

In the 80s, great attention was paid to technology strategy also by consultants and practitioners. Methodologies were developed, supporting some categories of decisions related to technology, in particular the selection of technologies. Among the others, widely used methodologies were those given by A.D. Little, Booz-Allen & Hamilton and Mc Kinsey, which will be here briefly described.

A.D. Little Methodology

A structured methodology was proposed by A.D. Little in 1980 and later refined in following works (Roussel et al., 1991; Floyd, 1997).
It is composed of the following steps:
- identification of the technologies required,
- definition of the strategic importance and the selection of the technology to achieve key success factors,
- determination of the firm's technological strengths and weaknesses,
- technology strategy formulation.

Identification of the technologies required. It is the result of the typical strategic planning process, starting with the identification of product/market segments, the identification of the bases of competition in each product/market segment (examples of principal bases of competition are product performance, price, quality, reliability, maintainability, availability and delivery response, customisation, after-sale service, compliance with international standards), the determination of the key factors for success and the matching of the technologies involved with the key success factors. The latter point is represented by a matrix (Figure 2.3) where crosses show that the corresponding technology is relevant to achieve the related key success factor.

Definition of the strategic importance and selection of the technology to achieve key success factors. Technologies are classified into four categories on the basis of their competitive impact: base (essential to be in the business, widely exploited by competitors, small competitive impact), key (embodied into products/processes, high competitive impact, generator of competitive advantage), pacing (under experimentation by some competitors, competitive impact likely to be high), emerging (at early research stage or emerging in other industries, competitive impact unknown but promising).

Determination of the firm's technological strengths and weaknesses. The firm's level of technological competence is classified into five categories: clear leader (the firm sets the pace and the direction of technological development and is recognised as such in the industry), strong (able to express independent technical actions and set new directions), able to sustain technological competitiveness in general and/or leadership in technical niches), tenable (unable to set independent course, continually in the catch up mode), weak (unable to sustain quality of technical outputs versus competitors, short fire fighting focus).

	Key Factors for Success														
Important Technologies	Price	Size	Power	Shock sentitivity	Erasable	Features	Reliability	WO	Integration	EMC	Assess Time	Data Rate	Storage Density	Data Integrity	Picture Quality
Light path	√√	√√	√√		√√		√	√√		√	√√	√√			
Physical support structure	√√	√	√	√√			√		√						
Data signal processing	√		√	√	√	√		√	√			√√	√	√√	
Tracking mechanism		√	√	√	√√		√			√	√	√	√		
Servo control	√		√	√√	√			√			√	√	√		
System control	√			√√	√	√		√	√		√			√	
System architecture		√	√	√	√	√		√			√	√		√	
MO system	√√		√		√√					√	√√				
Manufacturing	√	√√					√		√						
Support (sourcing and purchasing)	√	√													
Disc					√			√				√	√√	√√	

Figure 2.3. Technologies underpinning key factors for success – An example
(Source: Arthur D. Little (Floyd, 1997)).

Formulation of the technology strategy. The formulation of the technology strategy starts from the joint analysis of technological competence level and technology importance (Figure 2.4), which brings to identify the strategic implications of the firm's technology position. Then, matching the competitive impact of the technologies and the competitive position leads to the *formulation of the technology strategy* (Figure 2.5). The generic strategies are of five types: build, nurture, maintain, repair and invest selectively.

Technology significance	Level of Technology Competence				
	Clear leader	*Strong*	*Favourable*	*Tenable*	*Weak*
Base	Alarm signal for waste of resources		Industry average	Alarm signal for survival	
Key	Opportunities for present competitive advantage			Alarm signal for present	
Pacing	Opportunities for future competitive advantage			Alarm signal for future	
Emerging					

Figure 2.4. Joint analysis of technology competence levels and technology importance.

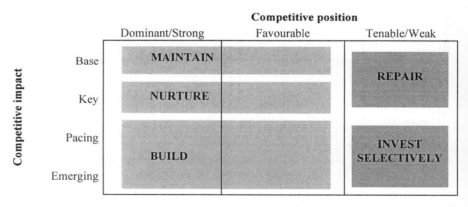

Figure 2.5. Generic strategies for technology development
(Source: Arthur D. Little (Floyd, 1997)).

Then the strategy is detailed into R&D projects (the process of definition, evaluation and selection is later treated in this book in chapter 4).

Booz-Allen & Hamilton Methodology

Booz-Allen & Hamilton (1981) developed a methodology to strategically manage technology. It is based on the following principles:

(i)　direction and timing of technology evolution need to and can be anticipated,

(ii) technology should be viewed as a capital asset,

(iii) the congruence of technology investment and business strategy is essential to successful technology management.

The technology strategy is the result of a four-step methodology:

- *technology situation assessment*, which is in turn composed of three phases: (i) identification of the technologies to analyse in a product/business area, (ii) assessment of the importance of the technologies to the specific products/businesses, (iii) definition of the firm's technology relative position (which requires scanning the external environment to pinpoint the investment patterns of competitors in each vital technology);

- *technology portfolio development*, which identifies the appropriate technology strategy of the business according to the two key dimensions which are technology importance (the extent to which the technology is vital to compete), and technology relative position (the position of the firm in that technology relative to competitors). The strategies (bet, draw, cash in, fold) are reported in the four quadrants of the grid (Figure 2.6);

- *matching business and technology strategy*, which jointly consider the business portfolio with the technology portfolio in such a way to identify the technologies supporting the best positioned businesses (in terms of competitive position and market attractiveness) (Figure 2.7);

- *define the technology investment priorities*, which provides the priorities of technology investments on the basis of the technology position in the quadrants of the grid (Figure 2.8).

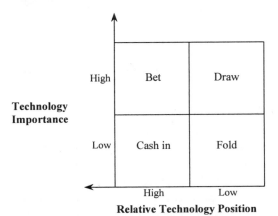

Figure 2.6. Development of the technology portfolio
(Source: Booz-Allen and Hamilton (Pappas, 1984)).

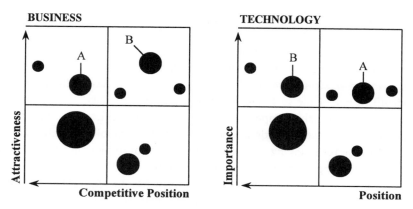

Figure 2.7. Matching business and technology portfolios
(Source: Booz-Allen and Hamilton (Pappas, 1984)).

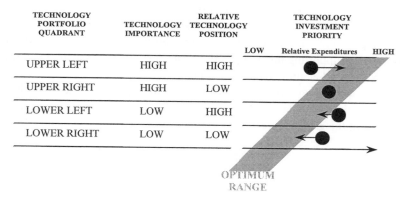

Figure 2.8. Technology investment matrix (Source: Booz-Allen and Hamilton (Pappas, 1984)).

McKinsey Methodology

Another well known contribution is that of Foster (1986) who focused on the problem of technological transitions and the ability of the firm to cope with that. He bases his analysis on the S-curve phenomenon. At the beginning of an R&D program, knowledge has to be acquired and problems solved, and the progress is slow, then the rate of progress picks up and finally the technology begins to be constrained by its limits and the rate of improvement begins to slow (Figure 2.9). It is time to move to other technologies managing a smooth transition to new technologies with superior performance improvement potential. This allows to cross technological discontinuities effectively. Foster suggests that it is critical to detect the technological decay of existing technologies. Symptoms of technological decay are:

- decline of firm's R&D productivity,
- trend towards missed R&D deadlines,
- a shift from product- to process-oriented R&D,
- dissension among the R&D staff,
- a shift in the source of sales growth, toward narrower market segments,
- tendency for significant variations among competitors in R&D spending to produce ever less significant results,
- dissatisfaction with the performance of a 'new broom' R&D manager,
- a trend among smaller weaker competitors in the industry to invest R&D effort in radical new approaches.

Once identified the potential for improvement of the concerned technologies, the R&D strategy has to be generated. Foster suggests that the appropriate R&D strategies should take into account the potential of technologies for productivity and yield improvements (Figure 2.10).

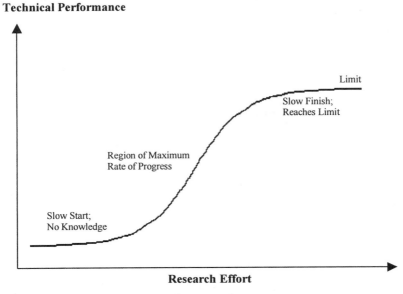

Figure 2.9. The S-curve phenomenon.

R&D Strategy and Organisation

These contributions provided methodologies and practical tools to carry out several steps of the technology strategy process, and support strategic decisions related to technology, especially the selection of the technologies on which to invest. Conceptually, they all lie upon the principles of the positioning approach to strategy. These are:

-   the starting point is the industry where a firm is competing or will compete;
-   the unit of analysis is the technology embodied or which can be embodied in the end product or process;
-   the basic concept is to understand how strategic decisions affect or are affected by changes in technology, how to embody technology in the strategy formulation process, how a technology program can support a given strategy and, ultimately, on how to gain competitive advantage through changing the technological solution for a certain product. Competition is seen as positioning the firm in a given competitive arena and technology as a support to a chosen competitive strategy;
-   the major decisions are taken sequentially: first, the selection of technologies, then, the timing of new technology introduction, finally, the mode of acquisition;
-   once selected the technologies to develop, the basic decision is whether to be leader or follower;
-   the mode of technology acquisition is not central and appears to be secondary to selection and timing decisions.

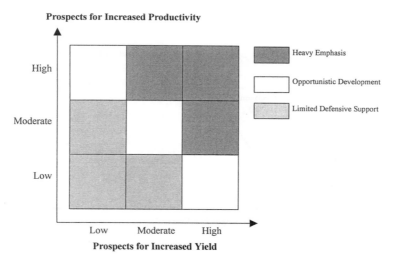

Figure 2.10. Defining priorities among technologies (Source: Foster, 1986).

2.2   THE RESOURCE BASED APPROACH TO STRATEGY

Unlike the positioning approach to strategy which focuses on market structure and positioning within an industry, the starting point of resource based approaches to strategy is the firm's competencies and resources. The background concept is that a firm's competence is the actual source of sustainable and long term competitive advantage. It is this firm-specific factor which mostly provides an explanation for significant performance differences among firms. Customer needs change much more rapidly than firm's competencies. Therefore, it is preferable that the strategy process starts from the latter and is seen as searching for ever new applications of such set of competencies and renewing the competencies themselves. Several contributions adopted this approach in the past (for example, Wernefelt, 1984). More recently it has been proposed under new forms by Prahalad and Hamel.

2.2.1   Prahalad and Hamel's Core Competence

Prahalad and Hamel (1989,1990,1993) view strategy as composed of the following fundamental elements:
(i)   identifying the evolutionary patterns of the concerned industries;
(ii)   define the strategic architecture;
(iii)   recognise that competition is played at different levels and that differentials should be achieved at each level.
(iv)   fix stretched objectives and leverage competencies (stretch and leverage);
(v)   design an appropriate organisation.

(i)   The turbolence and rapid change of markets, industry boundaries, customer needs, and products have brought to consider that these are not the appropriate reference points for strategy formulation. Successful firms are often those able to reshape competition and create new industries or to redefine the boundaries of existing industries, targeting latent needs or forcing changes in the purchasing attitude of customers. This means that positioning in existing industries may be not the appropriate perspective to assume in strategy formulation. This starts with the exercise of foreseeing future markets and needs in a long term perspective (5-15 years). Hamel and Prahalad emphasise that the *industry foresight* is a key issue and provide the required basis and the right direction to competence building and competition. Competence building requires a clear definition of how the context will be shaped and where the firm wants to be in the long term.

(ii)   On the basis of its long term view of competition, a firm has to define its strategic intent. It can be a fuzzy and weakly focused statement (Moenaert, 1992). However, it should address all firm's efforts. For example, Sony's founders intended from the beginning to apply "a mix of electronics and engineering to the consumer field". Hamel and Prahalad (1989) call this *strategic intent*. Then, the road to achieve the required objectives has to be designed in details. In fact, once identified the intent, the most critical aspect is to define the action to take and the trajectory to follow. This is called *strategic architecture* which establishes the competencies to accumulate to compete and how to acquire them. Of course it should be designed with the required degrees of freedom and flexibility. Each action should be referred to the satisfaction of customer needs, i.e. to the delivery of value. Products are viewed as the set of functions to be performed to match customer needs and provide value to customers (Abell, 1980). Product functions are more stable than technologies and products themselves. Therefore, product functions are the basis for an organisation to develop a long term strategy, and guide the company towards specific actions aimed to accumulate resources in a defined direction.

(iii) Competition is played at different levels (Figure 2.11). The focus of long term competition shifts from finding profitable product/market combinations to the inherent capability of a company to shape competition. The traditional competitive frame views strategy as selecting contexts appropriate to a firm's strengths and positioning favourably. The attention is paid to end products and their markets. In the competence-based competition competitive arenas are seen as factors which may be influenced and controlled by the firm. Roots of competitive advantage reside into a firm's existing resources and assets (competencies), and sustaining competitive advantage over time means to continuously create and develop new asset-based asymmetries beside the exploitation of the existing ones. End products become just the leaves of the tree of which the roots are the firm's intangible assets. These distinctive core competencies are the basis of long term competition, whilst end products are just the current (transient) embodiments of a firm's competitive advantage. The tangible link between core competencies and end products is the core product that is the physical embodiment of one or more core competencies; in other words, the core component that generates the value of the end products.

Core competencies have been defined in a variety of ways. They are viewed as a set of irreversible assets along which the firm is uniquely advantaged (Collis, 1991). Prahalad and Hamel (1990) have defined the core competencies as 'the collective learning in the organisation, especially how to co-ordinate diverse production skills and integrate multiple streams of technologies', stressing the role of technology. Other authors emphasise the role of the business processes as the building blocks of a competence-based strategy. Competitive success depends on transforming a company's key processes into strategic capabilities: 'core competence emphasises technological and production expertise at specific points along the value chain, capabilities are more broadly based, encompassing the entire value chain' (Stalk et al., 1992). Dosi and Teece (1993) define a firm's competence as the set of activities in which it excels, and its organisational competencies as 'the capabilities of an enterprise to organise, manage, coordinate or govern specific sets of activities'. Leonard-Barton (1992) views a firm's core capability as 'a knowledge set comprising four dimensions: employee knowledge and skills (1), technical systems (2), managerial systems (3) and values and norms (4).

All these contributions emphasise that competencies are the result of a cumulative resource development process and are based on skills and knowledge embedded in the organisation. Such skills are built incrementally via a series of learning cycles within a long term process of accumulating capabilities (Grindley, 1991). Knowledge and skills which are hard to imitate are source of lasting advantage. Prahalad and Hamel clearly state the key characteristics of competencies to be core:
- provide value for the customers;
- lead to a variety of applications;
- are hard to imitate.

(iv) Given that competition is often related with rivalry in new contexts, the positioning approach which is based on the concept of 'fit' appears to be no more appropriate. Establishing objectives consistent with the resources available is not enough; a 'misfit' should be introduced which stimulates to achieve ambitious and apparently unreachable objectives. This misfit or *stretch* is a major task of top management and is a key issue to create an organisation oriented to think different, reshape competition and proactively change the internal and the external context. Strategy is a consistent stream of efforts where resources are stretched and leveraged.

(v) This approach to strategy has a strong organisational impact. Competencies cross businesses and grow as they are applied and shared. A business-unit-oriented mind set imprisons the development of resources and competencies (Table 2.4). A business-unit-led process of technology strategy could lead to underinvest in developing core competencies and core products and bound innovation. Therefore, the traditional divisional structure seems to be inappropriate. New organisations have to be conceived and designed. How this is faced in R&D will be dealt with in the part II of the book.

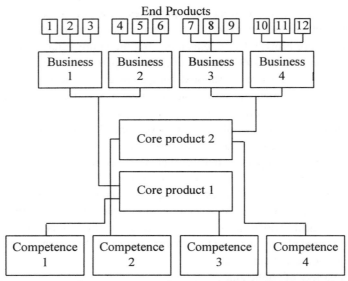

Figure 2.11. The 'core competence' tree (Source: Prahalad and Hamel, 1990).

Table 2.4. SBU orientation vs. competence based orientation. (Source: Prahalad and Hamel, 1990).

	SBU	Core competence
Basis for competition	Competitiveness of today's products	Interfirm competition to build competencies
Corporate structure	Portfolio of businesses related in product-market terms	Portfolio of competencies, core products, and businesses
Status of the business unit	Autonomy is sacrosanct; the SBU "owns" all resources other than cash	SBU is a potential reservoir of core competencies
Resources allocation	Discrete businesses are the unit of analysis; capital is allocated business by business	Businesses and competencies are the unit of analysis: top management allocates capital and talent
Value added of top management	Optimising corporate returns through capital allocation trade-offs among businesses	Enunciating strategic architecture and building competencies to secure future

2.2.2 D'Aveni Hypercompetition

D'Aveni (1994) emphasises that the dynamic character of competition is so deeply intrinsic that it can not be any longer considered as an afterthought to strategic thinking. He states that markets are so volatile and dynamic that the evolution is the dominant force in strategic action. On the line of the resource based thoughts, the most important aspect of competition is not a firm's current position but the changes created by the dynamic interaction between rival firms. The position offers only a temporary advantage. It is the firm's ability to manage a series of interactions successfully that determines the success of the company. Over long periods of time firms are forced to shift their positions.

From his framework it can be argued that there are three categories of arenas and competition:

(i) Arenas of which the boundaries are well defined where competition is played on two major dimensions: price and the perceived quality where the dimensions of the perceived quality are stable over time.

(ii) Arenas of which the boundaries are well defined where competition is played on two dimensions: price and perceived quality where the perceived quality changes over time. This means that the dimensions on which quality is perceived and therefore measured change over time.

(iii) Arenas where boundaries are weakly defined and competition is played on the ability to generate new product/market combinations.

These three categories also address three different ways of creating competitive advantage:

-    performing better than competitors on an already existing dimension of competition (either cost or already existing dimensions of quality);

-    establishing a new dimension of quality on which to compete;

-    creating a new product/market combination.

The first type of advantage means that a firm is able to create advantages providing a product of the same quality at lower prices or improving a certain performance, that is improving quality at the same price. However, this competitive cycle leads to the so named ultimate value position (low cost - high quality). When the ultimate value is reached, all the other positions are unviable. All firms tend to evolve to the same position; over time, the market becomes commodity-like and profitability very low. To escape from this cycle firms try to jump into a new market or introduce a new level of quality so improved or new that it reshapes the market and, in fact, create a new marketplace. In other words, it pursues new ways to create advantage which are the following.

A second type of advantage is the result of the creation of a new dimension of quality. The innovator introduces a new quality dimension and competitors are forced to take into account this new type of quality. The competitive arena is reshaped and redefined as the nature of the quality dimension changes. In other words, the way how quality is perceived by customers changes.

The third type of advantage relies on the creation of a new product/market combination.

D'Aveni states that innovations in product or process technology drive dramatic improvements in quality and reductions in cost. This makes the cycles of change (the moving towards the ultimate value) progressively shorter. Therefore, the other two types of advantage should be pursued. This means that it is the ability of the firm to manage the dynamic aspect of competition which matters rather than its static positioning.

Therefore, innovation (especially, technological innovation) should be used as the central instrument to escape the ultimate value and keep profitability high. In other words, competitive advantages should be pursued which are the result of innovations which change the basis to compete. The critical factors in such actions aimed to introduce an innovation (and therefore in such types of competitive advantages) are timing and know-how. As a matter of fact, these factors affect the sustainability of the competitive advantage. In fact, an innovation creates an advantage when there is a gap between the innovating firm and its competitors. This is essentially a knowledge and know-how gap. An innovation generates the reaction by competitors which try to imitate the innovator. Competitors' efforts are aimed to cover the knowledge gap. The larger gap of knowledge, the larger advantage to exploit. The appropriability of an innovation can be measured as the effort competitors should make to cover the knowledge gap. When the know-how gap is deep, competitors should make great efforts to cover it and this takes time and investments. The longer time required or (which is equivalent) the larger investments required, the more sustainable advantage. If the knowledge gap can be covered in a short time, the innovator can act as a monopolist and make profits from the innovation in the short term.

Another way is the exploitation of time advantages, which means staying ahead of competitors innovating continuously. The innovation may be the basis for a sustainable advantage if the firm is able to move on before or when followers are able to imitate. In this way, the innovator keeps the advantage innovating rapidly and continuously. The sustainability of the advantage is therefore related to the dynamics of competition and to the nature of the underlying innovation. The role of technology is central in this process of sustainable competitive advantage creation. D'Aveni's contribution emphasises that in highly dynamic competitive contexts the key principles of a strategy are the following:

- competitive advantages rely upon the capability to innovate continuously;
- the sustainability of a competitive advantage is strongly affected by the appropriability of the innovation, which in turn depend on know-how advantages;
- the sustainability of a competitive advantage is also related with the timing of introduction of the innovation.

2.2.3 Itami and Numagami's Review on Interaction between Technology and Strategy

Itami and Numagami (1992) made an interesting review of the dynamic interactions between technology and strategy which help view the approaches briefly described above in a comprehensive way. The types of interactions between strategy and technology are three:

- between current strategy and current technology;
- between current strategy and future technology;
- between future strategy and current technology.

The first case (identified by the statement: strategy capitalises on technology) focuses on the contemporaneous match between the strategy the firm wants to take and the technology it possesses. The underlying assumptions are that technology can act on strategy in three ways:

- a weapon to differentiate the firm from its competitors;
- a constraint to which firms must adapt;
- a threat firms have to guard against and cope with.

Current strategy should make the best use of current technology of the firm. This perspective is that taken by Porter and a number of other contributions (several quoted and described earlier in section 2.1 of this chapter). It is the traditional view of the interaction between technology and strategy as consistent matching of the two and the relationship between strategy and technology is a dynamic sequence of static matching.

The second perspective is that current strategic decisions have implications for future technology accumulation. It includes the first case (matching between strategy and technology) but it adds that the technology potential is greater than current short term needs. Strategy is designed to facilitate the development and accumulation of new knowledge in technological fields to be exploited in future competition. Various concepts are traced back by the authors to this approach: the experience curve, the core competence approach (and more generally the contributions based on intangible and invisible assets), the economies of evolution and economies of multi-projects.[a]

The third perspective is concerned with the effects of current technology on future strategy of the firm. Technology that the firm possesses now and/or the firm's current commitment to technological development affect human cognitive processes for strategy formation within the firm. Technology drives cognition of a particular strategy as it channels and activates idea generation processes and helps integrate fragmentary ideas. It is technology which drives the strategy formation process.

These three perspectives are different on several key dimensions:

- distinction between content and process of strategy;
- role of learning and human cognitive processes;
- strategic importance of technology.

Table 2.5 summarises the differences.

Table 2.5. Dynamic interactions between technology and strategy.

	Distinction between strategy content and strategy process	**Role of learning**	**Role of technology**
Traditional perspective (*static matching*)	separate (strategy drives implementation)	neglected (limited to experience curve)	tool to be used
Dynamic perspective I (*strategy cultivating technology*)	inter-related (strategy implementation affects future technology)	*learning by doing* is central	endogenous variable to be developed within an appropriate strategy
Dynamic perspective II (*technology as cognitive driver of strategy*)	total overlapping between *strategy formation* and *strategy implementation*, strategy as evolutionary process	all forms of learning are central	central (technology drives and provides the frame for strategy conception)

a   Economies of multiple projects and economies of evolution refer to the following concepts. The coexistence of multiple projects with different stages of technological evolution not only encourages technological transfer between projects but also creates new knowledge which would be hard to generate without this coexistence. Having two technologies at different evolutionary stages for the same product category at the same time speeds up the technological development for the advanced product and reduce costs for the less advanced product.

Itami and Numagami's contribution emphasise that the *dynamic* interaction between technology and strategy takes place in two ways:

- strategy is conceived as a set of actions which help cultivate technology critical for future competition; in other words, the cognition of how the context will shape should help identify the key technologies for the future and consequently an appropriate strategy should be conceived to develop such technologies;

- technology is the driver of strategy and, therefore, the technological competence base of the firm can be itself the starting point of the strategy formulation.

2.2.4 Technology Strategy in Dynamic Competition: Key Principles

The above contributions have all explored the basic principles and the key characteristics of the competition in dynamic contexts. Such principles provide the basis for formulating technology strategies under a different perspective from the positioning school of strategy. Actually, the comparison between the positioning approach and the resource based school of strategy allows to make some remarks:

- the positioning approach to the formulation of a technology strategy is appropriate in a limited number of industries and contexts. Especially industries where competition is played on a product's defined functional performance and cost, and industry boundaries are well defined. A different approach is needed in arenas with high innovation rates, very dynamic in which technology makes product paradigms obsolete in a short time and the introduction of new product/market combination is the basis for survival. The current product does not represent a sound reference;

- in highly dynamic environments, the continuity firms are searching for does not lean on product paradigms. Firms are forced to find a continuity in terms of skills and knowledge used for product application. Formulating a strategy means to define the trajectory by which resources are accumulated, acquired and used. The sustainability of the competitive advantage relates to the capability to develop technological competencies and resources along a given trajectory which is stable in the long term. Competence accumulation over time helps make skills and knowledge hardly imitable by competitors and opens unique innovative opportunities.

More in detail:

-   the unit of analysis of the technology strategy formulation can no more remain
    with the product and its constituent technologies, i.e. the technologies
    embodied into the product and the production process used to manufacture it,
    or, at most, the skills and disciplines applied to a particular product or process.
    In principles, this strongly limits the analysis and the formulation of a
    technology strategy to restricted conditions, in which the product (or
    production process) paradigm is stable over time. Only in this case, a strategy
    can be conceived relying on the analysis of the current technologies used and
    their potential substitutes. The units of analysis or the starting point of the
    strategy process should be, on the one hand, the customer needs and the
    related functions to be solved, and, on the other, the firm's base of
    technological competence;
-   the distinction between internal and external analysis (which are the typical
    initial steps of the positioning approach to strategy) is no more clear cut. It is
    the combination of both which supports understand the dynamic interaction
    between the firm's strategy and the context evolution. Learning is central and
    makes more difficult the distinction between internal and external analysis. In
    fact, learning is the process that allows a continuous adaptation of firm-
    specific competencies in the light of the experience and further information. In
    other words, 'the process of learning allows a continuous feedback between
    the content of a resource-based technological strategy and knowledge of the
    context outside together with the inner context within the firm and its
    competencies' (Pavitt, 1990);
-   it becomes central to the effectiveness of a strategy also the context within
    which - and the process whereby - technological strategies are generated,
    chosen and implemented (Pavitt, 1990). The positioning approach is content-
    centred; this view neglects the strategy process, i.e. how technological
    capabilities are fostered and managed so as to create the basis for competitive
    advantage and to reshape skills and structures of the organisation. The
    resource based view of strategy emphasises that the process by which strategy
    is generated is central to the strategy effectiveness. Therefore, the organisation
    of the technological activities becomes a central aspect of technology strategy;
-   the categories of decisions related to technology (selection, timing and
    acquisition mode) inter-relate each other. Given that the technology process,
    i.e. the implementation of technology, affects technology content decisions,
    how and by when technology is developed should influence the decisions
    about the technologies to invest on; also the opposite is true, the technology

selection should direct the mode of technology acquisition and influence the timing of technology development. More generally, selection of technologies, timing of new technologies introduction and acquisition mode should be seen as three dimensions of one strategic decision about technology;

- technology strategy is like designing a 'trajectory' that defines how to acquire and internalise technical resources and knowledge. Each step in a technology strategy is strongly dependent on previous actions and programs. Therefore, the matter is to understand how a certain step in a technology strategy, on the one hand, is linked with the previous ones, on the other hand, opens opportunities and creates options for future investments along the defined trajectory.

The chapter 3 of this book deals with the formulation of technology strategies in dynamic contexts and offers a tool supporting decision taking. The approach proposed attempts to match the features above outlined which characterise technology strategy formulation in dynamic environments. Before, it is necessary to make a clarification about the approach taken in this book.

2.3   ABOUT RATIONALIST AND INCREMENTALIST APPROACHES TO STRATEGY

Given that context conditions are highly turbolent and dynamic, a stream of thoughts argues that it is impossible to completely understand reality and grasp its complexity and change. The ability of strategists to predict the future and comprehend the present is highly limited. Therefore, firm has only very imperfect knowledge of its environment, of its strengths and weaknesses, of the likely rates and directions of change. Strategies are adapted in the light of new experience and information on the basis of a trial and error approach (Tidd et al., 1997). This stream of thoughts is that of the incrementalist approach to strategy, which has been opposed to the rationalist approach based on a systematic analysis of the inner and outer context.

This way of thinking and its contrast with the rational approach to strategy are, to a certain extent, outlined by Friar and Horwitch who identify two modes or paradigms of technology and innovation strategy. Mode I includes a strong commitment to a single narrow or focused technology area, a comparatively small, informal and changing organisational structure, a technological champion as head of the firm or part of the top management team, and an overall climate and style of entrepreneurship and risk-taking. It is the typical mode of small high-technology firms. Mode II is that of large scale corporation R&D operating in a multi-division, multi-product, multi-market contexts. Mode II includes strategic choices or trade-offs along a variety of dimensions: types of technological innovation, the specific technologies to develop, the timing or positioning of technology introduction into the marketplace. Then, a number of complex internal strategic activities including allocation of technological resources, monitoring and evaluation of technological undertakings, the design of an appropriate structure, the location of the innovating activity, internal technology transfer, the relationship between the early R&D work, the development work and the operating divisions. Mode I adopts an incremental approach, whereas Mode II is closer to the rational view.

The increasingly dynamic character of competition stresses that organisations are forced to combine the two in order to capture the benefits of both. Generally speaking, this means that large scale corporation, which are traditionally users of tools and techniques helping structure the problem, take decisions and solve trade-offs on the basis of a rational approach, are challenged to design organisations able to adapt and flexible. On the other hand, small firms, which by nature have an organisation very flexible and adapt to dynamic contexts, need to structure their approach to technology, which is often intuitive, and more extensively use tools and techniques supporting the decision making process.

Of course, conceiving strategies on the basis of tools and techniques which are inevitably not able to grasp the complexity and changing character of the (inner and outer) contexts becomes very difficult and often leads to wrong strategies. On the other hand, instruments, tools and techniques often help face a problem, identify the relevant variables and structure the process to design a solution. This is the aim of the techniques shown in this book, which, of course, do not have the ambition to provide a comprehensive understanding of and solution to the formulation of a technology strategy.

REFERENCES AND FURTHER READINGS

Abell, D.F., *Defining the Business: the Starting Point of Strategic Planning* (Prentice Hall, Englewood Cliffs, 1980).

Adler, P.S., McDonald, D.W and McDonald, F., Strategic Management of Technical Functions, *Sloan Management Review*, Winter (1992), 19-37.

Anderson, J., Fears, R. and Taylor, B. (Eds.), *Managing Technology for Competitive Advantage* (Cartermill International and Financial Times, London, 1997).

Ansoff, I. and Mc Donnell, E., *Implanting Strategic Management* (Prentice-Hall Int., Cambridge, 1990).

Asthana, P., Jumping the technology S-Curve, *IEEE Spectrum*, June (1995), 49-54.

Barker, D. and Smith, D.J.H. , Technology Foresight using Roadmaps, *Long Range Planning*, 28, 2 (1995), 21-28.

Bertelè, U. and Mariotti, S., *Impresa e Competizione Dinamica* (EtasLibri, Milano, 1991).

Bogner, W. and Thomas, H., From skill to technological competencies; the play out of resource boundless across firm, in Sanchez, R., Heene, A. and Thomas, H., *Dynamics of competence based competition: theory and practice in the new strategic management* (Elsevier, London, 1996).

Booz-Allen & Hamilton, The Strategic Management of Technology, *Outlook*, Fall-Winter (1981).

Carrubba, F., Reorganising R&D around business creation: making technology pay, in Anderson, J., Fears, R. and Taylor, B. (Eds.), *Managing Technology for Competitive Advantage* (Cartermill International and Financial Times, London, 1997).

Chiesa, V. and Barbeschi, M., Technology Strategy in Competence-Based Competition, in Hamel, G. and Heene, A. (Eds.), *Competence-Based Competition* (J. Wiley, 1994), 293-314.

Chiesa, V., Coughlan, P. and Voss, C.A., *Innovation as a Business Process*, Working Paper, London Business School, (1993).

Clarke, K., Ford, D. and Saren, M., Company technology strategy, *R&D Management*, 19,3 (1989).

Cohen, W.M. and Levinthal, D.A., Absorptive Capacity: a New Perspective on Learning and Innovation, *Administrative Science Quarterly*, 35 (1990), 128-152.

Collis, D., A resource-based analysis of global competition: the case of bearings industry, *Strategic Management Journal*, 12 (1991), 49-68.

D'Aveni, R.A., *Hypercompetitive rivalries - Competing in highly dynamic environments* (Free Press, New York, 1994).

Dosi G. and Teece D.J., *Organisational competences and the boundaries of the firm in market and organisation: the competitive firm and its environment*, Working Paper, Latapses, Nice and Iside, Rome (1993).

Floyd, C., *Managing technology for corporate success* (Aldershot, Gower, 1997).

Foster, R.N., Timing Technological Transitions, in Horwitch, M. (Ed.), *Technology in the Modern Corporation - A Strategic Perspective* (Pergamon Press, 1986).

Freeman, C., *The Economics of Industrial Innovation*, 2nd edition (Pinter Publisher, London, 1976).

Friar, J. and Horwitch, M., The Emergence of Technology Strategy: a New Dimension of Strategic Management, in Horwitch, M. (Ed.), *Technology in the Modern Corporation - A Strategic Perspective* (Pergamon Press, 1986).

Grindley, P., Turning Technology into Competitive Advantage, *Business Strategy Review*, Spring (1991).

Hall, R., The strategic analysis of intangible resources, *Strategic Management Journal*, 13 (1992), p. 135.

Hamel, G., Competition for Competence and Interpartner Learning within International Strategic Alliances, *Strategic Management Journal*, 13 (1992), 83-103.

Hamel, G. and Heene, A., *Competence Based Competition* (John Wiley & Sons, Chichester, 1994).

Hamel G. and Prahalad C.K., Strategic Intent, *Harvard Business Review*, 67, 3 (1989), 63-76.

Hamel, G. and Prahalad, C.K., Strategy as Stretch and Leverage, *Harvard Business Review*, March-April (1993), 75-84.

Hamel, G. and Prahalad, C.K., *Competing for the Future* (Harvard Business School Press, Harvard, 1994).

Hax, A.C. and Majluf, N.S., *Strategic Management: An Integrative Perspective* (Prentice Hall, Englewood Cliffs, 1984).

Hax, A.C. and Majluf, N.S., *The Strategic Concept and Process: A Pragmatic Approach* (Prentice Hall, Englewood Cliffs, 1991).

Hax, A.C. and No, M., *Linking Technology and Business Strategies: A Methodological Approach and an Illustration*, Working Paper No. 3383-92BPS, February (1992).

Hedlund, G. and Rolander, D., Action in Hetererchies: New Approaches to Managing the MNC, in Bartlett, C.A. and Doz, Y. (Eds.), *Managing the Global Firm* (Routledge, London, 1990), 15-47.

Heene, A. and Sanchez, R., *Competence-based Strategic Management* (J. Wiley, Chichetser, 1997).

Imai, K., Nonaka, I. and Takeuchi, H., Managing the New Product Development Process: How Japanese Companies Learn and Unlearn, in Tushman, M.L. and Moore, W.L. (Eds.), *Readings in the Management of Innovation* (Harper, Cambridge, 1988), 533-561.

Itami, H., *Mobilizing Invisible Assets* (Harvard University Press, Cambridge, 1987).

Itami, H. and Numagami, T., Dynamic interaction between strategy and technology, *Strategic Management Journal*, 13 (1992), 119-135.

Kay, N., The R&D function: Corporate Strategy and Structure, in *Technical Change and Economic Theory*, Dosi et al. (Eds.) (Pinter Publishers, London, 1988).

Leonard-Barton, D., Core Capabilities and Core Rigidities: a Paradox in Managing New Product Development, *Strategic Management Journal*, 13 (1992), 111-125.

Little, A.D., *The Strategic Management of Technology* (European Management Forum, Davos, 1981).

Maidique, M.A. and Patch, P., Corporate Strategy and Technological Policy, in Tushman, M.L. and Moore, W.L. (Eds.), *Readings in the Management of Innovation*, 2nd edition (Harper Business, 1978).

Mc Gee, J. and Thomas, H., Technology and strategic management progress and future directions, *R&D Management*, 19,3 (1989).

Mitchell, G.R., New Approaches for the Strategic Management of Technology, in Horwitch, M. (Ed.), *Technology in the Modern Corporation - A Strategic Perspective* (Pergamon Press, 1986).

Moenaert, R.K., *Firm Resources and the Meaning of Innovation Success*, International Workshop on Core Competence, Genk, Belgium, November (1992).

Nonaka, I., The Knowledge-Creating Company, *Harvard Business Review*, November-December (1991), 96-104.

Pappas, C., Strategic Management of Technology, *Journal of Product Innovation Management*, 1 (1984).

Pavitt, K., What We Know about the Strategic Management of Technology, *California Management Review*, 32, 3 (1990), 17-26.

Pavitt, K., Characteristics of the Large Innovative Firm, *British Journal of Management*, 2 (1991), 41-50.

Petroni, G., *Cultura tecnologica e sviluppo dell'impresa* (Cedam, Padova, 1997).

Porter M.E., *Competitive Advantage* (The Free Press, New York, 1985).

Porter, M.E., *Competitive Strategy: Techniques for Analysing Industries and Competitors* (The Free Press, New York, 1980).

Porter, M.E., The Technological Dimensions of Competitive Strategy, in *Research on Technological Innovation, Management and Policy*, AA. VV., vol.1 (JAI Press, Greenwich, Conn, 1983).

Prahalad, C.K. and Hamel, G., The Core Competence of the Corporation, *Harvard Business Review*, 68, 3 (1990), 79-91.

Price, G., Managing Uncertainty and risk using scenarios, in Anderson, J., Fears, R. and Taylor, B. (Eds.), *Managing Technology for Competitive Advantage* (Cartermill International and Financial Times, London, 1997).

Roussel, P., Saad, K. and Erickson, T., *Third Generation R&D* (HBS Press, Boston, 1991).

Sanchez, R., Heene, A. and Thomas, H., Towards the theory and practice of competence based competition, in Sanchez, R., Heene, A. and Thomas, H. (Eds.), *Dynamics of competence based competition: theory and practice in the new management* (Elsevier Press, London, 1996).

Senge, P. M., Team Learning, *McKinsey Quarterly*, 2 (1992), 82-93.

Stalk, G., Evans, P. and Shulman, L.E., Competing on Capabilities: The New Rules of Corporate Strategy, *Harvard Business Review*, March-April (1992), 57-69.

Steele, L.W., *Managing Technology - The strategic view* (Mc Graw-Hill, 1989).

Tidd J., Bessant J. and Pavitt K., *Managing Innovation – Integrating Technological, Market and Organisational Change* (John Wiley & Sons, Chichester, 1997).

Twiss, B., *Managing Technological Innovation* (Pitman, 1986).

Utterback, J.M., *Mastering the Dynamics of Innovation* (Harvard Business School Press, 1994).

Wernefelt, B.A., A Resource-Based View of the Firm, *Strategic Management Journal*, 5 (1984), 171-180.

CHAPTER 3

FORMULATING TECHNOLOGY STRATEGY
IN DYNAMIC CONTEXTS

This chapter defines a framework to formulate technology strategy in dynamic competitive contexts. In the previous chapter, there have been identified the basic principles and key characteristics of technology strategy formulation in dynamic environments.

An overall picture which more precisely illustrates the process of technology strategy in dynamic contexts is reported in Figure 3.1. Decisions are taken on the basis of information gathered on the future shape of competition and industries, the forecast technological progress and the evolution of the external and internal context of the firm. This information gathering provides the base for future scenarios which, in turn, are at the basis of strategy formulation. This phase is called *context foresight* and provides key inputs to the phase of decision taking. The key categories of decision in technology strategy (identified in the previous chapter) are *selection*, *timing* and *acquisition mode*.

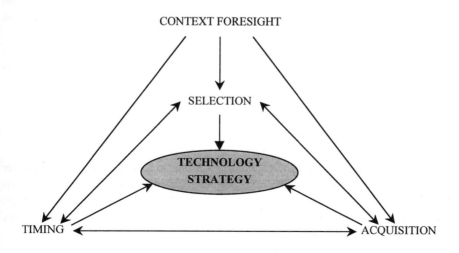

Figure 3.1. The dimensions of technology strategy.

Figure 3.1 emphasises that the decisions have to be considered jointly. The decision about the selection of the technologies on which to invest can not be kept separated from the mode of acquisition and the timing of technology development and introduction.

These three dimensions influence each other. Both the time length of technology development and the mode of acquisition influence the learning process about a new technology; therefore, they influence the effectiveness of strategy and should be taken into account in the phase of technology selection. For example, technology development programs with the same objectives and different time span (and, therefore, different level of investments) may result into different learning effects (slower programs facilitate more progressive and continuous processes of learning). The mode of acquisition affects the appropriation of the results of a certain development program and their exploitation potential. Moreover, as easily arguable, mode of acquisition and timing influence each other.

The output of the technology strategy is the definition of the long term technology policy of the firm. This is defined in broad action programs which identify the technologies to invest on (selection), fix the timing of new technology introduction and therefore when to start investing on the technologies selected (timing), define the acquisition policies of the technologies selected (acquisition). Of course, the long term technology policy should be generated having in mind the order of magnitude of the amount to be invested. Then, it follows a detailed yearly action program, which articulates strategy into projects (this will be treated in the next chapter).

In the following sections, the building blocks of the above framework (Figure 3.1) are analysed and, especially, the variables affecting a firm's technological choices are identified and examined.

3.1   CONTEXT FORESIGHT

The context foresight is the process by which firms, analysing their inner and outer contexts, attempt to identify the key characteristics of future competition. This provides the starting point of the process of formulation of a technology strategy. The context foresight is the result of the combination of two analysis, the externally driven and the internally driven.

The context foresight process can therefore be outlined as in Figure 3.2.

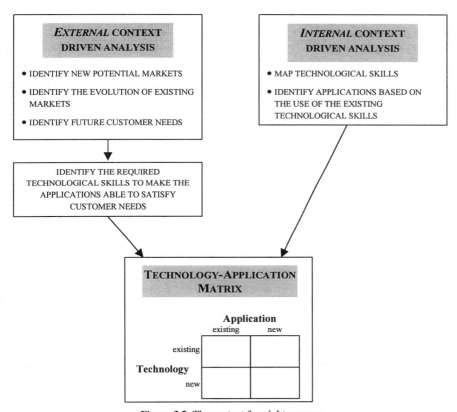

Figure 3.2. The context foresight process.

Externally Driven Context Analysis

This analysis sees market evolution and industry foresight as the drivers of the process of accumulation of the appropriate technological resources. It is articulated into two steps:

- the identification of the market shape and customer needs in the future and the related applications;
- the identification of the technologies required to make applications.

The first step is the identification of how markets will be shaped in the future and customer needs will evolve. The central factors are the value for the customer and the understanding of its evolution. The value for the customer is related with product functionality and critical performance. This functionally-based view of the product strongly differs from the view of the product taken in the traditional approaches to technology strategy. The product is seen as a transient technological solution to the satisfaction of customer benefits. Current technologies become just the components of the current dominant technological solution but they may not represent a reference for future solutions. The external analysis should therefore help understand the evolution of the dominant product paradigm able to satisfy customer benefits in the future. Benefits could concern not only the satisfaction of existing needs but also the creation or, to better say, the explicitation of latent or not articulated needs. Consumption patterns and consumer behaviours become a key input to the external analysis, helping identify the key future applications, fulfilling consumer needs. Of course, they can be both already existing applications and new applications.

Successively, there is the identification of the skills required to make the applications. This means to identify both technology needed to respond to future or not articulated customer needs and technology needed to meet current customers' needs which will evolve.

Internally Driven Context Analysis
This analysis is based on the view of technology as cognitive driver of strategy. It is again articulated into two steps:
-     the identification of the set of the technological skills available within the firm;
-     the identification of the applications which could be generated exploiting such skills.
Therefore, in this process, the starting point is the set of technological skills available within the firm. A first (not trivial) step of the process is the mapping of the firm's technological skills[a]. Then, efforts should be done to identify the applications (existing and new) which can be generated exploiting the technological skills available.

---

[a]   The use of the word technological skills rather than the simple word technologies wants to emphasise the nature of the inner context analysis. Such analysis should grasp the firm's potential in technology and how the firm's knowledge and know-how can be exploited. This often means to look at technologies not simply as solutions to fulfil a certain product function but as know-how. An example can clarify the difference. Laser technology is a technology and is used in a variety of applications. Using the laser technology develops a skills which is the ability to manage a beam in very limited spaces. Such skill can be used in other applications. For example it can be exploited to develop aligners to draw circuits on microchips, which is based on electron beam technologies (i.e. a different technology which exploits the same skill). In the rest of the book, for simplicity the word technology will be used; however, the meaning associated with it is the wider one of technological skill.

Box 3.1 - Techniques and practices supporting the external context analysis

Market forecasting. Market forecasting techniques help estimate the market potential of new applications and products. Marketing books provide wide reviews of techniques supporting market forecasting (see for example Kotler, 1997). The most common techniques concern: market characteristics determination, estimation of the market potential, market share analysis, sales analysis, industry development studies, competitors' products analysis, short term forecasting, acceptance and potential of new products, long term forecasting, price fixing studies.

Technology forecasting. Technology forecasting has been defined as the description or prediction of a foreseeable technological innovation, specific scientific refinement or likely scientific discovery, that promises to serve some useful function with some indication of the most probable time of occurrence. As mentioned in section 2.1.3, the technological progress follows an S-curve pattern (Figure 2.9). The main element to foresee is the timing of the progress. This is the main objective of forecasting techniques. Technology forecasting techniques are divided into three main categories: qualitative methods, quantitative and time forecasting methods, probability forecasting methods. Twiss provides a brief description of the techniques in each category:

- qualitative methods include creativity spurring methods (brainstorming, synetics, lateral thinking), time independent contextual mapping, analogies, morphological analysis, gap analysis, environmental surveillance and monitoring, scenarios;
- quantitative and time forecasting methods include attribute and parameter identification, time series (growth and logistic curves), envelop curves, precursor events and curves, substitution curves, relevance trees, quantified analogies, trend impact analogies, dynamic modelling;
- probability forecasting methods include Delphi techniques, cross-impact analysis, gaming methods.

Training. The participation to training programmes and courses is a source of information about technological progress.

Reverse engineering. It is the disassembly and systematic analysis of the components of the competitors' product conducted with the end of learning how competitors design and produce their products. It is often the basis for imitation processes which can be accompanied by the introduction of improvements of the competitors' products.

Monitoring lead users and key customers (market knowledge acquisition). Customers and users play a key role for innova-
(follows)

tion in a variety of industries. The work of Von Hippel (1988) emphasises this factor. Firms need to establish close and permanent relationships with their key customers and lead users which are often a major source of knowledge and ideas for technological innovation.

Technology scouting. Small units can be established simply to monitor the technological progress in a certain geographical area or at a certain technological centre. These units are often called listening posts or scanning units. They do not carry out technology development activities. They 'listen' to what happens outside and monitor technology evolution. Sometimes, the scouting is the task of one individual who is sent to work to technological centres (for example universities, research centres, etc.), where he/she takes part to certain projects. He/she mainly looks at what happens there in terms of technology development. Technology scouting is often a reason to locate units in foreign countries. This topic will be dealt with in chapter 6 on internationalisation of the R&D organisation.

Monitoring competitors. Another activity is that of monitoring competitors which has obvious difficulties. Large firms have often intelligence units dedicated to the monitoring of competitors' activities; for example, they systematically analyse journals, publications, announcements, publicity, advertising and all sources where information about competitors can be captured.

Monitoring suppliers. Suppliers represent a significant source of information about technology and themselves can be source of innovation. They can also provide information about competitors. Therefore, firms need to establish close relationships with suppliers.

Monitoring external technological resources. Especially when a certain technological area is not covered internally, a systematic monitoring of the resources available and accessible externally has to be done. Again, small units or few individuals can be assigned this task. Technological collaborations can also be undertaken with the objective of monitoring technological development at external sites (customers, suppliers, firms from other industries, etc.).

Networking. A major source of information in technology is networking. The scientific and technical community is something different from the business community; technical people often feel to be part of the former rather than the latter. Establishing and maintaining a network of relationship help capture information about technological progress. This is the result of informal meetings, attendance to conferences, reciprocal visits.

Box 3.2 - Techniques and practices supporting the internal context analysis

Technological capability audit – Benchmarking competitors and other firms on technology development resources. The evaluation of the internal technological capabilities is usually conducted through a comparison with major competitors on several dimensions. Traditionally these dimensions were aimed to define the appropriateness of the R&D resources relatively to competitors:

- the level of R&D expenditure;
- the quality of human resources employed in technology development activities;
- the breadth and depth of the technological knowledge available;
- the level of the equipment used in the R&D activity.

More recently, the process approach has been considered for a comprehensive technological audit (see section 1.2.2). Benchmarking consists of comparisons among competitors on specific dimensions in order to identify best practices in use. Therefore, great attention is paid to the process of technological innovation and practices in use to manage such process. The rational behind this is that not only the amount and quality of resources are important for innovation but also how they are used and how the underlying processes are shaped.

In their innovative capability audit framework, Burgelman et al. (1988) underline that both technological and functional capabilities should be audited and both formulation and implementation of innovation strategies addressed together with supportive organisational mechanisms. In their framework, they include five main dimensions:

- resource availability and allocation (level of R&D funding, breadth and depth of skills, distinctive competencies, allocation of R&D resources);
- understanding competitors' innovative strategies and industry evolution;
- understanding the technological environment;
- structural and cultural context (managing R&D projects, transferring them from R&D to manufacturing, integrating functional groups);
- strategic management capacity to deal with entrepreneurial behaviour.

Adler et al. (1992) have argued that technical functions need a way to benchmark not only their products but also their strategic management process. They provide a framework to assess the overall functional strategies of technical units. They set out three main elements of strategic management:

- direction setting (mission, objectives, strategic plan),
- policies,
- adjustment mechanisms (assessment of strengths and weaknesses, opportunities and threats).

(follows)

Within the policies they analyse the role of:
- processes (personnel management, technical project management, quality assurance management);
- resources (intellectual property, funding, facilities and equipment);
- linkages (structure, interfunctional linkages, external linkages, regulatory compliance).

They give a number of examples of successful innovative companies and associated with them the practices adopted.

At London Business School a research group developed a comprehensive benchmarking framework to audit a firm's technological capabilities (Chiesa et al., 1996). The benchmarking framework is based on the innovation model mentioned in chapter 1. The model views innovation as a process which includes four core processes (new product concept generation, technology acquisition, product development, production process innovation) and three support processes (leadership, resourcing, systems and tools). Each core and support process is then articulated into sub-processes (see table 1.2) on which a benchmarking exercise can be conducted. The framework can also be used to self assess the firm's capabilities in technology management and is built to carry out a performance audit too. In each process they have been identified metrics to measure its performance and evaluate the improvement over time. The framework has been used in a survey on the British manufacturing industry, and, later, on the Irish and the Australian manufacturing industries.

Knowledge management system (learning processes). Each learning process can contribute to the inner and outer context foresight. Learning can take place in a variety of forms: by doing, by using, by failing, by studying (Pavitt, 1991). Each system helping structure the knowledge accumulated during such processes of learning and make later use of it are actually instruments supporting the internal context foresight.

At the end of the two analyses, a matrix can be built, including:
- applications both existing and new;
- technologies both existing and new.

New is intended as new for the firm. The technology-application matrix (Figure 3.3) is the basis for taking decisions (Klein and Hiscoks, 1994).

The context foresight process can be done with the support of a variety of instruments and mechanisms aimed to grasp the appropriate information on both the external and the internal context. It is not the aim of this book to go in depth into these tools, as each would require a specific and dedicated analysis. A brief description of the objective, content and range of application of common instruments and tools are reported in the boxes 3.1 and 3.2.

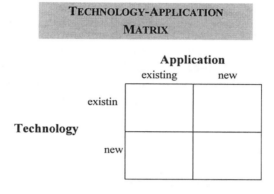

Figure 3.3. Technology-application matrix.

3.2 TECHNOLOGY STRATEGY DECISIONS

Once analysed the context and defined the matrix of existing and new (for the firm) applications and technological skills, which represent the unit of analysis of the strategic planning process, decisions need to be taken. As clarified above, the key decisions concern the selection of the technologies on which to invest, the timing of introduction of such technologies, and the acquisition mode.

Each dimension is now analysed in depth, putting into evidence the factors which influence the choice. Initially, the selection of the technologies on which to invest is analysed and then the timing and the acquisition mode.

3.2.1 Technology Selection

A first key decision is the selection of the technologies, i.e. the choice of the technologies on which to invest. The selection is affected by the following variables:

-    relevance of the technology;
-    risk associated with the development and application of the technology;

- appropriability;
- interdependencies with other technologies;
- option creation.

Relevance

The relevance of a technology addresses the extent to which the technology is able to create customer value. A technology is not good per se. Its value is measured by the extent to which it can be used in applications the firm can commercialise and the extent to which it contributes to satisfy customer needs. Therefore, the relevance of a technology, in turn, can be seen as the result of different factors:

- market potential;
- applicability;
- customer value creation.

Market potential. A first obvious factor influencing the relevance of a technology is the market potential of the applications in which the technology is used. This in turn depends on the market size and the firm's market share in each application market. Moreover, the market potential often depends on the timing of introduction. In other words, the size of the potential market depends on the ability to capture the window of opportunity and, therefore, is influenced by the time when the technology is commercialised. However, it should be noted that often the formulation of the long term technology policy occurs years before the market takes place and shape and, therefore, it is very difficult to understand how the timing will affect the market potential. Therefore, in this phase the market size and the potential market share are often the only variables which can be foreseen, supporting the estimation of the market potential.

Applicability. This factor concerns the range of applications in which the technology can be used. The value of a technology is related with the number of different applications in which it can be embodied. The variety of applications is a concept widely stressed in the resource-based literature and successful firms are often those able to control technologies leading to a variety of applications. Well known examples are Intel in semiconductor technology, Honda in engine technology, Casio in liquid crystal display technology.

Customer value creation. This factor concerns the contribution of the technology to the creation of customer value. In other words, it is related to the extent to which the technology is critical to fulfil the key product functions. The concept, already quoted, of core product is relevant to this end. It is the product part or component where the value for the customer is generated (the engine in a car, the cartridge in a laser printer or a copier machine, the chip and the software of a personal computer). The estimation of the customer value creation is of course qualitative. It relies upon the analysis of the key functional performance of the product and the identification of the technologies contributing to fulfil the required performance.

Risk

Another key selection criteria is the risk associated with the development of a certain technology. The dimensions of risk are three: technical, commercial, financial.

Technical risk. It is the risk that the technology does not achieve the desired level of performance and/or the development program does not end by the time required. The technical risk essentially depends on: (i) the firm's technological capabilities (internally available or externally accessed) in the concerned technology, and (ii) the 'distance' of the level of performance required from the state of the art. Therefore, the evaluation of the technical risk strongly lies upon the analysis of the firm's capability in that technology (in absolute terms and in comparison with other relevant firms). The evaluation of the technical risk is therefore supported by the techniques described to audit and benchmark the firm's technological inner context (Box 3.2).

Commercial risk. It relates to the risk that the associated applications in which the technology is embodied will fail on the market or will have a low economic return. Failures may occur because the market reveals much smaller than expected or not existing at all. In other cases, failures are due to the actions of competitors or other firms providing substituting products which strongly reduce the firm's market share (for example, a competitor is able to market its new product earlier than expected and acquire large market shares).

Financial risk. The financial risk relates to the amount to be spent to develop the technology and to bring the related innovation(s) to the market. As a matter of fact, an innovation can require an amount so great that the failure of the innovation itself could cause strong financial difficulties or the failure of the firm as a whole. The amount required concerns both the investment to be done to develop the technologies, and the investment to exploit the new finding and introduce it onto the market appropriately (manufacturing, marketing, after-sale services). The latter factor, which is identified as the complementary assets of an innovation, is often neglected. However, on the average, the cost of commercialisation of a new technology usually covers the seven tenths of the whole cost of a technological innovation, whereas the development of the technology covers the three tenths. Therefore, firms may undertake projects which are very promising and interesting from a technological point of view, but which requires huge investments (relatively to the firm's financial capabilities) in the commercialisation phase. If not aware, a firm can therefore be forced to stop good technological projects given that the exploitation phase can not be sustained. If aware of this, a firm can undertake projects of which the exploitation phase can not be sustained, with the clear objective (from the beginning) that, if successful, the technology will be sold, making business from selling the technology/know-how acquired.

Appropriability

This criterion reflects the extent to which the technical knowledge base which is behind the new applications can be protected against imitators. The degree of appropriability is the function of the firm's relative strength to competitors and the capability/opportunity to protect the firm's technical knowledge base against imitators. Means to protect the technical knowledge against imitators have been identified by Tidd et al. (1997). Here a summary is reported.

Secrecy. It is a form of protection especially in process innovations. Although information can be obtained from products and there is an inevitable leakage of know-how through a variety of channels (technical community, suppliers, etc.), firms can keep their innovation highly appropriable through secrecy. Michelin for example does not open its plants to anyone external to the firm and succeeds in keeping its own process innovations secret.

Accumulated tacit knowledge. If a firm's technical knowledge is strongly embodied into people and technical systems, relies upon the experience, and the knowledge accumulated in years is not explicit, the related technological innovations can result highly appropriable. The well known case of Italian small firms, often world leaders in niche markets and traditional manufacturing industries, is largely based on the accumulation of tacit knowledge. In very concentrated geographical areas (districts), there are networks of small firms which are strongly specialised in highly specific manufactures. Knowledge is, to a large extent, embedded in people living in that area.

Lead times and after-sale service. The ability of generating and putting new products on the markets quickly is a major source of protection against imitation. It helps establish brand loyalty and credibility, accelerate feedback from customer use, accelerate learning effects and consequently increase cost of entry for imitators. Intel bases its leadership on the ability to frequently provide new generations of products.

Learning curve. The cumulation of production also allows to accumulate knowledge which is tacit to large extent, and, therefore, is the basis to appropriate innovations. Learning curve advantages mainly refer to savings in production, thanks to fewer scraps, shorter idle times, incremental innovations. Such cumulative learning effect allows firms to exploit their innovations and stay ahead of competitors.

Complementary assets. The commercialisation of an innovation often depends on the availability of assets or competencies, such as production capabilities, marketing, distribution, after-sale service, which are complementary to the technological capabilities (Teece, 1986). These complementary assets are often determinants of the exploitation of an innovation and of the appropriation of the related benefits. On the other hand, they are often the reason of failures of the innovators, who, once generated the technological innovation, do not have the required complementary assets to exploit it or find themselves to spend large amounts to acquire them. Both these conditions may prevent the innovator from making profits from innovation. J&M Airframes, an aerospace manufacturer, reacted to the decline of the demand in the military market, moving to the civil market. The technological resources and capabilities required were the same. However, the firm had to strongly invest to acquire the capabilities necessary to survive in the civil market, such as increasing the variety of products produced and managing different customers. Also internally, the organisation was radically changed, innovating the planning and control systems and modifying the incentive system for employees.

Product complexity. In some sectors, the product complexity is a major barrier against imitators. The large electromechanical equipment industry or the aircraft industry are typical examples.

Standards. The acceptance of a firm's standard on a large basis opens the market and raises barriers against competitors. This is especially true in network markets, where the compatibility of a system with the others is a pre-requisite for the product success. Computing, telecommunication, consumer electronics industries show series of examples in which standard setting is a key factor to appropriate benefits from innovation.

Pioneering radical new products. If an innovation is radically new, i.e. represents a strong discontinuity with the existing products/processes/services and lies upon a base of knowledge which is completely different from that behind traditional products, the innovating firm is more protected against imitation. Potential imitators can not rely on the existing knowledge base to replicate the innovation. Michelin was the first to introduce truck tyres of which the structure was made of steel cord rather than textile fibres. It was a radically new product and the newness of the innovation prevented from imitation for decades.

Strength of patent protection. Patenting is also a major means to protect innovations. This is especially true in some sectors, chemical and pharmaceutical for example, where products can be clearly and rigorously described (often with a structural formula) and imitation by small differences is not easy as in most industries.

Interdependencies

Another factor is that of interdependencies between technologies. The value of a technology can be higher if other technologies are available. Therefore, this factor should be considered when technologies are selected. Actually, a mode of innovation is the technology fusion where innovations come from the combination of different technologies rather than from breakthroughs in specific technological areas. This means that firms can identify cluster of technologies which once put together are able to generate a variety of applications. Such integration knowledge can also result difficult to imitate as it concerns the blending of different technological disciplines. Canon's success is based upon the integration of precision mechanics, optics, and microelectronics, Nec's on the integration of computer and communication technologies. Japanese machine tool manufacturers were the first to introduce mechatronic solutions which were based on the use of components combining electronic and mechanical technologies. Such interdependencies can be of two kinds: technical and commercial. The technological dependencies concern the interrelations among the technical developments of different technologies. The success of the development of a technology depends on the availability of another technology. The commercial dependencies concern the fact that the success of a technology on the market (relevance) depends on the availability of another technology even if independent from a technical point of view (e.g. the relevance of the flat screen display in the hand-held telephone device is linked to the contemporary possession of the battery technology as nobody buys a mobile telephone with a wonderful screen but short talk time).

Option Creation

A further element affecting the technological choices is the option creation effects. Technologies can be of low value as they may not lead to marketable applications. However, the technical knowledge accumulated investing on them can allow to start a new technological trajectory, accelerate learning in certain technological disciplines, increase the ability to value external sources of knowledge in that technology, throw the seed for further technological developments. Early investments in communication technologies enabled computer firms to integrate the two areas and generate new equipment. Given the dynamic nature of competition and the importance of time, it is clear that early creation of options opens opportunities as it accelerates the accumulation of knowledge in a certain discipline.

3.2.2 Timing of Technology Development and Introduction

The importance of timing in new technology introduction is increasingly high. Competition is often based on time especially in high technology industries and therefore the ability to introduce new technologies at the right time is central. However, the role of time needs to be analysed in depth as traditional assumptions may be misleading. The traditional view of timing in innovation has been limited to the distinction between leaders and followers where followers include a variety of behaviours (see § 2.1).

The factors mentioned in § 2.1 (Porter, 1985) at the basis of the advantages of leaders and followers are of course still sound and to be taken into account in the choice of timing. They are reported and commented more extensively in Box 3.3.

Box 3.3 - First mover advantages and disadvantages

First mover advantages

First mover advantages are related to:

- reputation: a significant effect of a leadership strategy is creating a reputation as a pioneer in a certain business. It is an action which often requires marketing resources to be widely advertised. JVC recently advertises its products reminding to be the firm which introduced the VHS system in video-recording;
- positioning: first movers can position itself within the business, forcing competitors to other less favourable positions;
- switching costs: first mover can take advantages when there are high switching costs for the customers;
- selection of the distribution channel: first mover can select the most appropriate distribution channels or acquire the exclusive access to them;
- learning curve: first mover starts learning curve in advance and can advantages on this;
- access to input resources: first mover can take advantage from the access to scarce input resources;
- standard definition: first mover can set the industry standard;
- institutional barriers: first movers can raise institutional barriers against imitators such as patent policies, privileged relationships with governmental bodies, etc.;
- initial profits: in early phases of a product life prices can be high as products are scarce and high profits can be made.

First mover disadvantages

First mover have to bear disadvantages, which, of course, in turn can be seen as advantages of followers. They are related to:

- pioneering costs: pioneers have to sustain costs related to a variety of factors, such as the approval of governmental bodies, customer training, development of infrastructure, development of the required inputs if not available;
- facing uncertain market demand;
- changes in customers' needs: if customer needs change, first movers can be associated with the old technology;
- specific investments: first movers have to sustain investments specific to the new product/process which can not be easily converted to other uses;
- echnological discontinuities: if there are strong technological discontinuities, the position of pioneers may be attacked by competition of followers, whereas if the technological evolution is more continuous and gradual, pioneers can take advantage;
- imitation at low cost: pioneers have to face the competition of imitators at low cost.

Source: adapted from Porter (1985)

Such trade-offs between leadership and followership should be seen in the light of the dynamic character of competition which stresses two further aspects:
- the role of time as a competitive weapon (time based competition);
- the relation between time and learning.

Time Based Competition - Window of Opportunity

The usual distinction between *leadership* and *followership* becomes weaker and weaker. Competing on time means that there is a restriction of the *window of opportunity* useful to exploit an innovation, and this does not allow followers to invest much less in technology than leaders. Delays in new product commercialisation prevent from capturing large part of the profits (the average window of time to exploit an innovation in the electronic and computing industry is often less than one year). In the competitive environments with strong turbulence and rapid change as those of high technology industries, pioneering technological innovation has often become the key to control market dynamics and be successful. Otherwise, the fast followership is still pursuable, although it often requires amount and level of resources as much large and high-quality as leaders. In any case, late entry strategies can be followed even more seldom.

Time Compression Diseconomies (Relation between Time and Learning)

Technology development programs can be crashed to shorten duration. However, this can impact on the effectiveness of the learning processes during the project. Dierickx and Cool (1989) define this factor time compression diseconomies. If the time spent to develop a certain technology is shortened, the underlying learning may be less effective than in project achieving the same objective but longer. Short term results of the project may be the same but in the long term the program effects can be worse.

Moreover, it should be considered that when timing choices are considered, two different decisions are actually involved:
- the decision about the optimal time of development of a technology;
- the decision about the optimal time of introduction of a new technology.

The two decisions are obviously related each other as the minimum timing of introduction is constrained by the minimum time spent to develop a technology. However, it is not obvious that as soon as a technology is available and can be marketed it is actually commercialised.

The following factors provide explanations why the timing of introduction can differ from the time at which the product is available.

Time and Profitability Profile

A key factor affecting the choice of the timing of introduction is the requirement of the firm in terms of profitability over time. The introduction of new technologies can be accelerated or postponed in relation to that. New product introduction can be seen as a means to fill in the gap existing between the required profits and the total expected profit from the existing products (Figure 3.4). The firms can plan the introduction of new products when more appropriate to cover the gap. Of course, this depends on the degree of market control on the market and the actual possibility to postpone or accelerate the introduction without profit loss.

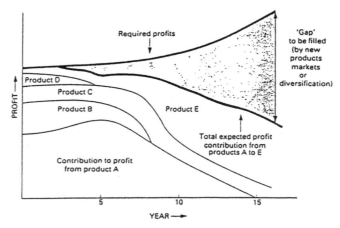

Figure 3.4. Profitability profile and new technology introduction (Source: Twiss, 1986).

Cannibalisation

A firm may delay the introduction of a new technology as this would erode the profits which could still be obtained from the commercialisation of old products. The erosion of the firm's own potential profits from old products with the introduction of new product is known as cannibalisation. Matsushita have reduced the rate of introduction of new product in the electrical equipment and white goods market as this eroded profits of earlier generation products.

Acceleration Trap

The time-based competition can lead to the so called acceleration trap. Von Braun (1997) has profoundly analysed the effect of an exaggerated time-based competition. If the speed at which the firm substitutes its products continuously accelerates, there is a point at which such speed can be no more increased (natural limit). When the firm starts to substitute its products at a rate constant over time, there is a decrease of sales and profits at a level which is equal to or below the level of sales when the acceleration started. It is equal if the cumulated volume of sales of each new product is constant (the area under the curve) although the life cycle gets shorter and shorter; it is below the initial level of sales, if the sales of the new products decline as life cycles get shorter. The overall result is given by the fact that the acceleration effect is essentially that of anticipating profits and sales. Therefore, firms could decide to decrease the rate of substitution to avoid too rapid decrease of sales and profits. The acceleration trap appears when firms introduce products which are close substitute of each other. The acceleration trap is avoided when the new product introduced is not the substitute of an existing one. Therefore, the rate of introduction of new product does not lead to this effect if the firm is able to continuously diversify.

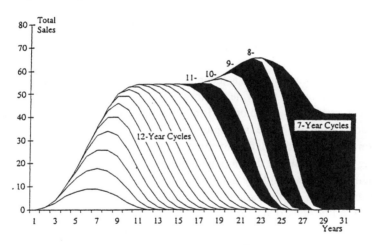

Figure 3.5. The acceleration trap (Source: Von Braun, 1997).

Standard Setting

The need to set standards in certain industries (especially the so called network markets) may strongly affect the timing of new product introduction. In the past, the establishment of a *standard de facto* was often the result of market fights with very bad consequences for losers. A well known example is that of VHS (of JVC-Matsushita) and Betamax (of Sony) in video recording. More recently, to avoid the risk of heavy losses, firms tend to find an agreement which leads to define and set standards before the introduction of the product on the market. This may occur during or at the end of the development of the new technology.

This may delay the introduction of new products on the market. An example is that of DVD of which the introduction is delayed as Philips and Toshiba (who are the leading technological companies) do not find an agreement on the standard to introduce.

Availability of Complementary Assets

The non availability of complementary assets by the innovator can be a reason to delay the introduction of a new technology. The innovating firm is forced to acquire such assets and therefore to postpone the introduction of the new technology. Otherwise, it can sell its innovation which is commercialised by other firms, or it can commercialise the product jointly with a firm which provides the required complementary asset.

3.2.3   Technology Acquisition Mode

The third critical dimension of a technology strategy is the mode of technology acquisition, which means to define whether to develop technologies through internal development, cooperating with other firms or institutions, or buying the technology. This section deals with the strategic factors affecting a firm's choice of the acquisition mode and the relation of this with the selection of the technologies and the timing of technology development and introduction. The selection of the appropriate form of technology acquisition and the organisational implications of the different modes of technology acquisition from external sources are deeper treated later in this book (Chapter 7).

When technology acquisition is considered, actually, a distinction should be made between technology development and technology introduction. In the phase of technology development, external sources can be accessed to acquire the required technological competencies. In the phase of technology introduction the decision concerns whether to acquire the resources necessary to commercialise a technology. Whereas in technology development the decision concerns whether to develop the technology internally, to cooperate or to buy the technology from external sources, in the phase of technology introduction the decision concerns whether to resort on internal resources, to cooperate with other firms to access the required resources or to sell technology. Therefore, although there may be inter-relations between the two decisions, there are factors which are relevant to the development activity and others which are relevant to the introduction phase. The two topics are here treated separately.

Acquisition of Technology from External Sources (Make vs. Buy vs. Cooperate)

In technology development, the following variables affect the decision about whether to develop internally, cooperate or buy.

Availability and Level of External Sources

A first obvious factor and a pre-requisite for the external acquisition of technology is the availability and the quality of the external sources of the concerned technology. Especially, if the results the firm is aimed to achieve are already available elsewhere and can be acquired, it looks rather obvious to avoid a strain on the firm's funds and access such findings.

Time

The mode of acquisition strongly affects the time spent to develop a technology. The external acquisition usually shorten the development time. Purchasing the technology is the quickest form of acquisition. In general, cooperative development is shorter than internal development. However, the lesser time spent to develop the technology can be consumed by the time spent to set up the cooperation agreement. The more formalised and integrated the organisational form of collaboration, the longer set up time (see chapter 7 for a discussion about set up time in technological collaboration). Moreover, the ability to exploit effectively and quickly the technology acquired externally depends on the capability available internally on that technology. The lesser defined and more fuzzy object and organisation of the collaboration, the higher internal capability required to effectively exploit the result of the collaboration in a short time.

Appropriability

External acquisition of technology affects the appropriation of the benefits from innovation. Collaborating may lower the appropriability of the technology as it means to share the results of the technological innovation activity. Internal development ensures there is higher appropriability.

Learning Acceleration

Accessing external sources of technology is a major means to learn and quickly accumulate knowledge. The learning effect of a collaboration strongly depends on the firm's approach to the technological collaboration. Hamel (1991) emphasised that firms may approach collaborations with primary objectives of learning or with primary objectives of obtaining financial returns from the collaboration. The former approach allows higher appropriability of collaboration results. This factor has of course to be taken into account in the selection of the partner, as there are firms who are well known to be able to deeply learn from other firms during collaborations.

Costs

Costs of technology acquisition usually decreases if the acquisition takes place accessing external sources. The sharing of resources among partners reduces development costs. However, this reduction may be significantly lower than expected if the time (and therefore the resources) spent to set up the collaboration is long. The cost of buying a technology may strongly vary, depending on the contractual power and the type of contract (exclusiveness, property rights, etc.) .

Technical Risk and Familiarity with Technology

Cooperation during the development phase of a new technology allows a firm to share the technical risk with partners. The risk relates to the capability available internally. The lesser adequate resources available internally, the higher technical risk. Therefore, a firm is forced to cooperate rather than develop a technology internally because of limited or no familiarity with the technology concerned. Firms tend to develop a technology internally if familiar with it. On the other hand, cooperate can be simply a means to increase the amount of resources to allocate to a certain development project. Enlarging the amount of resources reduces the technical risk of the project. Buying a technology eliminate the risk of technology development.

Table 3.1 summarises the factors affecting the decision about make, cooperate or buy in the development of a technology (three stars identify the most appropriate choice to meet the objective, one star the least appropriate).

Table 3.1. Factors affecting the decision about the acquisition mode in technology development.

	Acquisition modes		
Factors	MAKE	COOPERATE	BUY
Development time	*	**	***
Appropriability	***	**	*
Learning	**	***	*
Development costs	*	**	?
Technical risk and familiarity	*	**	***

Acquisition of Resources for Technology Introduction (Make vs. Sell vs. Cooperate)

In technology introduction, the key decision concerns whether to ally in the new technology introduction or not. A further alternative is to sell the technology. The following are the most important factors affecting such decision.

Availability of Complementary Assets

Firms can be forced to collaborate in the phase of technology introduction as they lack assets complementary to the innovation. If they lack production, distribution, after-sale service capabilities they may choose to cooperate in the commercialisation phase of a technology. Often the collaboration between small and large firms is based on such exchange. Small firms develop innovations they are not able to exploit and commercialise, and large firms provide the required complementary assets.

Commercial Risk and Familiarity with Market

Relying on external resources can be a major means to share risk with other firms in the commercialisation of a new technology. Accessing manufacturing capacities, distribution channels, after-sale service networks of other firms allows to share the risk of commercial failure. The commercial risk can be high because the market knowledge available internally is low. As a matter of fact, the market knowledge is as much important as technical knowledge in innovation. If the innovation process leads to products/services and the firm is not familiar with the markets of such products/services, the innovating firm can choose to cooperate in the introduction of the new technology. It offers its partner the technological finding to commercialise and accesses the market knowledge of the partner.

Standard Setting

Another factor affecting the decision about whether to cooperate or not in the introduction of a new technology is the standard setting process. Introducing compatible products may mean to accelerate the market growth. Therefore, firms may be forced to collaborate to facilitate the adoption of their product as standard and favour the taking off of the market. These collaborations may involve agreements related purely to the commercialisation of the new technology: OEM agreements, licensing, distribution agreements.

Sometimes, collaborations of such kind may also involve joint technological collaboration activity and not only collaboration purely in the introduction of a new technology. However, usually firms who decide to collaborate are well ahead in the development of a certain product and start cooperate when they realise that their timing of introduction would be similar. In this case they may decide to join their efforts, define a shared standard and introduce it into the market rather than take the risk of a standard war once products have been introduced (which would mean significant losses in case of defeat).

If the firm is not able to commercialise the technology on its own or to find partners with whom to share the introduction of the new technology on the market, a further alternative is to sell the technology. Selling a technology can be appropriate when:

- it is financially the most valuable strategy. Selling can be done in a variety of ways. For example, it may occur that revenues of the acquiring company are linked to royalty payments;
- the commercialisation of the technology would mean to enter a new business area which is not considered a future core business for the firm;
- it is a means to access the required distribution capabilities. It may occur that a firm sells a technology to another firm who embodies the technology as part of it own product but has not and can not get the control of this technology. This is a way to access the distribution capabilities of the acquiring firm and therefore the market. The cartridge technology in laser printers and copiers has been diffused by Canon through licensing its technology to Apple and HP.

3.2.4   Formulating the Firm's Technology Strategy: the Output

The output of the strategic technology planning process consists of three elements:
- the identification of the technologies on which to invest;

- the identification of the window of opportunity for each selected technology to be effectively exploited (which determines the latest time when to start the development program of that technology);
- the definition of the mode how technologies are developed, i.e. the broad indication of the mode of acquisition (whether internally developed or through accessing external sources).

Although treated separately and in such order, the three decisions are strongly interrelated each other, as mentioned above. Figure 3.6 shows the major inter-relations between the three decisions which should be seen as three dimensions of one decision, which is the definition of the firm's long term technology policy.

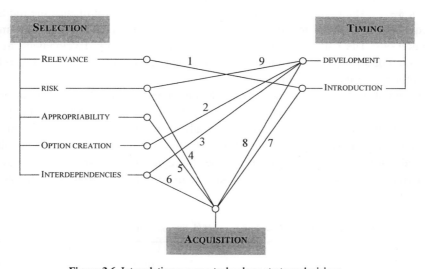

Figure 3.6. Interrelations among technology strategy decisions.

Different links can be identified between the three dimensions of a technology strategy:

Link 1 -   The relevance of a technology is strongly inter-related to its timing of introduction as the timing affects the market potential of that new technology;

Link 2 -   The timing of development is influenced by the presence of interdependencies among technologies, as different technologies may need to be available at the same time;

Link 3 -   If a technology creates options for future opportunities, the required development time can be affected by the time by which future technologies need to be available;

Link 4 -   The risk associated with a technology is affected by the mode of acquisition, as collaborative forms of development allow to share risk;

Link 5 -   The appropriability of a technology is affected by the mode of acquisition, as internal development ensures that there is higher appropriability than external acquisition forms;

Link 6 -   The presence of interdependencies may affect the mode of acquisition. For example, if the value is in the integration of different technologies, the acquisition of each individual technology can be external whereas the integration activities are kept internal;

Link 7 -   The timing of introduction of a technology can influence the mode of acquisition, as it has to rely upon external resources;

Link 8 -   The timing of new technology development can influence the mode of acquisition as external acquisition may be chosen to shorten the development time;

Link 9 -   The risk is affected by the timing of technology development, as the duration of a program of technology development impacts on learning and therefore on program effectiveness and results.

The output of the strategic technology planning process is the formulation of broad action programs which define the technologies on which to invest, the timing, i.e. the time when technologies should be ready to be effectively exploited and the acquisition policy. At this stage, also the policy concerning the new technology introduction should be examined, whether through internal resources or accessing external resources. A table like 3.2 should be filled in as the output of such stage of the R&D strategy process.

Table 3.2. Broad action programs (technology selected, timing, acquisition mode).

TECHNOLOGIES SELECTED	TIMING	ACQUISITION MODE (in both technology development and introduction)

The technology strategy conceived can be outlined on the technology-application matrix. The next section describes five types of technology strategies on the basis of their positioning on the technology application matrix.

3.3   TYPES OF TECHNOLOGY STRATEGIES

The types of technology strategies can be identified on the technology/applications matrix. Five major categories of technology strategies can be identified: *competence deepening, competence fertilising, competence refreshing, competence comple-menting* and *competence destroying* (Figure 3.7). The content and the meaning of these strategies are described below. Each strategy addresses a mode of acquisition which seems appropriate (Table 3.3).

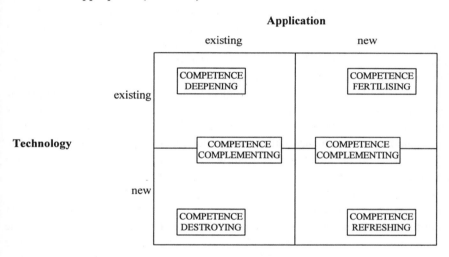

Figure 3.7. Types of technology strategy.

Competence   deepening.   Such   strategy   means   investing   on   the technology/applications which are fundamental to the firm's current strategy. Concentrating investments on them would mean to found a firm's technology strategy on the deepening of the current base of knowledge and reinforce a firm's current technology base. This strategy is feasible if the existing skills are likely to remain highly appropriable, and are already widely applied. The critical element is how long they will remain   appropriable. Undertaking such strategy means to strongly rely on the current critical technologies and on maintaining the knowledge gap with respect to competitors. A risk associated with such strategy is to keep the technical knowledge base too limited.

As far as the mode of acquisition is concerned, it should be taken into account that these technologies are already part of the firm's competence. There is a wide and diffused tacit knowledge throughout the organisation, and advantages on competitors are expected to come from the firm's capability to improve the performance of the current applications. In this strategy, the most appropriate mode of acquisition is in-house R&D.

Competence fertilising. Competence fertilising actions concern technologies already available within the firm which show strong potential to create new applications. The development of these new applications could provide cross-fertilisation effects with the existing applications, as they use the same technological base. Problems may raise on the commercialisation side, depending on the degree of familiarity of the firm with the markets of the new applications. In technological terms, investing on these technologies would mean to strongly reinforce the current competence base through providing a wider range of opportunities associated with it. Again this strategy is feasible if the current technological base is likely to remain appropriable in the future. It is advisable when the range of application of the current technology base needs to be broadened. As far as the acquisition mode is concerned, again, as these technologies are already part of the technological knowledge base of the firm, they are likely to be developed and cultivated through internal R&D programs. Alliances or joint ventures may concern the commercialisation phase if the firm is weakly familiar with the markets for the new applications.

These remarks actually provide suggestions also for divestment decisions. Whether or not to divest from a certain activity should not be taken only on the basis of the financial results. A certain technological base can be source of new applications different from the existing ones. Therefore, before a firms divests from a certain business, which means also divesting from a certain technological base, the potential of exploitation of such technological base should be evaluated. An example is that of the VCR for Sony. Although Sony has been and is still not profitable in this business, the knowledge gained from staying in the VCR business and following the technological pace is critical to build the capabilities for future applications in the consumer electronics industry. Therefore, they keep on investing in this area.

Competence complementing. Investing on competence complementing technology/application combinations means to acquire new technologies to be integrated with the current set of technologies in order to open new market opportunities. This strategy underlies a key process to progressively shift the technological base from the current to a new one. As a matter of fact, it relies upon the integration of available technologies with new technologies to generate new applications or new modes of doing existing applications. The combination of new and existing technologies reduces the technological risk related to the applications. The use of the combination of such technologies for the development of existing applications reduces the associated commercial risk, as the firm is familiar with the related markets. Therefore, if correctly conceived and applied, this strategy helps change the firm's technological knowledge base gradually. Some acquired technologies become part of the future critical technology base and could be used in the future together with further new technologies to generate new applications and so on. In other words, investing on them means to make the first step to move to a new competence base. Of course in this case the new technology acquired should show a high degree of appropriability and wide application potential.

They can be conceived competence complementing actions which may have lower strategic impact. They can concern new technologies which are not expected to become part of the future critical technological base. They simply allow to open new application opportunities at the moment, leaving that the firm's advantage is still based on the current technology base. In other words, it may occur that the new technologies are simply acquired to generate new applications but are not part of the future technology base. In this case a high degree of appropriability of the new technology is not required.

An example of the latter kind is the current policy of NEC and Northern Telecom in areas such as software engineering, artificial intelligence and knowledge based systems through collaborations with Universities and research institutions.

An example of the first kind is that of Canon. Competence complementing investments are leading to the production of aligners for the laying out of Dram (Dynamic random access memory) chips. Aligners require that the current competence of the firm on laser beam technology and the related manufacturing skills are combined with new skills concerning X-ray technologies and electron beam technologies. The latter has been acquired through the acquisition of Lepton, a small company founded by researchers from the Bell Labs. The new competence resulting from the integration of the two should generate a series of profitable innovations in the future (applications in semiconductors, screens, TV sets, telecommunication equipment) and is a first step to enter the business of personal computers when the optoelectronic paradigm will replace the electronic one.

Therefore, the investment strategy may follow different patterns. In the first case, new skill and technological knowledge are acquired mostly from external sources through alliances, licences, etc. In the second case, also internal capabilities need to be built. A certain absorptive capacity is created to establish a base of knowledge internal to the firm in the field, and value the knowledge to be acquired from external sources. In turn, absorptive capacity can be created through acquisition of small firms or internal ventures.

Competence refreshing. Such investments are aimed to acquire new technologies which have the potential to generate a cluster of new applications in the future. Their potential to create a new technology base depends on the degree of appropriability associated with them. Undertaking competence refreshing may be highly risky as they involve the change of the technology base and concern new applications.

If this new technology base is highly promising, the mode of acquisition is that of acquiring companies that have developed know-how in that area. The aim may be that of creating an absorptive capacity to be able to understand how the technology will evolve and how it may contribute to build future competencies. In the case the technology base shows a strong potential but is still in an embryonic phase, internal ventures or venture capital investments could be appropriate in the initial phase. Internal R&D can be undertaken in later phases.

Competence destroying. The strategy conceived may also point out that certain technologies may erode the set of knowledge required for certain existing applications to be performed in the future. In other words the set of technologies required to operate certain businesses shifts and these new technologies are likely to prevail in the long term. If the firm recognises that there are no opportunities to shift its knowledge base to stay in the same application range, it needs to refresh its current technological base. The earlier the firm recognises that a competence destroying set of technologies is emerging, the earlier can attempt to refresh its competence. This process can be speeded up through alliances and joint ventures that reduce the cost of refreshing competence, but may also reduce the degree of appropriability. On the other hand, a firm can undertake competence destroying strategies aimed to build a new technology base and remain in the same application range. Conceptually competence refreshing and competence destroying actions do not differ. They both attempt to create a new technology base. The result is different, as competence destroying strategies lead to replace the existing base to realise the same set of applications, whereas competence refreshing strategies lead to create a new technology base but for new applications and therefore they do not lead to replace the existing one. Therefore, the first are risky as they replace the current set of competence without opening new opportunities and cannibalise the current set of skills. On the contrary, competence refreshing strategies may be risky if there is a limited familiarity with both technologies and markets for the new applications.

The technology-application matrix also helps define a long term technology strategy appropriate for dynamic environments. The central element of a resource-based approach is to define a strategy as a trajectory, which means that a continuity in technology actions should be found. This matrix helps identify the elements of continuity which could characterise the firm's behaviour over time. An appropriate cycle of action programs to be conceived at a given time is shown in Figure 3.8.

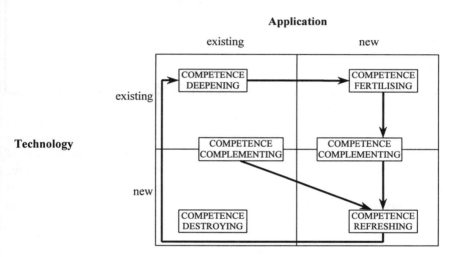

Figure 3.8. Technology strategy actions cycle.

Conceiving a trajectory means that at a given time a firm should conceive and define its long term program of actions and understand how they are related each other. It should start investing on competence deepening and fertilising strategies and accompany competence complementing strategies with them. Competence fertilising strategies nurture the current competence and help acquire familiarity with new application and therefore new markets, whereas competence complementing strategies help acquire technologies which could be critical in the future. This could make easier realise a continuous process towards the refreshment of the current competence in a second phase. In fact, the technologies acquired through competence complementing strategies could then be combined with other technologies. Therefore, a firm can progressively change its base of technology and refresh it. This refreshed competence becomes the new current base and the cycle restarts.

Table 3.3. Type of technology strategy and acquisition mode.

Type of technology strategy		Acquisition mode
Competence deepening		Internal R&D
Competence fertilising		Internal R&D
Competence complementing	complementary	Licences, alliances and joint ventures
	strategic	Acquisitions Creation of internal R&D groups to build absorptive capacity
Competence refreshing and competence destroying		Acquisitions Venture capital or internal ventures Creation of internal groups to build absorptive capacity

The action programs should be conceived searching for this continuity. Of course, it may occur that a firm is forced to jump on a new knowledge base as the existing is realised to obsolete. This radical shift should be avoided. Making the process of strategic technology planning regularly (for example, on a yearly basis) helps give continuity to actions and gradually move to a new base of competencies. This makes the process of technology planning a revision of the plan already in place and helps keep the technological direction of the firm stable over years.

APPENDIX - CASE STUDY

It is often difficult to conduct a process so complex as the technology strategy formulation taking into account all the dimensions mentioned above. In this appendix, a tool helping structure the problem, obtain an objective evaluation, and conceive a technology strategy is presented. It is applied to the case of Philips in the multimedia business. The case is focused on the process of selection of technologies, then some considerations are made on the mode of acquisition of the technologies selected. Some preliminary information are given on how the first step - the context foresight - is carried out in Philips.

Context Foresight: the 'Imaging the Future' Process

The process of context foresight is recognised as a key aspect of strategic planning of technology in Philips. It is called 'Imaging the Future', to emphasise that the investigation goes beyond the firm's current activities and technologies, exploring emerging businesses and technologies as well. Most Philips activities, traditionally separated, are now converging in one business: content production (Polygram), consumer electronics (Philips Sound and Vision), services and software (Philips Media), professionals equipment (Philips Business Electronic) are all converging in the multimedia business. Multimedia is seen as the future core business of Philips and, as a consequence, a great attention is paid to foresee its future evolution.

Three different units participate to the process of 'Imaging the future': Philips Research, the Strategic Planning Board Staff and Philips Corporate Design.

- Philips Research studies the evolution of technologies. It is responsible for the Multimedia Industry Foresight of the digital, microelectronics, display technologies. It identifies whether and how advancements in the technologies studied in the firm's labs allow to create new applications, new products and services for the customer. Philips Research benchmarks the progress of the research activities of Philips with competitors. In particular, researchers participate to specialised conferences where they can meet colleagues from competing firms and other institutions and evaluate the level of knowledge accrued in Philips laboratories with respect to them. Philips Research also evaluates whether the existing technologies can be exploited for other (new) applications;

- the Board Staff attempts to foresee the evolution of the social, economic, demographic and political world environment. The 'space' observed goes well beyond the context of the current competition, and includes all the areas which can potentially affect, in the future, the Philips' activities and performance. The observed tendencies contribute to image further applications and the progress of new technology development, stimulating and suggesting new combinations for future products;

- Philips Corporate Design, created in 1994 by the Philips Board and based in Eindhoven, started the 'Vision of the Future' project in 1995. This project concerns the identification of socio-cultural developments, aimed to image people interests and desires in the next decade (the time horizon was ten years 1995-2005). "A 10-years foresight allows to undertake in advance the steps required to respond to future human needs" (Philips Corporate Design Report, 1996). Multi-disciplinary working groups were created with the participation of anthropologists, economists, sociologists, engineers, designers of different countries. Working groups were given two key inputs: socio-cultural trends and emerging technologies. The former were provided by RISC (Research Institute for Social Change) who focuses on emerging socio-cultural behaviours, interests, objectives in the modern society. The latter were the output of the activities of Philips Research, and of research institutions from key country markets like Japan and Germany. In a series of creative workshops, the groups developed some 300 scenarios. Each scenario is characterised by a set of new products/applications, embedding specific technologies. Such scenarios, and the related products/applications, were later analysed on the basis of four main criteria:

  1.   Are the advantages for the customers clear and real?
  2.   Are the products within the Philips business scope?
  3.   Are the applications technically feasible?
  4.   Are the products suited to the socio-cultural area identified?

  The 300 scenarios were thus reduced to 60 'concepts', representing the Philips foresight of the multimedia market.

The industry foresight elaborated by Philips Research, by the Board Staff and by Philips Corporate Design is then submitted to a committee, composed of members of the Board of Directors, and chaired by Frank Carrubba, president of Philips Media, who is directly responsible for the validation of the Multimedia Industry Foresight. Once evaluated and validated by the committee, the Foresight becomes the reference for developing the Philips technology strategy.

The evolution foreseen in the case of the multimedia business can be summarised as in Figure A.1.

Past	Future
one media	multimedia
analogic	digital
traditional separated businesses: computer communication consumer electronics content production	businesses converge computer communication consumer electronics content production
one mode: print / text / audiovisual	multiple modes integrated: text, sound and visual combined
passive use by user	user has more control, choice and interactivity

Figure A.1. The Multimedia Industry Evolution.

Accordingly, Philips identified the (new) potential applications. The most important are:

- instant access to the latest information and images;
- wandering around museums;
- playing games;
- reliving soccer's World Cup;
- browsing in an encyclopaedia;
- watching programs about anatomy or pregnancy;
- paying bills;
- enjoying favourite films;
- shopping;
- consulting with customers, colleagues or suppliers;
- medical specialist in London watching an operation place in San Francisco;
- English schoolchildren talking with their counterparts in the United States.

The products able to support these new applications are both updated traditional products like TVs (becoming Web-TV), communication systems, audio and videorecording systems, and new products like the Multimedia CD-DVD, the Set Top Box, the Multimedia PC (MMPC), the HDTV, the PDA, the Network Computer (NC), the Smart Card[b].

---

b   They here follow the descriptions of the multimedia products mentioned:
- Web-Tv: it is the evolution of the traditional TV that upgraded with specific devices is able to surf in the WWW like a home PC. It enables applications like teleshopping, home-banking, teleservices, etc.;
- Cd+Dvd: they are the optic disks with high storage capacity that allow multimedia applications such as hypermedia encyclopedia;

The success of these products strongly depends on the opportunity for the user to connect with the so named information superhighways. Philips Corporate Design thus identified different scenarios, corresponding to a different diffusion of such infrastructure. These scenarios cannot be described in detail for confidentiality reasons.

Applications	Web Tv	Cd+Dvd	Audio Syst.	Videorec.	Comm syst.	Monitors	MM Pc	STB	PDA	Smart Card	N.C.	Hdtv
Percentual Weight (%)												

Technologies	Normalised Importance											
1) Analogical												
2) Display technologies												
3) Microelectronics												
4) Optics												
5) Magnetics												
6) Mechanic												
7) Digital (trasm, compress, encript.)												
Check Sum												

Legenda: Percentual Weight = Product Sales in 2000 / Total Sales

Figure A.2. The Technology-Application matrix.

- Audio systems: they are all the audio consumer devices; these devices are being converted from analogical technology to digital (e.g. DCC, Minidisk, DAB radio);
- Videorecording: the video cassette recording systems;
- Communication systems: home telephone, cordless and cellular devices;
- Monitors: the graphic interfaces of terminals;
- Multimedia PC (MMPC): the PC upgraded with audio-systems, video-cameras and microphone that enables multimedia communications through the network;
- Set Top Box (STB): the device that permit to the traditional Tv to receive digital signals converting them in analogical signals;
- Personal Digital Assistant (PDA): a pocket assistant device able to surf in the net;
- Smart Card: card with a chip inside to store a lot of information;
- Network Computer (NC): a very simple and cheap terminal that works network connected;
- High Definition TV (Hdtv): the new television devices with high resolution image system.

Here, as examples, two scenarios are considered:
Scenario 1: the users connected to broad band network will be less than the expected, and the multimedia market will take off at low growth rate;
Scenario 2: the users interconnected to the broad band network will be considerable and there will be a large diffusion of multimedia products.
The foresight has also identified the competencies required. These are both competencies already available within the firm (such as display technologies, microelectronics, optics, magnetics) and other new to the firm (analogical, mechanics and digital). The technology-application matrix is therefore that reported in Figure A.2.

Selection of Technologies

It is here reported the application of an experimental methodology for technology selection, based on the Philips' experience and tested by the author in the Philips Italian R&D unit in collaboration with the responsible of the unit. The methodology is described taking the perspective of the decision maker in 1995 who selects the technologies to be developed in the multimedia business. The analysis has been conducted in relation with the two scenarios previously identified in the context foresight.
The first step of the methodology consisted of the estimation of the value of future products in the multimedia business and of the importance of the various technologies in each. The tool used is the technology-application matrix (Figure A.2).
Matrixes to be filled in are as many as the scenarios developed.
The upper section of the matrix lists the applications the firm is willing to sell in the future. The value of future applications can be measured with the size of its potential future market. Other measures can be used, such as the margin, the added value, etc. However, the potential turnover of the product in a given scenario seemed to be the easiest and the most realistic to forecast. It is very difficult to estimate other indicators than turnover of products to be sold in 5-10 years. The potential sales of the multimedia products in the early 21st century have been estimated, also considering forecast of market research centres and trend studies published by leading institutions. Then, these values have been modified according to the specific scenario considered: for example, in scenario 1 the potential sales of the products requiring broad band connection have been reduced (the values used are not reported in absolute terms for confidentiality reasons).

The bottom section of the matrix shows the technologies to be embedded within products. These technologies were identified in the 'Imaging the future' process. For each technology, the relative Importance (M) for the future success of the products is evaluated. Maix is the Importance of technology a for product i in the scenario x; higher importance reflects higher provision of customer value given by that technology. Evaluating the importance of a technology is obviously very complex. In Philips, the Importance is assessed by the R&D managers and specialists, directly involved with the multimedia technologies, and marketing people. The attempt is to create teams able to evaluate the relation between technology and product performance. The Importance is assigned using a scale from 1 to 10 where 1 means low importance and 10 maximum importance[c].

At this stage, the selection process starts. The selection process is based upon the evaluation of two factors for each technology: the Relevance and the Success Probability (Risk).

Evaluating the Relevance of the Technologies

In order to evaluate the Relevance of the technologies, each application (listed in the matrix) is assigned a weight, and each technology a Normalised Importance.
The *weight* is the ratio between the turnover of a specific application in a scenario and the total turnover. Therefore, W_{ij} is the weight associated to product i in scenario j and is defined as:

$$W_{ij} = \frac{V_{ij}}{\sum_i \sum_j (V_{ij})}$$

where:
- V_{ij} is the potential turnover of the application i in the scenario j;
- $\sum_i \sum_j (V_{ij})$ is the sum of the turnovers of all applications in all the scenarios identified.

---

[c] To make the quantitative evaluation of such variables more reliable, they can be used more sophisticated techniques such as the fuzzy method, which helps translate qualitative evaluation given to variables into scores. See for example Zimmerman (1992).

Thus, the Weight[d] indicator of each application is a percentage.

The *Normalised Importance* represents the relative contribution (in terms of benefit for the customer) that a definite technology k gives to application i in a specific scenario j. It is defined as:

$$I_{ijk} = \frac{M_{ijk}}{\sum_k (M_{ijk})}$$

The Normalised Importance is thus based upon the Importance (M) estimated above. It is defined in such a way that $\sum_k (I_{ijk}) = 1$, that means that the sum of the Normalised Importance of all the k technologies relevant to application i in scenario j is equal to 1 (if only one technology is relevant, its importance will be 1).

Scenario 1: multimedia low diffusion

Applications	Web Tv	Cd+Dvd	Audio Syst.	Videorec.	Comm syst.	Monitors	MM Pc	STB	PDA	Smart Card	N.C.	Hdtv
Percentual Weight (%)	3.9	3.6	4.9	2.4	4.5	3.5	16.7	1.5	2.4	4.7	2.3	0.3

Technologies	Web Tv	Cd+Dvd	Audio Syst.	Videorec.	Comm syst.	Monitors	MM Pc	STB	PDA	Smart Card	N.C.	Hdtv
	Normalised Importance											
1) Analogical	0.2		0.25	0.3	0.15							
2) Display technologies	0.4				0.2	0.4			0.25			0.3
3) Microelectronics	0.35	0.1	0.3	0.2	0.3	0.2	0.25	0.3	0.25	0.25	0.35	0.2
4) Optics		0.35		0.1								
5) Magnetics				0.1	0.15	0.1	0.4	0.35	0.25	0.4	0.45	0.2
6) Mechanic		0.25	0.25	0.3			0.1					
7) Digital (trasm., compress., encript.)	0.05	0.3	0.2		0.2	0.3	0.25	0.35	0.25	0.35	0.2	0.3
Check Sum	1	1	1	1	1	1	1	1	1	1	1	1

Legenda: Percentual Weight = Product Sales in 2000 / Total Sales

Figure A.3. Weights and normalised importance (scenario 1).

---

d   The underlying hypothesis here is that all scenarios have the same probability to occur. If the various scenarios are not equi-probable, the Wij can be multiplied by the probability of occurrence of their respective scenario.

Figure A.3 and Figure A.4 respectively show the Weights of each product and the Normalised Importance of each technology in scenario 1 and 2.

Weight and Normalised Importance are finally used to evaluate the *Relevance* of each technology, as follows:

Relevance of the technology k $= (R_k) = \sum_i \sum_j (W_{ij} \times I_{ijk})$

Scenario 2: multimedia *cornucopia*

Applications	Web Tv	Cd+Dvd	Audio Syst.	Videorec.	Comm syst.	Monitors	MM Pc	STB	PDA	Smart Card	N.C.	Hdtv
Percentual Weight (%)	4.9	2.9	4.9	2.0	4.5	3.6	12.5	1.5	2.4	4.7	4.5	1.5

Technologies	Normalised Importance											
1) Analogical	0.05		0.1	0.3								
2) Display technologies	0.2				0.25	0.4			0.25			0.4
3) Microelectronics	0.2	0.1	0.3	0.2	0.25	0.2	0.25	0.25	0.25	0.25	0.3	0.15
4) Optics		0.35		0.1								
5) Magnetics	0.2			0.1	0.2	0.1	0.4	0.35	0.2	0.4	0.4	0.15
6) Mechanic		0.25	0.25	0.3			0.1					
7) Digital (trasm., compress., encript.)	0.35	0.3	0.35		0.3	0.3	0.25	0.4	0.3	0.35	0.3	0.3
Check Sum	1	1	1	1	1	1	1	1	1	1	1	1

Legenda: Percentual Weight = Product Sales in 2000 / Total Sales

Figure A.4. Weights and normalised importance (scenario 2).

The Relevance indicator thus shows how much the technology contributes to the future turnover of the firm. In fact, the weight W_{ij} is the part of the whole turnover that the application i provides in scenario j. The I_{ijk} is the contribution of the technology k to the success of the product i in scenario j. Therefore, the relevance of technology k is the 'turnover' the technology provides in the various products in which it is embedded and creates value.

Technology	Relevance	Norm. Rel.
1) Analogical	4.7%	0.1807692
2) Display Technologies	9.3%	0.3576923
3) Microelectronics	24.7%	0.95
4) Optics	2.7%	0.1038462
5) Magnetics	24.1%	0.9269231
6) Mechanic	8.3%	0.3192308
7) Digital	26.0%	1

Figure A.5. The Technology Relevance.

The Relevance of the technologies is then normalised to 1 (in such a way to have the Relevance of the most relevant technology equal to 1).

The result is a technology list with the associated Relevance. Figure A.5 shows the Relevance of each technology in the multimedia business, and then the Relevance normalised to 1.

Evaluating the Success Probability (Risk) of the Technologies

The other key factor in the selection process is the *risk* associated with a technology, i.e. the probability that the technology will not bring the desired success for the firm in the future. Two major components of risk are considered: the technical risk and the commercial risk.

The *Commercial risk* of a technology is the probability that, in the future, the application incorporating the technology cannot have an economic return (e.g. a software house that develops an excellent architecture that will not become a world standard widely used). The commercial risk is estimated measuring the dispersion of the Relevance of a technology in the various scenarios.

Two steps are used to evaluate the commercial risk:
- calculate for each technology k its Relevance R_{kj} in the scenario j, as

$$R_{kj} = \sum_i (W_{ji} \times I_{ijk}) ;$$

- calculate the dispersion of the R_{kj}, as the Standard Deviation of the R_{kj}.

The commercial risk of a technology is thus defined as the Dispersion of the technology Relevance (R_{jk}). These values are then normalised to 0.5.

This indicates how much the Relevance of the technologies varies in the different scenarios. If the technology is equally or similarly relevant for the firm in any future scenario, the standard deviation of its Relevance is low and the commercial risk is low; otherwise, the relevance significantly changes in the various scenarios, and the commercial risk is high.

The *Technical risk* is defined as the probability not to develop the technology by the time required and/or in such a way to achieve the desired level of performance. The estimation of the technical risk takes into account the firm's technological capabilities in that technology, the state of the art of that technology and its 'distance' from the level of performance required. The technical risk has three components:

(i)   level of progress of the technology in the firm: the risk is high if the technology has not been explored yet by the firm;

(ii)   difficulty of the objectives: the technological risk is high if the target is far from the state of the art;

(iii) resource adequacy, which depends on several factors:

- specialisation of resources: the experience of the people involved in the project about the technology to develop;
- equipment resources: availability of well tested equipment to be used in the R&D activity;
- project leadership: the personal capability and charisma of the people charged of the responsibility to develop the technology;
- degree of integration of the R&D with the other functions;
- availability of external resources from other firms and institutions.

Each of the three components is assigned a score between 0 and 10, where 0 means minimum   probability of success and 10 maximum probability of success. The probability of technical success is then calculated as:

(Resource adequacy × Level of progress of the technology × Difficulty of the objectives) /1000.

The technical risk is equal to (1 - Probability of technical success).

These values are then normalised to 0.5.

Combining the commercial and technical risks, Philips comes to an estimation of the Success Probability of a technology (Figure A.8). This is:

Success Probability = 1 - (Commercial Risk + Technical Risk).

Being both the technical and the commercial risk normalised to 0.5, the highest value of risk is 1 and consequently the Success Probability is 0, and the lowest value of risk is 0 and the Success Probability in that case is 1[e].

Figure A.6 shows the relevance of the technologies in scenario 1, the relevance of the competencies in scenario 2, the commercial risk in absolute terms (calculated as the standard deviation of the relevance), and the commercial risk normalised to 0.5.

Technology	Relevance in scenario 1	Relevance in scenario 2	Commercial Risk	Commercial Risk normalised
1) Analogical	3%	1%	0.010	0.313
2) Display technologies	5%	5%	0.001	0.028
3) Microelectronics	13%	12%	0.005	0.141
4) Optics	2%	1%	0.001	0.045
5) Magnetics	12%	12%	0.003	0.093
6) Mechanic	5%	4%	0.004	0.109
7) Digital (trasm, compress, encript.)	11%	15%	0.017	0.500

Figure A.6. Technology Commercial Risk

Figure A.7 shows the scores of the three components of the technical risk (levels achieved in the technology, target easiness and resource adequacy), the technical risk, and the technical risk normalised to 0.5 of each technology. The Success Probability is reported in Figure A.8.

---

[e] Normalising both the risks to 0.5 means that the importance of the two risk factors is equal. If a source of risk is higher or more relevant, then the risk indicators can be normalized differently (for example, normalizing to 0.7 the commercial risk and to 0.3 the technical risk means that the commercial risk is more relevant than the technical).

Technology	Level already accrued	Target Easiness	Resource adequacy	Technical Risk	Techn. risk normalised
1) Analogical	8	4	9	0.71	0.394
2) Display technologies	8	6	8	0.62	0.341
3) Microelectronics	8	6	9	0.57	0.314
4) Optics	5	7	8	0.72	0.398
5) Magnetics	6	8	6	0.71	0.394
6) Mechanic	7	7	8	0.61	0.336
7) Digital (trasm, compress, encript.)	2	6	8	0.90	0.500

Legenda: Evaluation scores between 1 and 10

Figure A.7. Technology Technical Risk.

Technology	Technological risk normalised	Commercial risk normalised	Success Probability
1) Analogical	0.394	0.313	0.29
2) Display Technologies	0.341	0.028	0.63
3) Microelectronics	0.314	0.141	0.55
4) Optics	0.398	0.045	0.56
5) Magnetics	0.394	0.093	0.51
6) Mechanic	0.336	0.109	0.56
7) Digital	0.500	0.500	0.00

Figure A.8. The Technology Success Probability.

The financial risk was also considered. In general terms the management evaluated that the amount requested to operate the multimedia business could be borne by the company and that the required assets to produce, commercialise and distribute the multimedia products were available.

Selecting the Core Technologies

In order to select the technologies to be developed, the Relevance and the Success Probability of each technology are jointly considered in a matrix (Figure A.9).

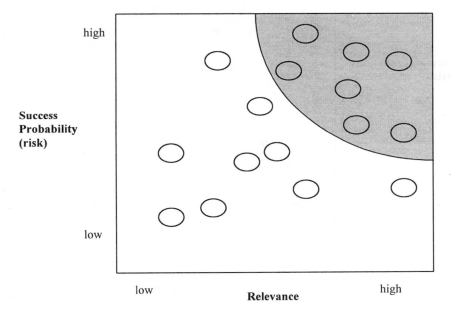

Figure A.9. The selection of the core technologies.

The grey area (high relevance - high probability of success) identifies the future core technologies, i.e. those the firm has to develop for its future leadership. The grey area is obtained considering the amount of money necessary to develop the technologies and including the best technologies (high relevance-high probability of success) using the whole budget available.

The Relevance and the Success Probability of each technology in the multimedia business are represented in Figure A.10. The grey area includes the technologies selected.

Figure A.10 shows the case of a risk neutral firm. Actually, the shape of the selected area depends on the risk propensity of the firm. If the firm is risk taking the selected area has the shape reported in Figure A.11 (including high relevance competencies, although they show low probability of success).

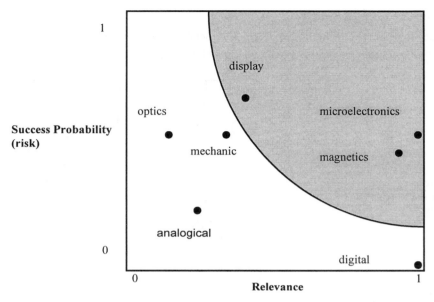

Figure A.10. The selection of the core technologies in Multimedia.

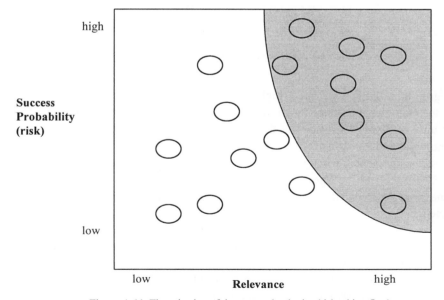

Figure A.11. The selection of the core technologies (risk taking firm).

If the firm is risk adverse, the selected area is that of Figure A.12.

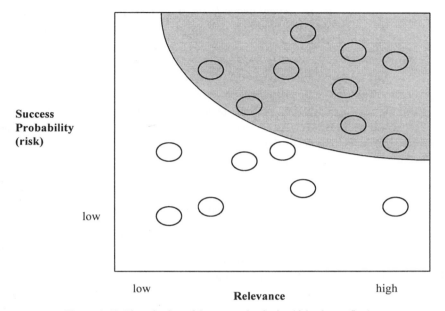

Figure A.12. The selection of the core technologies (risk adverse firm).

The technologies included in the grey area are the core technologies, whereas the technologies in the white area are non core.

So far the selection has taken into account two key variables (relevance and risk) of the technologies. Some consideration have been done also in relation to the other three: appropriability, option creation and interdependence.

Interdependence. The analysis starts considering interdependencies. So far, each technology (with its own Relevance and Success Probability) is considered separately. However, it is clear that several interdependencies exist among the various competencies, which need to be considered as well. In Philips two types of inter-dependencies have been considered: the technological dependencies and the commercial dependencies.

- *technological inter-dependencies* refer to the interrelations among the technical development of different technologies. The success of the development of a technology depends on the availability of another technology. The technological dependence between two technologies 'a' and 'b' is classified in two types:

- *'one way' technological dependence,* if the development of 'b' needs that 'a' is available (the symbol a → b means that b depends on availability of a);

- *'mutual' technological dependence,* if the technical developments of 'a' and 'b' are mutually dependent (the symbol is a ←→ b) ;

- *commercial inter-dependencies* concern the fact that the Relevance of a technology depends on another technology even if independent from a technical point of view. As a matter of fact, if competencies 'a' and 'b' are considered, it may occur that both I_{ijb} (i.e. the importance of technology 'b' in product i and scenario j) and I_{ija} are high. This means that the Relevance of technology 'a' in product i and scenario j is actually dependent on the contemporary possession of technology 'b', as also I_{ijb} is high. In other words, if the technology 'b' would not be available, the product would not have a fundamental characteristic for its success and, as a consequence, the relevance of 'a' would also be affected. Therefore, there is commercial dependence when two technologies are important in the same products.

The identified dependencies among technologies can be put into evidence in the selection space drawn before (Figure A.13).

It may occur that a technology selected depends or is interrelated with another technology which is in the white area (non selected). The evidence is provided by the arrows from the white area (non selected technologies) into the grey area (selected technologies). This is an alert flag that should force to do the process of ranking and selecting the technologies again, modifying some variables. To face this point, the following approach has been defined.

First, the calculation of the Relevance and the Success Probability indicators should be revised. In fact, if a technology with high Success Probability and high Relevance depends on a technology with low Success Probability and low Relevance, it may be that the Relevance of the latter is not so low. This means that the Importance values need to be revised and then the selection process done again.

Second, if there are still dependencies between selected and non-selected technologies, the Relevance of the technologies selected are re-calculated in the case the technologies inter-related with them and in the white area (non selected) would not be developed. Then, the Relevance-Success Probability matrix is re-drawn. This allows to understand to what extent the Relevance of the technologies in the grey area decreases (for example, whether or not these competencies go outside the grey area). The lesser decrease of the Relevance of the technology (ies) selected, the lesser importance of the technologies non selected, the lesser need to develop the latter.

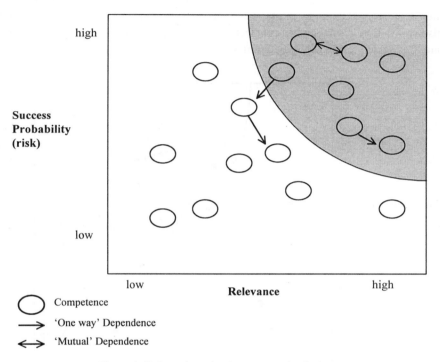

Figure A.13. Inter-dependencies among technologies.

Third, if this revision does not lead to a satisfactory solution, other factors are considered:

- re-define the budget and increase the amount available so to develop a wider range of technologies (including those in the white area interrelated with those in the grey area);
- acquire technologies through accessing external sources of technology rather than through internal development (which lowers the cost of technology acquisition). If the external acquisition is taken into consideration, other variables account, for example, whether the external acquisition allows to achieve that technology by the time required, or whether there are appropriability factors limiting the involvement of third actors in this process.

Inter-dependencies among the competencies in the multimedia business are showed in Figure A.14.

A 'mutual' dependence among the digital, microelectronics and magnetic technologies emerges. This is a natural effect of the technological convergence of the 3C sectors (Communication, Computer, Consumer Electronics). Figure A.14 also shows that Digital and Microelectronics are dependent on Display technologies and the Mechanics on Microelectronics.

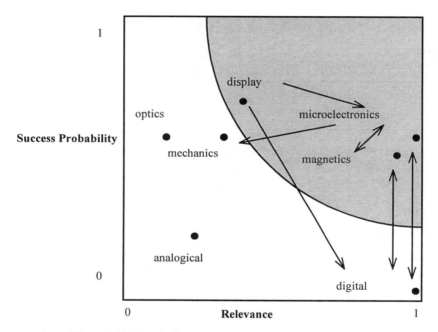

Figure A.14. The selection of the core technologies of Philips in Multimedia.

Figure A.14 shows that the core technologies for Philips in multimedia industry are Microelectronics, Digital, Magnetics and Display technologies. The Digital technology which is outside the grey area is included because of the inter-dependencies with Magnetics and Microelectronics. Philips is here supposed risk neutral.

Digital technology is the object of cooperation with other firms as it is not core itself and the firm's capabilities are very low (as mirrored by the very low success probability). All the other technologies are to be developed internally.

Appropriability. As far as the appropriability is concerned, the management evaluates that it is rather high as the applications are the result of the blending of various technologies and only leading firms in the consumer electronic industry will be able to match the window of opportunity and commercialise such products effectively. The existing base of knowledge in all the technologies required apart digital technology and the complementary assets required to enter the multimedia business protect against low cost imitators.

Option creation. As far as the option creation is concerned, investing in collaborations in the digital technology is considered a means to acquire initial knowledge in that critical technology and create options for future applications and technological developments.

Finally, the trajectory to be followed was considered to check whether there is a coherence and continuity between the previous, current, and future technological bases. Actually, when seen on the matrix it is clear that the only critical technology to be acquired is the digital one. The other core technologies for future competition (display, microelectronics and magnetics) are already available and will be developed by internal R&D activities. Therefore the introduction of the digital technology is a technology complementing action which allows to gradually move to the new base of knowledge and create opportunities for future developments.

		TV	Cd	Cd-i	CVd-Rm	Audio	Videorec.	Comm. Syst.	Cd Dvd	TV Web	Man.	MM PC	STD	PDA	SC	NC	MDTV
Existing	Optics					X	X		X								
	Display						X		X	X		X					X
	Microelectronics				X	X	X		X	X	X	X	X	X	X	X	X
	Magnetics					X	X				X	X	X	X	X	X	X
New	Digital					X			X	X	X	X	X	X	X	X	X
	Analogue				X	X	X		X								
	Mechanics				X	X			X			X					

Figure A.15. Type of Technology strategy of Philips in multimedia.

The following table summarises the steps to be followed to apply the methodology.

Step	Brief description	Operative actions
Mapping the technologies	- mapping the future products and the embedded technologies in each scenario; - estimating the value of future products (potential turnover or value added or margin, etc.) - assessing the importance (M) of the technologies for the product value	-build the product / competencies matrix - build the product / turnover matrix - qualitatively evaluate the M_{kij}
Evaluating the relevance of the technologies	- for each product, evaluating its relative contribution to the total turnover (weight W) - for each technology, evaluating its relative contribution to the value of the product (normalised importance I); - evaluating the relevance (R) of each technology as weight by normalised importance	- calculate $W_{ij} = V_{ij}/\Sigma_i\Sigma_j(V_{ij})$ - calculate $I_{ijk} = M_{ijk}/\Sigma_k M_{ijk}$ - calculate $R_k = \Sigma_i\Sigma_j (W_{ij} * I_{ijk})$
Evaluating the success probability of the technologies	- evaluating the commercial risk (as the dispersion of the Relevance of a technology in the different scenarios) - evaluating the technological risk (TR) as a function of the resource adequacy, the level of progress of the technology and the difficulty of the objectives - evaluating the success probability (SP)	- calculate the standard deviation of the $R_{kj} = \sigma(R_{kj})$ - calculate TR = 1- (resource adequacy * level of progress of technology * difficulty of the objective)/1000 - calculate SP = 1 - [$\sigma(R_{kj})$ + TR]
Selecting the core technologies	- jointly considering the relevance and success probability of each technology - considering the budget available - considering the firm's attitude towards risk - considering the interdependencies among competencies - selecting the core technologies	- build the relevance /success probability matrix - fix R&D investments - define the firm's risk attitude (neutral, risk taking, risk adverse) - evaluate the commercial and technological interdependencies - identify the best performing competencies (high relevance - high success probability) within the relevance /success probability matrix
	- conducting the portfolio analysis	- evaluate whether the portfolio selected is satisfactory and, if not, change endogenous variables and redo the selection process

Legenda: i= product i; j= scenario j; k= technology k; V = turnover or other indicator of the product value

REFERENCES AND FURTHER READINGS

Context foresight

Adler, P.S., McDonald, D.W. and McDonald, F., Strategic Management of Technical Functions, *Sloan Management Review*, Winter (1992).

Boardman B., Finding the Person who Knows, *Research Technology Management* (1995).

Burgelman, R.A., Kosnik, T.J. and van den Poel, M., Toward an Innovative Capabilities Audit Framework, in *Strategic Management of Technology and Innovation*, Burgelman, R.A. and Maidique, M. (Eds.) (Irwin, 1988).

Chiesa, V., Coughlan, P. and Voss, C.A., Development of a Technical Innovation Audit, *Journal of Product Innovation Management*, 13 (1996).

Coombs, R., McMeekin, A. and Pybus, R., Benchmarking tools for R&D project management, *R&D Management Conference Proceedings*, Manchester, July (1997).

Floyd, C., *Managing technology for corporate success* (Gower, Aldershot, 1997).

Hamel, G. and Heene, A., *Competence Based Competition* (John Wiley & Sons, Chichester, 1994).

Hamel, G. and Prahalad, C.K., *Competing for the Future* (Harvard Business School Press, Harvard, 1994).

Hax, A.C. and Majluf, N.S., *Strategic Management: An Integrative Perspective* (Prentice Hall, Englewood Cliffs, 1984).

Hax, A.C. and Majluf, N.S., *The Strategic Concept and Process: A Pragmatic Approach* (Prentice Hall, Englewood Cliffs, 1991).

Hax, A.C. and No, M., *Linking Technology and Business Strategies: A Methodological Approach and an Illustration*, Working Paper No. 3383-92BPS, February (1992).

Heene, A. and Sanchez, R., *Competence-based Strategic Management* (J. Wiley, Chichester, 1997).

Kotler P., *Marketing management: analysis, planning and control* (Prentice Hall, Englewood Cliffs, 1997).

Moenaert, R.K., Deschoolmeester, D., De Meyer, A. and Souder, W.E., Information styles of marketing and R&D personnel during technological innovation projects, *R&D Management*, 22, January (1992).

Pavitt, K., What We Know about the Strategic Management of Technology, *California Management Review*, 32, 3 (1990), 17-26.

Pavitt, K., Characteristics of the Large Innovative Firm, *British Journal of Management*, 2 (1991), 41-50.

Prahalad, C.K. and Hamel, G., The Core Competence of the Corporation, *Harvard Business Review*, 68, 3 (1990), 79-91.

Roussel, P., Saad, K. and Erickson, T., *Third Generation R&D* (HBS Press, Boston, MA, 1991).

Sanchez, R., Heene, A. and Thomas, H., Towards the theory and practice of competence based competition, in Sanchez, R., Heene, A. and Thomas, H., *Dynamics of competence based competition: theory and practice in the new management* (Elsevier Press, London, 1996).

Souder, W.E., *Managing new product innovations* (Lexington Books, Lexington, 1987).

Tidd, J., Bessant, J. and Pavitt K., *Managing Innovation - Integrating Technological, Market and Organisational Change* (J. Wiley, 1997).

Twiss, B., *Managing Technological Innovation* (Pitman, London, 1987).

von Hippel, E., *The Sources of Innovation* (Oxford University Press, 1988).

Wolff, M.F., Scouting for Technology, *Research Technology Management* (1995).

Technology selection

A.D. Little, The Strategic Management of Technology (European Management Forum, Davos, 1981).

Booz-Allen & Hamilton, The Strategic Management of Technology, *Outlook*, Fall-Winter (1981).

Bower, J.L. and Christensen, C.M., Disruptive Technologies: Catching the Wave, *Harvard Business Review*, January-February (1995).

Cohen, W.M. and Levinthal, D.A., Absorptive Capacity: a New Perspective on Learning and Innovation, *Administrative Science Quarterly*, 35 (1990).

Dierickx, I. and Cool, K., Asset stock accumulation and sustainability of competitive advantage, *Management Science*, December (1989).

Foster, R.N., Timing Technological Transitions, in Horwitch, M. (Ed.), *Technology in the Modern Corporation - A Strategic Perspective* (Pergamon Press, 1986).

Hax, A.C. and Majluf, N.S., *Strategic Management: An Integrative Perspective* (Prentice Hall, Englewood Cliffs, 1984).

Hax, A.C. and Majluf, N.S., *The Strategic Concept and Process: A Pragmatic Approach* (Prentice Hall, Englewood Cliffs, 1991).

Hax, A.C. and No, M., *Linking Technology and Business Strategies: A Methodological Approach and an Illustration*, Working Paper No. 3383-92BPS, February (1992).

Itami, H., *Mobilizing Invisible Assets* (Harvard University Press, Cambridge).

Klein, J.A. and Hiscocks, P.G. (1994), Competence-based Competition: A Practical Toolkit, in Hamel, G. and Heene, A. (Eds.), *Competence-Based Competition* (J. Wiley, 1987).

Kodama, F., Technology Fusion and the new R&D, *Harvard Business Review*, 70, 4 (1992).

Kodama, F., *Emerging Patterns of Innovation* (Harvard Business School Press, Boston, 1995).

Leonard-Barton, D., Core Capabilities and Core Rigidities: a Paradox in Managing New Product Development, *Strategic Management Journal*, 13 (1992), 111-125.

Mitchell, G.R., New Approaches for the Strategic Management of Technology, in Horwitch, M. (Ed.), *Technology in the Modern Corporation - A Strategic Perspective* (Pergamon Press, 1986).

Pappas, C., Strategic Management of Technology, *Journal of Product Innovation Management*, 1 (1984).

Roussel, P., Saad, K. and Erickson, T., *Third Generation R&D* (HBS Press, Boston, 1991).

Timing

Axelrod, R., Mitchell, W., Thomas, R.E., Bennett, D.S. and Bruderer, E., Coalition Formation in Standard-setting Alliances, *Management Science*, 41, 9 (1995).

Besen, S.M. and Farrell, J., Choosing How to Compete: Strategies and Tactics in Standardization, *Journal of Economic Perspective*, 8, 2 (1994).

David, P.A. and Greenstein, S., The economics of compatibility standards: an introduction to recent research, *Economics of Innovation and New Technology*, 1 (1990).

David, P.A. and Steinmuller, W.E., Economics of compatibility standards and competition in telecommunication networks, *Information Economics and Policy*, 6 (1994).

Foster, R.N., Timing Technological Transitions, in Horwitch, M. (Ed.), *Technology in the Modern Corporation - A Strategic Perspective* (Pergamon Press, 1986).

Freeman, C., *The Economics of Industrial Innovation* (Frances Pinter Publisher, London, 1978).

Maidique, M.A. and Patch, P., Corporate Strategy and Technological Policy, in Tushman, M.L. and Moore, W.L. (Eds.), *Readings in the Management of Innovation*, 2nd edition (Harper Business, 1978).

Porter, M.E., *Competitive Advantage* (The Free Press, New York, 1985).

Twiss, B., *Managing Technological Innovation* (Pitman, London, 1987).

Utterback, J.M., *Mastering the Dynamics of Innovation* (Harvard Business School Press, 1994).

von Braun, C.F. (1997), *The Innovation War*, Prentice Hall PTR.

Zimmerman,H.J., *Fuzzy Sets Theory and Its Applications* (Kluwer Academic Publisher, Boston, 1992)

Acquisition

Axelrod, R., Mitchell, W., Thomas, R.E., Bennett, D.S. and Bruderer, E., Coalition Formation in Standard-setting Alliances, *Management Science*, 41, 9 (1995).

Bidault, F. and Cummings, T., Innovating through Alliances: Expectations and Limitations, *R&D Management*, 24, 1 (1994).

Brockhoff, K., Research and Development cooperation between firms. A Classification by Structural Variables, *International Journal of Technology Management*, 6, May-August (1991), 3-4.

Bruce, M., Leverick, F., Littler, D. and Wilson, D., Success Factors for Collaborative Product Development: A Study of Suppliers of Information and Communication Technology, *R&D Management*, 25, 1 (1995).

Chatterje, D., Accessing External Sources of Technology, *Research Technology Management*, March-April (1996).

Chatterji, D. and Manuel, T.A., Benefiting from External Sources of Technology, *Research Technology Management*, November-December (1993).

Chesbrough, H. and Teece, D.J., , When Is Virtual Virtuous? Organizing for Innovation, *Harvard Business Review*, January-February (1996).

Coombs, R., Richards, A., Saviotti, P.P., Walsh, V. (Eds.), *Technological Collaboration - The Dynamics of Cooperation in Industrial Innovation* (Edward Elgar Publishing Limited, Cheltenham, 1997).

David, P.A. and Greenstein, S., The economics of compatibility standards: an introduction to recent research, *Economics of Innovation and New Technology*, 1 (1990).

David, P.A. and Steinmuller, W.E., Economics of compatibility standards and competition in telecommunication networks, *Information Economics and Policy*, 6 (1994).

Davidow, W.H. and Malone, M.S., *The Virtual Corporation* (Harper Business, New York, 1992).

Doz, Y.L., The Evolution of Cooperation in Strategic Alliances: Initial Conditions or Learning Processes?, *Strategic Management Journal*, 17 (1996).

Farr, C.M. and Fischer, W.A., Managing International High Technology Cooperative Projects, *R&D Management*, 22, 1 (1992), 55-67.

Forrest, J.E. and Martin, J.C., Strategic Alliances Between Large and Small Research Intensive Organisations: Experiences in the Biotechnology Industry, *R&D Management*, 22, 1 (1992).

Gersony, N., Sectoral Effects on Strategic Alliance Performance for New Technology Firms, *The Journal of High Technology Management Research*, 7, 2 (1996).

Hagedoorn, J., Understanding the Rational of Strategic Technology Partnering: Interorganisational Modes of Cooperation and Sectoral Differences, *Strategic Management Journal*, 14 (1993).

Hakansson, H., Technological Collaborations in Industrial Networks, *European Management Journal*, 8, 3, September (1990).

Hamel, G., Competition for Competence and Interpartner Learning within International Strategic Alliances, *Strategic Management Journal*, 12 (1991).

Harris, R.C., Insinga, R.C., Morone, J. and Werle, M.J., The Virtual R&D Laboratory, *Research Technology Management*, March-April (1996).

Hendry, J., Culture, Community and Networks: The Hidden Cost of Outsourcing, *European Management Journal*, 13, 2 (1995).

Hennart, J.F. and Reddy, S., The Choice between Mergers/Acquisitions and Joint Ventures: The Case of Japanese Investors in the United States, *Strategic Management Journal*, 18 (1997).

Kotabe, M. and Swan, K.S., The Role of Strategic Alliances in High-Technology New Product Development, *Strategic Management Journal*, 16 (1995).

Kreps, D.M., Milgrom, P., Roberts, J. and Wilson, R., Rationale Cooperation in the Finitely Repeated Prisoners, *Journal of Economic Theory*, 27 (1982).

Millson, M.R., Raj, S.P. and Wilemon, D., Strategic Partnering for Developing New Products, *Research Technology Management*, May-June (1996), 41-49.

Mitchell, W. and Singh, K., Survival of Business Using Collaborative Relationships to Commercialise Complex Goods, *Strategic Management Journal*, 17 (1996).

Noria, N. and Eccles, R.G. (Eds.), *Networks and Organisations - Structure, Form and Action* (Harvard Business School Press, Boston, Massachusetts, 1992).

Quinn, B. and Hilmer, F.G., Strategic Outsourcing, *Sloan Management Review*, Summer (1994).

Roberts, B. and Berry, C.A., Entering New Businesses: Selecting Strategies for Success, *Sloan Management Review*, Spring (1985).

Robertson, P.L. and Langlois, R.N., Innovation, Networks and Vertical Integration, *Research Policy*, 24 (1995).

Rothwell, R., Towards the Fifth-Generation Innovation Process, *International Marketing Review*, 11, 1 (1994).

Teece, D.J., Profiting from Technological Innovation: Implications for Integration, Collaboration, Licensing and Public Policy, *Research Policy*, 15 (1986).

Teece, D.J., Competition, cooperation and innovation - Organisational arrangements for regimes of rapid technological progress, *Journal of Economic Behavior and Organization*, 18 (1992).

Upton, D.M. and McAfee, A., The Real Virtual Factory, *Harvard Business Review*, July-August (1996).

Venkatesan, R., Strategic Sourcing: To Make or Not To Make, *Harvard Business Review*, November-December (1992).

CHAPTER 4

R&D PROJECT PORTFOLIO DEFINITION

Once formulated the long term technology strategy indicating (i) the technologies which are critical for the firm's competitiveness, (ii) the time by when the technologies need to be introduced on the market and (iii) the mode of acquisition, more detailed plans of actions have to be defined. The multiyear broad action programs formulated in the technology strategy should be articulated into R&D projects. This is the second phase of the planning process which is the R&D project portfolio. The R&D project portfolio is composed of various steps:

- *fixing the R&D budget*, the phase when the amount of expenses in R&D for the current year is fixed;
- *R&D project definition*, which includes the generation of R&D projects and the definition of the characteristics of R&D projects (such as objectives, resources, time, organisation) submitted to the evaluation phase;
- *R&D project evaluation*, when the various projects are evaluated;
- *R&D project selection*, when projects are ranked and selected;
- *R&D project portfolio analysis*, aimed to adjust and optimise the portfolio of projects.

4.1   FIXING THE R&D BUDGET

The setting of the R&D budget is usually the result of negotiations between top management and R&D managers. In the past, negotiation was essentially all about the amount devoted to the R&D activities and top management was not involved in considering the content of the activities and the projects to be carried out. More recently, especially in technology- or research-intensive industries, top management directly participates to the strategic technology planning process and is often involved in the definition of the R&D projects content and in technology management. Therefore, the budget is fixed on the basis of the real content of the activities to be done in a certain year rather than on other basis. However, traditionally there is a number of allocation bases which are commonly used to fix the budget and which are usually accepted by all parties as starting points[a]. They are:

- inter-firm comparison. This method takes into account the R&D expenditure of direct competitors as reference point to determine the R&D budget. Usually, indications from companies operating in other industries are not likely to be significant. However, this method may present problems. In fact, it is rather difficult to know the real level of R&D investments of a competitor. This figure is seldom contained into official publications. Moreover, the R&D expenditure often includes different types of activities from firm to firm and makes comparisons unreliable. When available, it usually concerns a company as a whole whereas it would be necessary to have the figure related to an individual business or to a limited set of businesses. Therefore, the availability of reliable figures on the investment level of competitors is largely dependent on the ability of the firm's intelligence to find them;

- a fixed relationship to turnover. This method relates the R&D budget to turnover as a fixed percentage. It is a widely used criterion. Its advantage is that it makes the level of R&D investment grow proportionally to the firm's growth. The main disadvantage is that in such a way the level of R&D investment which affects the future competitiveness of the firm is related to past activities;

- a fixed relationship to profit. This method relates the R&D budget to profit. It is rarely used as the wide oscillations of profit are mirrored into the level of R&D investment which, on the contrary, needs to remain stable over time;

- reference to previous level of allocation. The basis of allocation is often the level of investment of the previous year;

- the costing of an agreed program. The budget is based on the funding program of specific projects on which top management has to give its consensus. This method, as mentioned above, is becoming largely used in technology-intensive firms.

These are the most widespread criteria used as basis to fix the R&D budget. Independently from the criteria used to fix the budget, there are some principles which should be taken into account in setting the R&D expenditure. They are:

- the R&D investment level has to be consistent with the firm's long term objectives and plans;

---

a   A summary can be found in Twiss (1986).

- the R&D activity requires stability to be fruitful. Both rapid decreases or increases in the amount of R&D investments are likely to generate difficulties as the R&D activity is labour- and especially brain-intensive. The organisational and managerial impact of rapid and sharp changes can be relevant;
- the distortion introduced by large projects should be considered. Cuts or adds to the R&D budget can be justified when large projects have been carried out in the past or are to be undertaken in the future respectively.

Generally, managers (both R&D and top) agree that budgets are better fixed when all these principles are considered. They recognise that the budget has to be the result of a joint analysis (involving the main firm functions concerned) of the firm's technology program rather than only a negotiation for money.

4.2   R&D PROJECT DEFINITION

This activity starts with the R&D project generation. The generation of R&D projects is the result of both bottom up and top down processes.

On the one hand, there is a continuous and non-organised phase in which R&D project ideas are proposed and put forward. It is a process involving the R&D function as well as other functions. There are projects which are generated by R&D people as the output of their thoughts, discoveries and research. Moreover, the manufacturing function typically provides ideas for incremental changes into products and production processes; the marketing function gives idea captured from the customers or other companies. This continuous process is bottom-up and allows to collect the ideas of people from different functions at various hierarchical levels.

On the other hand, there is the top down process which generates projects on the basis of the strategic inputs of top management. In other words, the long term technology strategy (chapter 2) provides the key inputs and the agreed direction where to invest. As a consequence, most projects have to be consistent with that strategy and formulated accordingly[b].

The project definition defines and describes the key characteristics of the project. Its aim is to clearly state the objectives of the projects and provide the information

---

b   Generally, a small amount of the budget is used to fund projects which are not in line with the agreed strategy. Allowing researchers to spend (a small portion of their) time on the development of their own ideas is recognised as a means to enhance the organisation creativity, motivate R&D people, find and open new lines of research. This underpins the bottom up process of R&D project generation.

necessary to the project feasibility evaluation. Three project variables should be in particular estimated and defined:
-       the duration of the project;
-       the resources (type and amount) required by the project;
-       the output of the project.

The type of project output differs if the project is in the development phase or in the research phase. The output of a development project is a new product or an innovative production process in use. Its measure is the estimation of the product market potential (of the new product or of the product produced with the innovative production process in use). If possible, it should identify the profits generated by such innovation. A research project can be described as a knowledge improvement in a certain disciplinary area. The estimation of the output can be a qualitative evaluation of what the project is able to produce: quality of people trained or acknowledged in a certain discipline, ability in the use of certain equipment, performance of a certain prototype or pilot plant.

The three characteristics (duration, costs and output) are related each other.

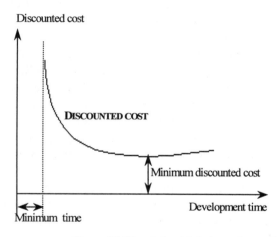

Figure 4.1. The relationship between time and cost of an R&D project.

First, there is a relationship between costs and duration which is graphically reported in Figure 4.1. It shows that the R&D cost curve of a project has a U shape in relation to time. If duration has to be shortened, the project has to be crashed, which means that costs[c] raise significantly. The curve shows a minimum level of costs and then goes up as consequence of longer duration. Long duration often means that the productivity of researchers decreases and/or the project may need to be redefined as the context changes or the objectives are revised. For these reasons, costs tend to increase.

Second, the margin generated by the project decreases with the length of the project, as the market window shortens. The margin is given by the difference between revenues and operating costs, where operating costs include all costs excepting R&D costs. Revenues and operating costs, as well as R&D costs, are discounted. It should be observed that the increasing importance of time as competitive weapon shortens the window of opportunity. This means that the margin curve often goes sharply down with the increasing duration of the project.

Third, the minimum level of R&D expenses does not identify the optimum level of R&D investment. This is identified by the maximum profit, i.e. the maximum difference between the margin curve and the R&D cost curve. The effect of the time-based competition is that the maximum profit point tends to move leftwards, as a consequence of the sharp decrease of the margin with the project length (Figure 4.2).

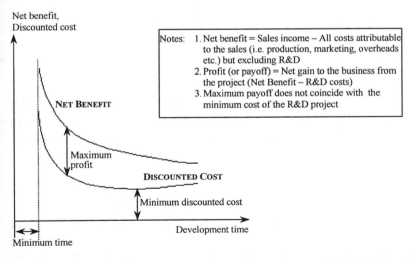

Figure 4.2. Relationship between project duration, project costs and profitability (Source: Twiss, 1985).

---

c   Here, costs are meant as discounted costs.

Fourth, there is an intangible factor to be considered when solving the trade-offs among duration, costs and profits. In fact, the output of a certain project in terms of acquired capabilities in a certain technological area changes if the time devoted to such acquisition or absorption process varies. Dierickx and Cool (1989) have defined this factor as "time compression diseconomies". This means that maintaining a given rate of spending over a certain time span produces a larger increment to the stock of R&D know-how than, for example, maintaining twice this rate of spending over half the time span. Therefore, crashed R&D programs are less effective than programs where annual R&D outlays are lower but spread over a proportionally longer period of time. In other words, if the time of an R&D program is shortened, the effect in terms of acquired skills is poorer.

The profile of the project (in terms of duration and costs and expected output) influences the type (meant as the quality) of resources to be involved. Therefore, in several organisations different versions of the project are prepared, each corresponding to a certain duration, R&D cost, market potential, profile of resources used. This helps the following evaluation phase (section 4.3).

Finally it should be added that the project definition phase should also provide a definition of the project organisation, identifying the project manager and/or the project champion and some early organisational aspects. These aspects concern project management factors and techniques which are not dealt with in this book[d].

4.3   R&D PROJECT EVALUATION

Once defined, the project is then subject to a formal evaluation procedure. This section presents different techniques used in the evaluation of R&D projects. Before the different techniques are described, it is worth to list the general principles to consider in the evaluation, whatever technique is used. They are the following.

(i)   The evaluation of a project should consider the impact on the overall business, i.e. on the firm as a whole (including R&D and all the other functions), as well as the potential return from the market. Although the R&D phase is often far from commercialisation, the evaluation of an R&D project should take into account the effect of the project on the whole set of activities involved, from R&D to the

---

[d]   To deepen further this aspect see among the others: Allen (1976), Roussel et al. (1991), Clark and Fujimoto (1991).

marketing of the output. This means that the value of a project can significantly vary from firm to firm. A project, which can be fully exploited by a firm where the resources required downstream (distribution capabilities, logistics, marketing channels) are available, is of minor value (or even unsuccessful) in another firm, which lacks the required resources (or should invest a large amount of money to acquire them). In the innovation management theory, it has been clearly emphasised that to exploit an innovation it may be necessary to have complementary assets which are needed to bring the innovation appropriately onto the market (Teece, 1986). Chapter 3 (§ 3.2.1) mentions that failures may occur because the innovating firm lacks the required assets complementary to innovation which prevent it from appropriating the benefits of the innovation.

(ii)   The effect of each project on the other R&D projects should be considered. The output of a certain project can be the pre-requisite to undertake another project; in other words, the knowledge developed provides the basis to generate and develop new projects in a certain technological discipline. Two concepts are related to this approach:
-    the absorptive capacity (Cohen and Levinthal, 1990),
-    the option theory applied to R&D.
The concept of absorptive capacity emphasises that the capacity of a firm to value and utilise outside knowledge is largely a function of the level of prior related knowledge, i.e. of the skills available within the firm. This means that a project can be undertaken to create or enrich a firm's knowledge in a certain area, in order to increase the capacity to value the external knowledge in that area. A second concept largely applied to the case of R&D projects is that of seeing them as options for future exploitation of technical knowledge. This will be treated later as there is a category of evaluation techniques which lie upon the option theory.

(iii)   R&D projects are intrinsically risky. The risk of a technological project relates to the probability that the project reveals to be not feasible technically (technical risk) or that a technically successful project fails on the market (commercial risk). The probability that the project is not successful is therefore equal to:

$1 - P_t \times P_c$

where:
-    P_t is the probability of technical success;
-    P_c the probability of commercial success.
Evaluation techniques of R&D projects have therefore to consider the risk factor.

(iv) The appropriate unit of analysis is the project. The projects subject to evaluation are both new projects and projects in progress whose potential has to be evaluated at each stage (where stage means every year if there is a yearly review of the R&D project portfolio or the project milestone which is a key decision point at which the go/no-go decision has to be taken).

(v) When projects in progress are evaluated, it has to be considered that the concept of sunk costs is central. Costs already sustained should not influence the evaluation of the project. The evaluation of the project has to be based only on costs and benefits the project will generate from now. Therefore, although a project has so far required a large amount of expenses, if the evaluation of the project now reveals that its financial return is negative, the project has to be killed. The fact that a relevant amount of money has been already spent is not a justification to go on. On the contrary, if a project has so far required large expenses, this is not a justification to stop the project. If the project from now on reveals to have positive financial results it has to be carried on. In both cases the wrong evaluation is due to the fact that sunk costs (the amount already spent for the project) are considered. Costs already sustained can not be modified by the decision to be taken today. The project should be evaluated on the basis of its financial impact from now.

(vi) The aim of an R&D project is to reduce the uncertainty about a certain discipline or technology or application. As a matter of fact, the progress of the project work increases the stock of information and knowledge available and reduces the uncertainty. The higher information, the lower uncertainty, the more reliable evaluation. In other words, information gathering costs; and the progress of the project itself is a major source of information; such wider information is the basis for more accurate and reliable evaluation of the project. This explains why projects already in progress have to be evaluated: the result of the R&D activities itself improves the stock of knowledge available for evaluation and makes this more reliable.

4.3.1. R&D Project Evaluation Techniques

There are different categories of techniques which can be used to evaluate R&D projects. Three major categories can be identified:
-      Discounted Cash Flow (DCF) techniques (Net Present Value, Profitability Index);

- Option-based techniques;
- Non-financial techniques.

DCF Techniques

A first category is that of the DCF techniques, the most common financial techniques used for investment evaluation. Given that an R&D project involves risk, DCF techniques under uncertainty conditions have to be applied. This means that the variables used to calculate the indicators (Net Present Value, Profitability Index) are stochastic and not deterministic. Each variable is therefore associated a probability of occurrence. In turn, the Net Present Value (NPV) is a stochastic variable. The NPV is the following:

$$NPV = \sum_t \frac{NCF(t)}{(1+i)^t}$$

where:
NCF(t) is the Net Cash Flow generated by the project in year t [e];
i is the risk free rate and is used as hurdle rate (the rate used is the rate in absence of risk as the risk is implicitly taken into account in NCFs which are stochastic variables).

The NPV allows to evaluate both the relevance and the risk of the R&D project.
The expected value of the NPV measures the relevance of the project, i.e. whether and to what extent the project is fruitful.

---

[e] The Net Cash Flow of year t is obtained as:

[*(Revenues - Cash costs)* $(1-t^*)$ + *(Depr. + Amort.)* t^*] - *Inv.*

where:
- *Revenues* are the incremental revenues generated by the innovation (new product or use of new production process) generated by the project;
- *Cash costs* are the incremental cash costs sustained for producing and selling the innovation (material, labour, rents);
- *Depr.* is the depreciation of the investments in tangible (fixed) assets acquired for the project;
- *Amort.* is the amortisation of the investments into intangible assets (R&D expenses, brand names, patents) sustained for the project;
- t^* is the fiscal rate;
- *Inv.* are the investments into assets and working capital.

The risk of the project can be measured in three different ways:
- the range of the possible future project results (measured by the dispersion of the NPV: the NPV of the project is a stochastic variable and its dispersion is calculated with indicators such as the dispersion coefficient, the variance, the standard deviation);
- the probability that the firm undertaking the project reduces its value, i.e. the probability that the project generates a negative result (measured as the probability that the NPV is negative);
- the probability that the firm undertakes a project which threats the firm's survival (measured by the worst event, i.e. the case in which the firm sustains the initial investment and has no returns).

Alternatively, it can be used the Profitability Index which is linked to the NPV by the following relation:

$$PI = 1 + \frac{NPV}{I}$$

where I is the amount of discounted investments required by the project.

The PI is a stochastic variable and its expected value measures the project relevance. The risk can be calculated in the three modes described above respectively as:
- the dispersion of the PI values;
- the probability that PI is less than 1;
- the worst event (loss of the whole investment).

Example

A two years R&D project is aimed to develop a new product. The year after the end of the R&D project is spent to install the plant required to produce the new product and then the product is commercialised. The market life of the product is four years. The R&D project costs 1000 every year for two years (amortisation in two years starting from the year after), the building and setting up of the plant costs 5000 (depreciation in four years from the year after). Values and probability of occurrence of revenues and operating cash costs of each year of the product life are reported in the table below. The fiscal rate is 45%, the cost of capital is 15%, the risk free rate is 5%.

REVENUES		COSTS	
Values	Probability	Values	Probability
2000	0.3	1500	0.25
3000	0.5	2000	0.45
4000	0.2	2400	0.30

Therefore, every year, the expected difference between revenues and operating costs is the following (each difference is associated a probability which is obtained multiplying the probability of occurrence of the corresponding cost by the probability of occurrence of the corresponding revenue).

REVENUES

		2000	3000	4000	Prob. Costs
COSTS	1500	500 (p=0.075)	1500 (p=0.125)	2500 (p=0.05)	0.25
	2000	0 (p=0.135)	1000 (p=0.225)	2000 (p=0.09)	0.45
	2400	- 400 (p=0.09)	600 (p=1.15)	1600 (p=0.06)	0.30
	Prob. Revenues	0.3	0.5	0.2	

The NCF associated with the first scenario (revenues = 2000, costs = 1500) are:

Year	NCF
0	Revenues = 0 Costs = 0 Inv (R&D expenses) = 1000 Amort = 0 NCF = -1000
1	Rev. = 0 Costs = 0 Amort = 500 Inv (R&D expenses) = 1000 NCF = $500 \times 0.45 - 1000 = - 775$
2	Rev = 0 Costs = 0 Amort = 500 + 500 Inv (plant) = 5000 NCF = $1000 \times 0.45 - 5000 = - 4550$
3	Rev = 2000 Costs = 1500 Amort = 500 Depr = 1250 Inv = 0 NCF = $500 \times 0.55 + 1750 \times 0.45 = 1062.5$

(follows)

4	Rev = 2000
	Costs = 1500
	Depr = 1250
	Inv = 0
	NCF = 500 × 0.55 + 1250 × 0.45 = 837.5
5	As year 4
	NCF = 500 × 0.55 + 1250 × 0.45 = 837.5
6	As year 4
	NCF = 500 × 0.55 + 1250 × 0.45 = 837.5

The NPV can be obtained from:

$$NPV = -1000 - \frac{775}{(1+0.05)} - \frac{4550}{(1+0.05)^2} + \frac{1062.5}{(1+0.05)^3} + \frac{837.5}{(1+0.05)^4} + \frac{837.5}{(1+0.05)^5} + \frac{837.5}{(1+0.05)^6}$$

This value of NPV has associated a probability of occurrence equal to 0,075, which is the probability of occurrence of the related revenues and costs.

Similarly, the other NCFs and the related eight NPVs can be calculated. NPV is therefore, in turn, a stochastic variable with an associated probability distribution. The expected value of the NPV which is obtained as:

$$E(NPV) = \sum_t \frac{E(NCF(t))}{(1+i)^t}$$

where:

E (NCF (t)) is the expected values of the NCFs

or (which is the same) as

E(NPV) = NPV × p(NPV)

where *NPV* is the Net Present Value corresponding to certain values of revenues and cost, and

p(NPV) is the probability of occurrence of that NPV.

The expected value of the NPV measures the project relevance.

The risk can be measured in each of the three ways above mentioned:

-   the dispersion of the NPVs (the variance, standard deviation or dispersion coefficient);
-   the probability that NPV is lower than zero;
-   the worst event (the minimum value of NPV).

The variance can be calculated as

$$\sigma^2_{NPV} = E\ [(NPV - E(NPV))^2]$$

therefore,

$$\sigma^2{}_{NPV} = \sum_t \frac{\sigma^2{}_t}{(1+i)^{2t}} + 2\sum_j\sum_k \frac{\sigma_j\sigma_k\rho_{jk}}{(1+i)^{j+k}}$$

where:

σ_{NPV} is the standard deviation of the NPV;

σ_t is the standard deviation of the NCF of year t;

ρ_{jk} is the coefficient of linear correlation between the NCFs of year j and k.

The linear correlation coefficient measures the extent to which net cash flows of different years are correlated each other. Theoretically, its value varies from -1 to +1; however, in the evaluation of R&D projects the values vary from 0 to 1, where 0 means that value of the NCF in a given year does not influence (or is independent from) the values of the net cash flows in other years[f]. If greater than 0, it means that if the NCF is above (below) the average in a year, the probability that they are above (below) the average in other years increases. Usually, it is very difficult to measure the values of the linear correlation coefficient. Therefore, usually, the variance is calculated in the cases of correlation equal to 0 and correlation equal to 1, which are the minimum and the maximum values of the variance of NPV.

This approach can be used when the number of stochastic variables composing the NPV is limited. In the above case they are only revenues and operating costs. If the number of variables is high (for example if each type of cost, such as material, labour, etc. is a stochastic variable), simulation techniques can be used.

Option Based Techniques

Several contributions suggested that options pricing theory should be applied to the evaluation of R&D. The general concept is that an R&D investment is analogous to an investment into a call option. A call option for a common stock can be seen as a contract where the purchaser of the option obtains the right to buy at a specified price on a specified future date. When the future date arrives, the holder of the option can decide whether to exercise or not the option. The holder will exercise the

---

[f] Negative values of the linear correlation coefficient would mean that if the NCF is above (below) the average in a year, the probability that it is below (above) the average in the other years increases. This seems to be not the case of such projects.

option if the market price of the stock is higher than the price specified in the option contract. He will obtain a profit proportional to the difference between the market price and the option price. If the market price of the stock is lower than the option contract price, the option holder will allow the option to expire and the loss will be limited to the amount of money originally invested in the option. The equivalent situation occurs for an R&D program. A corporation can decide not to make the follow-up investment necessary to capitalise on the R&D program. The equivalent loss is the cost of the R&D program, which in general is smaller than the follow-up investments.

It has been argued that the view of uncertainty changes. Volatility (or uncertainty) has a reverse impact on a call option, as the risk is limited to the cost of the option. If the volatility of the stock price is zero, the value of the option is zero. Increased volatility in the stock price increases the chance that it may exceed the exercise price before expiration. The R&D program is similar: an R&D program which shows high impact opportunities with a modest or low probability of success does not imply higher risk.

Also time has a reverse effect than for usual investments. For a call option, increasing the time by which the option may be exercised increases the probability that stock price may exceed the exercise price during this period and thus increases the value of the option. The analogy is still sound. The R&D program which provides the opportunity to make a series of investments over a period of time or offer the flexibility in the timing of subsequent investments are preferred to those requiring a short-range limited window of application. Mitchell and Hamilton (1988) emphasised that an R&D program has an advantage over the call option. Whereas the purchase of a stock option has no direct effect on the exercise price or the future price of the stock, the major purpose of an R&D program is to influence the future investment favourably either by lowering the costs or by increasing returns.

Example

A pharmaceutical firm has to decide whether to invest 0.5 M$ in an R&D project in 1997. This may lead to a patent of which the exploitation is estimated to start three years later, in 2000. The production and commercialisation of the new product requires an investment of 4 M$ at the year 2000. The time in between is requested to obtain the authorisation from the regulatory body. The foreseen discounted cash flows generated by the exploitation of the patent at year 2000 are the following:

Scenario	Discounted cash flows at year 2000	Probability
Market is small	1 M$	0.6
Market is big with strong competition	6 M$	0.1
Market is big with no competition	10 M$	0.3

The cost of capital is 15%.

The use of the traditional DCF technique would lead to the following evaluation. The expected value of the exploitation phase is:

$$0.6 \times (1 - 4) + 0.1 \times (6 - 4) + 0.3 \times (10 - 4) = +0.2$$

and the overall evaluation would be

$$NPV = -0.5 + \frac{0.2}{(1+0.15)^3}$$

In reality, the decision to launch the product is postponed to the year 2000. The R&D program is an option to launch a new product on the market three years later. The exercise price of the option is 4M$, i.e. the investment to be made at year 2000. However, the decision to exploit the option and go ahead will be taken at year 2000. Therefore, if the scenario will be pessimistic at that time, the firm will decide not to launch the product. Therefore, the expected value of the exploitation phase is:

$$0.6 \times 0 + 0.1 \times (6 - 4) + 0.3 \times (10- 4) = 2$$

and the overall evaluation is:

$$NPV = -0.5 + \frac{2}{(1+0.15)^3}$$

Also the evaluation of risk strongly changes. With the traditional technique, the risk of the investment estimated with the worst event is equal to:

$$worst \ \ event = \min(NPV) = -0.5 - \frac{3}{(1+0.15)^3}$$

corresponding to the R&D project expenses and the worst case of market failure, whereas with the option technique the risk is equal to:

worst event = min(NPV) = -0,5

corresponding to the expenses of the R&D project.

Non-Financial Methods

There are different non-financial methods commonly used to evaluate R&D programs. The main three categories are:
- profile methods;
- checklists;
- scoring methods.

Profile methods. It is the simplest method (with checklists) to evaluate an R&D program. A set of criteria is defined to evaluate the project which are considered key factors in determining the success or failure of the project. Projects are qualitatively evaluated against these criteria. Each project is assigned a qualitative judgement (for example high, medium, low) which mirrors the performance of the project against that criterion. Finally a profile is drawn which shows the profile of the project. An example is reported in Figure 4.3.

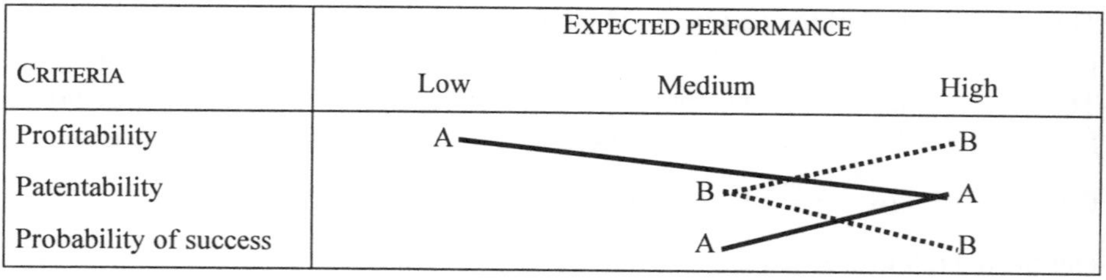

CRITERIA	EXPECTED PERFORMANCE		
	Low	Medium	High
Profitability	A		B
Patentability		B	A
Probability of success	A		B

Figure 4.3. Profile method - An example.

Checklists. It is similar to the profile method. A set of criteria is fixed and projects are evaluated against these criteria. The difference is that each project is assigned a yes/no evaluation according to the fact that the project is satisfactory against the criterion or not. An example is reported in Figure 4.4.

Both the profile method and the checklist are very simple to be used. Moreover, they help evaluate projects of which a quantitative evaluation would be arbitrary and unreliable. However, there are also disadvantages. Profile methods do not lead to a synthetic measure of the goodness of the project as they show the profile but do not provide a merit figure to be associated to the project. Checklists may lead to a merit figure which is obtained summing the number of criteria satisfied by the project. This remains a rather poor method to obtain a synthetic measure and also does not consider that criteria may have different importance.

CRITERIA	Project A	Project B
Profitability	0	1
Patentability	1	0
Probability of success	0	1
Totals	1	2

Figure 4.4. Checklist method - An example.

The fig. 4.4 shows a very simple checklist.
However, the list of criteria which can be used to evaluate the project is very wide. Figure 4.5 shows an exhaustive list taken from Twiss (1986).

A.   Corporate objectives, strategy, policies, and values
1. Is it compatible with the company's current strategy and long range plan?
2. Is its potential such that a change in the current strategy is warranted?
3. Is it consistent with the company's "image"?
4. Is it consistent with the corporate attitude to risk?
5. Is it consistent with the corporate attitude to innovation?
6. Does it meet the corporate needs for time-gearing?
B.   Marketing criteria
1. Does it meet a clearly defined market need?
2. Estimated total market size.
3. Estimated market share.
4. Estimated product life.
5. Probability of commercial success.
6. Likely sales volume (based on items 2 to 5).
7. Time scale and relationship to the market plan.
8. Effect upon current products.
9. Pricing and customer acceptance.
10.Competitive position.
11.Compatibility with existing distribution channels.
12.Estimated launching cost.

(follows)

C.   Research and development criteria
1. Is it consistent with the company's R&D strategy?
2. Does its potential warrant a change to the R&D strategy?
3. Probability of technical success.
4. Development cost and time.
5. Patent position.
6. Availability of R&D resources.
7. Possible future development of the product and future applications of the new technology generated.
8. Effect upon other projects.
D.   Financial criteria
1. Research and development cost:
(a) capital;
(b) revenue.
2. Manufacturing investment.
3. Marketing investment.
4. Availability of finance related to time scale.
5. Effect upon other projects requiring finance.
6. Time to break-even and maximum negative cash flow.
7. Potential annual benefit and time scale.
8. Expected profit margin.
9. Does it meet the company's investment criteria?
E.   Production criteria
1. New processes involved.
2. Availability of manufacturing personnel – numbers and skills.
3. Compatibility with existing capability.
4. Cost and availability of raw material.
5. Cost of manufacture.
6. Requirements for additional facilities.
7. Manufacturing safety.
8. Value added in production.
F.   Environmental and ecological criteria
1. Possible hazards – product and production process.
2. Sensitivity to public opinion.
3. Current and projected legislation.
4. Effect upon employment.

Figure 4.5. Checklist for R&D project evaluation (Source: Twiss, 1985).

Scoring methods. Scoring methods are based on the same architecture as the previous two. The application of a scoring method requires the following steps:

-     fixing the criteria, on the basis of which the projects are to be evaluated;
-     assigning each criterion a weight, which mirrors the relative importance of the criterion (weights are normalised so that their sum is equal to one);
-     assigning the project a score in relation to each criterion, which mirrors how the project behaves against that criterion.

The score of the project is:

$$T_i = \Sigma_j \, W_j \times S_{ij}$$

where:

W_j is the weight of criteria j

S_{ij} is the score of the project i against criteria j.

Advantages of the scoring methods are the following:
-      the criteria can be as many as required and changed according to the specific project evaluated;
-      weights allow to assign criteria different importance;
-      projects can be easily ranked on the basis of their merit figure;
-      non financial criteria can be used;
-      the method can be easily adapted.

Disadvantages are:
-      the merit figure is useful when used to compare different projects, but in absolute terms it has not any meaning;
-      it does not give the possibility to identify a range of results;
-      criteria need to be carefully fixed as they have to be independent from each other;
-      it does not help ex-post audit (as any non financial method);
-      it is highly subjective and dependent on the individual characteristics of people who develop and use it;
-      given its subjectivity, it is often difficult to support certain decisions with other people and convince top management of the goodness of a project.

Box 4.1 - Scoring method – Example

This box reports a method used in a large European chemical company. Scoring methods are used to evaluate both basic research projects and applied research projects. The method is designed to separately evaluate two key dimensions: the project attractiveness and the firm's capability in that area (which is a proxy of the project risk).

The method for applied research and development projects is the following.
The project attractiveness is the result of:
- the strategic relevance which includes:
    - strategic importance of the technological area concerned;
    - the range of applicability of the project results;
    - benefits to the firm's positioning in the business;

(follows)

- relevance of the business(es) where the project results would be utilised;
- economic relevance:
  - revenues;
  - costs;
  - return on investment;
  - probability of commercial success;
- time-to-market;
- robustness:
  - normative factors;
  - technological factors;
  - economic factors;
- indirect benefits:
  - industrial benefits;
  - environmental benefits;
  - scientific benefits.

Firm's capability is measured assigning scores against the following variables:
- resource adequacy, including:
  - project leadership;
  - team specialisation;
  - integration of R&D with other functions;
  - availability and appropriateness of the equipment;
- soundness and originality of the idea, including:
  - technical feasibility;
  - originality;
- project definition, including:
  - clarity of the final objective;
  - clarity of the intermediate objectives;
  - market benefits;
  - patenting;
- engineering phase, including:

- criticality of resources needed in the engineering phase;
- constraints to the industrial exploitation;
- firm's strength in the technologies used in the exploitation phase;
- industrialisation experience;
- transfer to manufacturing and scale up;
- willingness to exploit the project results.

The method for basic research projects is the following.
The attractiveness is estimated on the basis of:
- strategic relevance, including:
  - relation with the core technologies of the firm;
  - the range of applicability of the project results;
  - consistency of the project objectives with the business objectives;
  - relevance of the business(es) where the project results would be utilised;
- expected benefits, including:
  - potential applications;
  - creation of a base of knowledge;
  - impact on other projects;
- time and costs:
  - project duration;
  - project costs.

The firm's capability is related to the following factors:
- resource adequacy, including:
  - project leadership;

(follows)

- team specialisation;
- commitment of the team;
- access to external sources;
- soundness:
  - feasibility;
  - technical strengths of the project;
  - peer reviews;
- originality:
  - newness;
  - patenting;
- project definition:
  - potential benefits;
  - soundness of the theoretical background;
- awareness of the current knowledge;
- project programming.

The method allows to place the project on a bi-dimensional matrix, where six areas have been identified (Figure 4.6):
- area of the most important projects;
- area of important projects;
- area of not interesting project;
- area of projects to abandon;
- area of incremental projects.

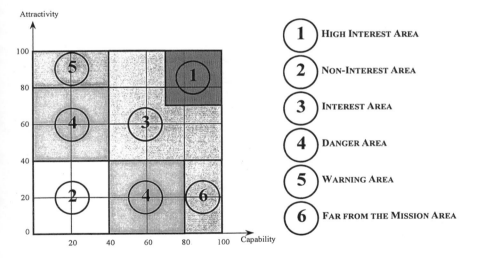

Figure 4.6. Matrix and classification areas.

Scoring methods can be made less subjective and more reliable with the introduction of appropriate techniques. A widely used technique is that of the *Analytic Hierarchy Process* (*AHP*), developed by Saaty during the 70s which has been largely used to support decisional problems. It is a method which helps decompose a complex decisional problem building a multi-layer hierarchical structure. Its main benefit is to make scoring methods more reliable and less subjective, as it helps make more reliable the subjective judgement of the decision maker(s).

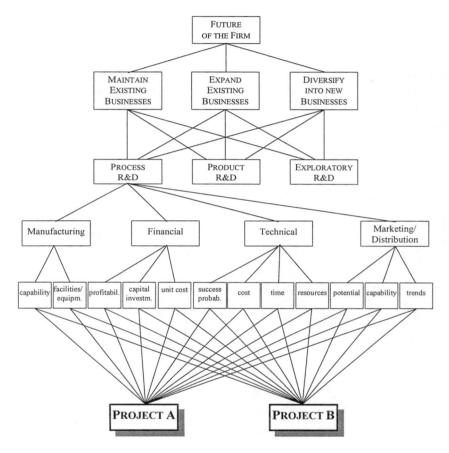

Figure 4.7. An AHP application to the evaluation of R&D projects (Source: Liberatore, 1987).

It is based on five steps:

-   building the hierarchy. The decisional problem is disaggregated into multilevel hierarchy. At the top of the hierarchy there is the objective. Then, there is a first level of decisional attributes, each of which can be subdivided into attributes and so on. Each attribute at a given level influences the higher level.

The last level is composed of the n alternatives to be evaluated to achieve the objective;

comparing the attribute at the same level. Attributes at the same level are pair wise compared. Usually the scale used is from 1 to 9. If a_{ij} is the importance of the attribute i compared with the attribute j in influencing the attribute at the higher level, $a_{ij} = 1$ means that i has the same importance as j, $a_{ij} = 3$ means that i is weakly preferred to j, $a_{ij} = 5$ means that i is preferred to j, $a_{ij} = 7$ means that i is strongly preferred to j, $a_{ij} = 9$ means that i is absolutely preferred to j. A square, positive, reciprocal matrix is built on these comparisons;

a_1/a_1	a_1/a_2	a_1/a_3	....	a_1/a_n
a_2/a_1	a_2/a_2	a_2/a_3	....	a_2/a_n
....	....	....	....	....
a_n/a_1	a_n/a_2	a_n/a_3	....	a_n/a_n

assigning a weight to each attribute. The weight of each attribute is calculated as the result of the pair wise comparisons. This is the real newness and strength of the method. Weights are assigned as the result of the pair wise comparisons between attributes rather than through the direct assignment of a weight to each attribute. The weights are obtained calculating the eigenvector associated with the above square matrix. The eigenvector shows the priorities (rankings of the attributes at that level). The method verifies whether there are consistencies among the comparative evaluations given (Saaty, 1980);

identifying the importance of each attribute with respect to the objective. Multiplying the importance (weight) of an attribute in influencing the higher level attribute by the importance (weight) of the higher level attribute, it can be calculated the composed weight of each attribute which is the importance of the attribute in influencing the objective. The composed weights which show the importance of an attribute at a certain level k with respect to the objective at level 1 is obtained from:

$$C[1,k] = \prod_{i=2;k} B_i$$

where:

B_i is the matrix of which the rows are the eigenvectors (n_i is the number of attributes at level i);

C[1,k] is the vector of the composed weight of the elements at level k with respect to the objective (level 1);
- evaluating the alternatives. As the last level n is composed of the alternatives, the components of the vector C[1,n] are the scores associated with the alternatives and represents the evaluation of the alternatives against the objective. In other words, the vector associated with the last level shows the overall scores of the different alternatives.

The AHP is therefore a methodology which supports the determination of priorities of a set of alternatives. It allows to face complex decisional problems where both quantitative and qualitative factors account in the evaluation. It also allows to deal with interdependencies among factors and suggests whether there are inconsistencies in the judgements.

An example of the application of the AHP technique to the evaluation of the R&D projects has been provided by Liberatore (1987). Figure 4.7 shows the hierarchy of the AHP model for R&D project selection.

4.3.2. Range of Application of Financial and Non-Financial Techniques

The techniques shown above are usually applied to projects of different nature in R&D. Development projects usually can be evaluated through financial techniques. Basic or exploratory research projects are evaluated with non-financial techniques. The variables cannot be estimated quantitatively. Pre-development or early development or feasibility or prototype projects (i.e. projects in which the potential innovation has already been defined and the project is aimed at evaluating the feasibility) can be evaluated through option based techniques.

TYPE OF PROJECT	EVALUATION TECHNIQUES
Development project	DCF techniques
Early development	Option based techniques
Research	Non financial technique

Non-financial techniques can be used in two ways:
- they can lead to a synthetic measure including both relevance and risk in one measure. This means that the variables used to evaluate a project include both relevance and risk factors in one merit figure;

- they can be used to separately evaluate relevance and risk. In the latter case, a profile, checklist, or score is given for relevance and risk separately. This allows to make portfolio analysis (see the section 4.5) as well as when financial techniques are used.

4.4   R&D PROJECT SELECTION

In the phase of project selection the decision taker defines whether a project has to be undertaken or not on the basis of the evaluation made. A clear distinction should be done between large or strategic projects and small projects.

Large or Strategic Projects

Large projects usually concern strategic investments such as the development of a new product or a new product generation, or the building of a new plant based on new technologies.

Examples are a new car or a new product platform in the automotive industry, a new generation in the chip industry, a radically new product, the building of a new plant in the chemical industry adopting a new process technology.

These projects are usually evaluated individually and not as part of the portfolio[g]. The decision whether to undertake the project or not is based on its relevance and risk. They are projects on which the firm's strategy is based. Given that they require large investments, risk is usually measured with the worst event approach. Risk is measured with the financial exposure required to undertake the project and therefore the whole amount requested and lost in case of failure. This means that risk is related to the firm's survival itself as the failure of the project can lead to significant losses or the failure of the firm.

Small Projects

Given that firms operate in limited budget conditions, small projects are seen as alternative to each other and, therefore, they should be selected as they were mutually exclusive. The selection process depends on the techniques used in the evaluation phase.

---

[g]   It is of course true that undertaking such projects means to consume a large part of the budget and firms may consider whether this prevents from undertaking other technological initiatives. However, firms usually evaluate such projects and decide whether to undertake it or not separately from the process of selection of other projects.

Financial techniques. When financial techniques are used, the Profitability Index has to be used rather than the NPV. It can be demonstrated that PI is appropriate when selection takes place in limited budget conditions and allows to select the most profitable portfolio of projects.

The selection is based on the two factors defined in the evaluation process: the relevance and the risk. Therefore, the decision should take combinedly into account these two factors. This makes difficult to establish the superiority of a project on another one. Three ways can be used:
- stochastic dominance;
- utility theory;
- subjective decision of the decision taker.

Stochastic dominance. It is the case when there is clear dominance of some projects on the others. When two projects A and B are considered, there is stochastic dominance when:
- PI_A has an expected value greater than the expected value of PI_B, and the risk of A (measured with one the three ways above mentioned) is lower than the risk of B;
  or
- between the two distribution functions FA (x) and FB (x) there is a relation by which, whatever x is taken, the probability that PI_A is greater than x is greater than the probability that PI_B is greater than x.

In other words, project A is clearly superior to project B.

If there are projects which are clearly superior to the other in terms of both relevance and risk, the selection can take place using the stochastic dominance[h]. Projects are therefore ranked on the basis of this criterion and the first ranked using the budget available are those selected.

Utility theory. This approach is based on the definition of an 'utility function' which identifies combinations of relevance and risk equivalent for the decision taker. The utility function has an analytical expression and its use can be analytically treated. The use of the utility theory is here treated showing its graphical application.

The selection process takes place as follows (Figure 4.8).

---

[h] For a discussion on the application of this criterion see Suresh and Meredith (1986).

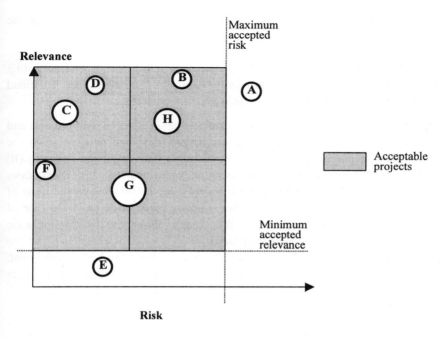

Figure 4.8. The selection of R&D projects with the utility function.

Projects are classified according to their characteristics of relevance and risk. Only the projects are considered of which the relevance overcomes a certain threshold value and risk is minor than the maximum risk accepted. These projects are then represented in a relevance-risk diagram with a circle of which the diameter is proportional to the amount of investment requested. The utility function is represented by the straight line (for simplicity). The slope of the line mirrors the risk propensity. If the line has a slope which is greater than 45°, the decision maker is risk adverse, as he/she accepts projects of low relevance provided that it has low risk. On the contrary, the utility function with a slope smaller than 45° means that the decision maker is a risk taker, as he/she accepts projects with high risk, provided that they have high relevance. Starting from the upper left corner, the line is moved towards the bottom right corner. An area in the upper left corner is identified by the utility function. Projects, which are progressively intersected by the line, have a decreasing utility. The movement towards the bottom right corner stops when the whole budget is used (i.e. when the sum of the investments requested by the projects included in the upper left area equalise the budget available). Projects in the area are those selected.

Subjective evaluation. The decision taker subjectively selects the projects according to the most preferable (for him/her) profiles of relevance and risk. A rank is defined and the first consuming the budget available are those selected.

Non financial techniques. Non financial techniques again allow to rank projects and then select the most relevant. As mentioned above, there are two cases: (i) the technique leads to one synthetic evaluation including both relevance and risk, (ii) the techniques lead to separate evaluations of relevance and risk. In the first case, the decision is simple as the rank is given by ordering the projects on the basis of their merit figures. In the second case, the selection takes place as in the case of financial techniques, adopting one of the criteria above described (stochastic dominance, utility theory, subjective decision).

Therefore, these techniques allow to rank the projects from the best to the worst. The selection is done considering the amount of investment each project requires and going from top to the bottom of the list. The projects selected are the first which utilise the whole budget available.

4.5   R&D PROJECT PORTFOLIO ANALYSIS

The phase of selection often requires a further step which is the portfolio analysis. It may occur that the set of projects selected in the selection phase does not constitute an appropriate portfolio of projects. The portfolio analysis essentially evaluates whether the set of projects selected is balanced against certain variables. The main reasons to conduct a portfolio analysis are the following[i].

(i)   A first factor against which the portfolio of projects selected have to be balanced is time. It may occur that a large majority of the projects selected shows a time-to-completion very short or, on the contrary, very long. Usually it is preferred to have a portfolio with a certain distribution over time in order to have a continuous pipeline of projects, each stage of the innovation process appropriately fed, and potential for innovation over both short and long term. The portfolio

---

[i]   In this section, reference is made to the use of the relevance-risk diagram as in the utility theory. This helps view how the changes of the project profiles impact on the relevance and risk profile of the projects and, consequently, on the position of the project in the diagram. Of course, any other selection method can be used.

analysis helps identify whether the time profile of the project portfolio is appropriate. A simple tool to be used is the diagram in which the budget spent and the time to completion of the projects selected are shown. It gives an idea of the temporal distribution of the budget.

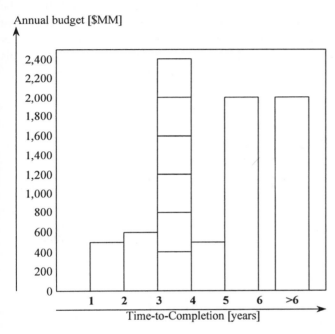

Annual budget [$MM]

Time-to-Completion [years]

Figure 4.9. Annual budget and time-to-completion of R&D projects.

If the portfolio is judged unbalanced, the profiles of certain projects should be modified. Changing the duration of a project means to change the amount (and often the type) of the resources required. Therefore, the project characteristics change and its position in the relevance-risk diagram changes.

(ii) Another reason to conduct the portfolio analysis is that the process of selection has not yet taken into account whether there are or not inter-dependencies among projects. Interdependencies can be of two types:
- results of a project are the pre-requisite to undertake another project;
- projects are inter-linked each other and results are reciprocally dependent.

This can be represented in the relevance-risk diagram (Figure 4.10). The one-way arrow means that a project is the pre-requisite of another. The two-ways arrow means that the results of the two projects are inter-dependent.

It may occur that a project interdependent with another has been excluded in the selection process. This means again that the portfolio has to be modified. It may be decided that the project depending on the non-selected one is not selected and therefore there is an amount available to fund other projects. On the contrary, it may be decided to undertake the pre-requisite project originally non selected. This requires that project characteristics are modified or that the budget is enlarged.

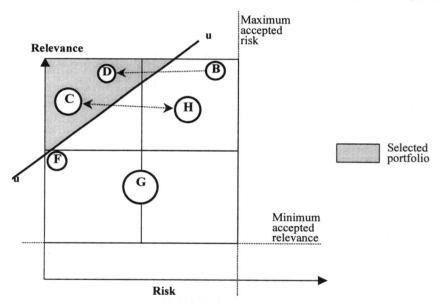

Figure 4.10. Interdependencies between projects.

(iii) There may be conflicts on resources among projects. Actually the selection process has not taken into account that projects may require the use of the same resources. When there are conflicts on resources among projects, again the project characteristics have to be changed. The profile of the projects in terms of types of resources used is modified and this may change the duration, the results, and the organisation of the projects themselves.

(iv) It may occur that the projects selected are all very risky. As a matter of fact, although the selection above is done considering the quadrant corresponding to a minimum level of relevance and a maximum level of risk, it may occur that the projects selected are mostly close to the maximum level of risk. The decision taker can be not satisfied with that, and can, therefore, decide to change the project characteristics in order to have a more balanced set of projects.

(v) It may occur that the number of projects selected is too low. The decision taker can find desirable to undertake a wider number of projects, in order to allocate resources on a larger variety of potential innovations. This means that projects need to be smaller and/or that the budget available needs to be enlarged.

The portfolio analysis can therefore make necessary to review the projects and change their characteristics in order to achieve a more balanced set of projects.[j]
The need to change the portfolio may lead to different choices:

- increasing the amount of resources available. This means that the utility function line can be moved further towards the bottom right corner, and, more generally, that a larger number of projects can be selected;
- increasing the productivity of (a) project(s). This means that there is a reduction of the amount of resources required by the concerned project(s). As a consequence the relevance of these projects increases. Moreover, the utility function line moves further to the bottom right corner and can include other projects;
- reducing the risk. These can be related to a better control and management system of projects or to a diversification of the firm's markets and areas of application. The result is the reduction of the slope of the utility function line;
- increasing the project relevance with an increase of the project risk. This can be obtained, for example, establishing higher objectives (such as shorter time to market) or enlarging the scope of the work. This change is useful if the slope of the move of the project in the diagram is sharper than the slope of the utility function line;
- reduction of the risk of the project with a reduction of the project relevance. This change is useful if the slope of the move of the project in the diagram is less sharp than the slope of the utility function line.

---

j   However, it should be noticed that project changes can dramatically impact on the organisation. If a project is delayed, there may be strong consequences on the morale of the team, and the charisma and power perceived in the organisation of the people involved in the team is also affected.

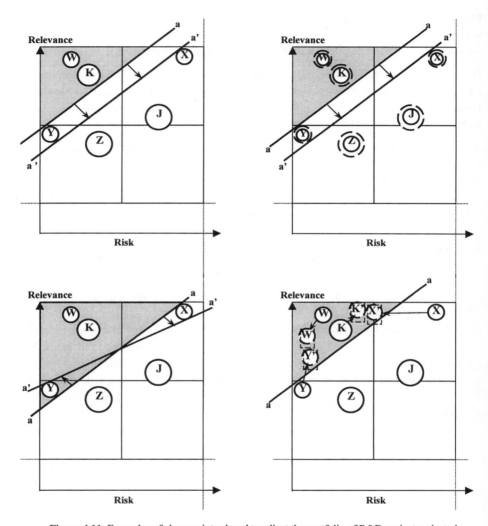

Figure 4.11. Examples of changes introduced to adjust the portfolio of R&D projects selected.

Once introduced these changes, projects are evaluated and selected again. The set of projects selected is subject to a portfolio analysis and the process is iterated until the portfolio obtained is satisfactory.

The project portfolio analysis ends the process of R&D project planning and sets the projects to be carried on during the year.

REFERENCES AND FURTHER READINGS

Allen, J., *Managing the Flow of Technology*, (MIT Press, Cambridge, 1976).

Boer, F.P., Linking R&D to growth and shareholder value, *Research Technology Management* (1995), 16-22.

Brown, M.G. and Svenson, R.A., Measuring R&D productivity, *Research Technology Management*, July-August (1988), 11-15.

Clark, K.B. and Fujimoto, T., *Product Development Performance* (HBS Press, Boston, 1991).

Cohen, W.M. and Levinthal, D.A., Absorptive Capacity: a New Perspective on Learning and Innovation, *Administrative Science Quarterly*, 35 (1990), 128.

Collier, D.W., Mong, J. and Conlin, J., How effective is technological innovation ?, *Research Management*, September-October (1984), 11-16.

Cooper, R.G., Edgett, S.J. and Kleinschmidt, E.J., Portfolio Management in New Product Development: Lessons from the Leaders-I, *Research Technology Management*, September-October (1997).

Cooper, R.G., Edgett, S.J. and Kleinschmidt, E.J., Portfolio Management in New Product Development: Lessons from the Leaders-II, *Research Technology Management*, November-December (1997).

De Maio, A., Bellucci, A., Corso, M. and Verganti, R., *Gestire l'innovazione e innovare la gestione* (Etaslibri, Milano, 1994).

Dierickx, I. and Cool, K., Asset stock accumulation and sustainability of competitive advantage, *Management Science*, December (1989).

Ellis, L.W., Managing financial resources, *Research Technology Management*, July-August (1988), 21-38.

Faulkner, T.W., Applying 'Options Thinking' to R&D valuation, *Research Technology Management*, May-June (1996), 50-56.

Foster, R.N., Linden, L.H., Whiteley, R.L. and Kantrow, A.M., Improving return on R&D – I, *Research Management*, 28, 1 (1985), 12-17.

Foster, R.N., Linden, L.H., Whiteley, R.L. and Kantrow, A.M., Improving return on R&D – II, *Research Management*, 28, 2 (1985), 13-22.

Grady, D. and Fincham, T., Making R&D pay, *The McKinsey Quarterly*, 3 (1990), 161-175.

Halliday, R.G., Drasdo, A.L., Lumley, C.E. and Walker, S.R., The allocation of resources for R&D in the world's leading pharmaceutical companies, *R&D Management*, 27, 1 (1997), 63.

Kester, W.C., Today's options for tomorrow's growth, *Harvard Business Review*, March-April (1984).

Liberatore, M.J., An extension of the Analytic Hierarchical Process for Industrial R&D Project Selection and Resource Allocation, *IEEE Transactions on Engineering Management*, February (1987), 12-18.

Mandakovich, T. and Souder, W.E., A flexible hierarchical model for project selection and budget allocation, *R&D Management*, 15, 1, January (1985), 23.

Martino, J. P., *R&D Project Selection* (John Wiley & Sons, New York, 1995).

Meredith, J.R. and Suresh N.C., Justification Techniques for Advanced Manufacturing Technologies, *International Journal of Production Research*, 24, 5 (1986), 1043-1057.

Mitchell, G.R. and Hamilton, W.F., Managing R&D as a strategic option, *Research Technology Management*, May-June (1988), 15-22.

Morbey, G.K. and Reithner, R.M., How R&D affects sales growth, productivity and profitability, *Research Technology Management*, January-February (1990).

Newton, D:P: and Pearson, A.W., Application of option pricing theory to R&D, *R&D Management*, 24,1 (1994), 83-89.

Pappas, R.A: and Remer, D.S., Measuring R&D productivity, *Research Management*, May-June (1985), 15-22.

Roussel, P., Saad, K. and Erickson, T., *Third Generation R&D* (HBS Press, Boston, 1991).

Saaty, T.L., *The Analytic Hierarchy Process* (Mc Graw-Hill, 1980).

Scholefield, J.H., The allocation of R&D resources, *R&D Management*, 24, 1 (1994), 91.

Schumann, P.A., Ransley, D.L. and Prestwood, D.C., Measuring R&D performance, *Research Technology Management*, May-June (1995), 45-54.

Steele, L.W., Selecting R&D programs and objectives, *Research Technology Management*, March-April (1988), 17-36.

Szakonyi, R. (1994), Measuring R&D effectiveness – I, *Research Technology Management*, March-April, 27-32.

Szakonyi, R., Measuring R&D effectiveness – II, *Research Technology Management*, May-June (1994), 44-55.

Teece, D.J., Profiting from Technological Innovation: Implications for Integration, Collaboration, Licensing and Public Policy, *Research Policy*, 15 (1986).

Tipping, J.W., Zeffren, E. and Fusfeld, A.R., Assessing the value of your Technology, *Research Technology Management*, September-October (1995), 22-39.

Twiss, B., *Managing Technological Innovation* (Pitman, 1985).

Zimmerman, H.J., *Fuzzy Sets Theory and Its Applications* (Kluwer Academic Publishers, Boston, 1992).

PART II

R&D ORGANISATION

The introductory section of this book emphasised that the approach to R&D management has been subject to an evolution. Different generations mirroring different styles of management of R&D have been identified (Chapter 1 includes a summary of the key characteristics of each style of management). Accordingly, the organisation of R&D has been subject to changes. The latest generation of the R&D management highlights that the management and organisation have to meet two key requirements.

- risk and temporal horizon of R&D investments need to be appropriately balanced. This means that, on the one hand, R&D has to support time-based competition and needs to be strongly integrated with manufacturing and marketing; on the other hand, R&D has to ensure that long term technology development is not put under time pressure. This strongly challenges the design of the R&D organisational structure. R&D can no more be kept in one function/unit. Therefore, different units may play different missions. The criteria at the basis of the design of the organisational structure of a certain unit is determined on the basis of the mission of the unit itself. Moreover, the R&D activities need to be distributed in different units located at different hierarchical levels within the firm's organisation. This hierarchical distribution of R&D activities raises the point of the balance between central control and decentralisation of R&D;

- the amount of investments requested to technologically innovate and the range of technologies to be covered force R&D departments to rely on external resources and balance the use of internal resources with the resort on external sources of technology. This means that an R&D organisation should also be designed to interact with external sources of knowledge and technology.

The latter, in turn, calls for two key factors of the modern organisation of R&D:

- cooperating with external sources of technology;
- locating units close to external sources of technology.

The first factor addresses the issue of cooperation in technology development, of how much to spend in external collaborations and of the selection of the appropriate organisational form of collaboration. The second factor addresses the issue of the delocalisation of R&D units, i.e. the geographical distribution or internationalisation of R&D, in order to interact with a certain external context.

Therefore, the structural dimensions of the R&D organisation are:

- the structure of R&D units, i.e. the criteria used to design the R&D structure of R&D units;
- the hierarchical distribution of the units, i.e. the balance between centralisation and decentralisation;
- the geographical distribution of the internal R&D resources;
- the balance between the use of internal and external resources and the organisation to acquire technology from external sources.

The following chapters will discuss these key dimensions of the organisation of R&D. Chapter 5 deals with the organisational structure of R&D activity and addresses the first two dimensions of the R&D organisation, i.e. how to structure a unit and where to locate the R&D units within the firm's overall organisation. Chapter 6 deals with the internationalisation of R&D and the problem of locating an R&D unit abroad; finally, Chapter 7 deals with the organisation of technological collaborations[a].

---

a   The structural dimensions of an R&D organisation are treated in this chapter. It is not the aim of this book to go in depth with the management of R&D. For example, R&D project management is not dealt with; however, project management factors which may influence the R&D organisation are mentioned. For further issues on project management applied to R&D, see for example Allen (1976), Clark and Fujimoto (1991).

CHAPTER 5

THE ORGANISATIONAL STRUCTURE

This chapter addresses the point of how to organise the R&D activities. It initially deals with the organisation and structure of an individual unit. Then, it faces the problem of the balance between centralisation and decentralisation of R&D activities, which addresses the point of how to distribute resources within the corporation and how to link the activities of the R&D units at different hierarchical levels. Finally, it is treated the point of the separation between R and D which is an emerging trend of the R&D organisations, especially in the pharmaceutical industry.

5.1   THE STRUCTURE OF R&D UNITS

In advance, it is worth to clarify the approach taken in this chapter on the structure of the R&D organisation:

(i)   the organisational structure here described concerns the individual R&D unit. As said above, the overall structure is composed of a variety of units often placed at different levels in the firm's hierarchy (section 5.2 deals with the distribution of R&D resources between corporate and business units level and the degree of centralisation/decentralisation).

(ii)   the organisational structures described represent the pure versions. The reality shows that structures are often adapted to the specific internal and external context of the firm (the boxes with the case studies and the examples provide evidence of the variety of forms the structures can assume in different firms).

As far as the structure of R&D units is concerned, two basic criteria can be used: the input-oriented and the output-oriented. The input-oriented are structures in which the basic criterion is the type of inputs required for innovation. These inputs can be the type of R&D activity or the type of scientific/technological discipline (or technical area). The output oriented are structures in which the criterion is the output of the R&D activity. The basis can be the product line (an R&D unit is articulated into as many sub-units as the product lines of the firm) or the project (an R&D unit is articulated into as many sub-units as the individual projects of

innovation). Finally, there is the matrix organisation which attempts to combine the two criteria creating a unit which is organised on the basis of a twofold dimension. Therefore, the basic criteria to design the structure of R&D units are:
- input-oriented organisation:
    - by scientific discipline or technical area;
    - by activity;
- output-oriented organisation:
    - by product line;
    - by project;
- matrix organisation.

5.1.1 Input-Oriented Organisation

As said above, there are two different input-oriented organisations. The organisation by scientific discipline or technical area and the organisation by activity.

Organisation by Scientific Discipline or Technical Area

The unit is organised by scientific or technological disciplines. Scientists, researchers and engineers are grouped on the basis of their technical specialities. This mirrors the usual organisation of university and research centre labs (Figure 5.1).

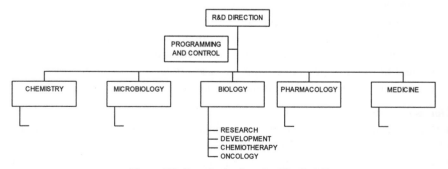

Figure 5.1. Organisation by scientific discipline.

This structure has several advantages:
(i)   favours the autonomy of the scientists and researchers;

(ii)   provides the ground for an increasing specialisation of competencies;

(iii)   well suites cases in which innovation is the result of the R&D activity in one discipline;

(iv)   facilitates the introduction of new people in the structure, as anyone easily recognises the piece of organisation with his/her specific knowledge and easily feels comfortable with the structure;

(v)   favours communication and interaction with colleagues sharing the same technical competence. This is often achieved also ensuring that there is physical proximity to colleagues who share the technical speciality;

(vi)   is adapt to the acquisition of new knowledge in a specialist field as this brings to add a leg in the R&D organisation;

(vii)   makes easier the career development of R&D specialists;

(viii) helps achieve economies of scale as the R&D activity is organised in each discipline at best. This ensures that the appropriate critical mass is achieved and potential synergies among activities within the same discipline are exploited.

There are also clear disadvantages:

(i)   the focus on technological innovation which is the commercialisation of technical change is weak. Focus on technical disciplines may detract the attention from the real aim of technical projects, i.e. the innovation;

(ii)   the integration of different disciplines is rather difficult. As said above the technology integration or technology fusion is often source of innovation. This structure separating the various disciplines generates obvious obstacles to the mixing and blending of different specialist knowledge;

(iii)   it is rather difficult to create a sense of urgency and time pressure, which are proper of innovation project;

(iv)   it does not help the coordination usually required in innovation project;

(v)   it is rather rigid and not flexible.

An example of input-oriented organisation by scientific discipline is that of Centro Ricerche Fiat, the corporate lab of the Fiat group. Its organisational structure is shown in Figure 5.2.

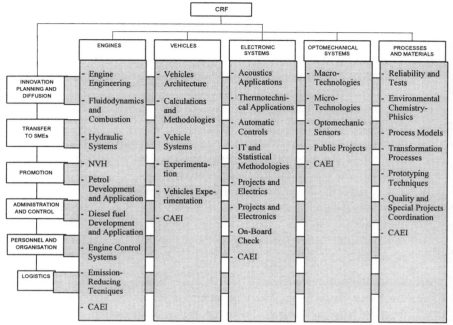

Figure 5.2. The organisation of Centro Ricerche Fiat.

Box 5.1 - The case of Centro Ricerche Fiat

The structure is by technological areas. There are five technological areas: engine, vehicles, electronic systems, optomechanical systems, processes and materials. There is a large staff articulated into different units. They are: Innovation Planning and Diffusion, Transfer to Small and Medium Enterprise, Promotion of Research Activities, Administration and Control, Personnel and Organisation. The first three are clearly oriented to increase the external orientation of the unit. In other words, the staff attempts to compensate the strong input orientation of the structure. Especially, within the Innovation Planning and Diffusion unit, there is the External Diffusion of the Innovation (EDI) group, aimed to identify potential customers for the research activities and the innovations developed. To this end, within each technological area unit, there are Coordinators of External Activities who support the EDI to find customers. The structure is evolving towards a matrix form. The idea is to create a sort of business units named External Business Units (EBU), each dedicated to individual market segments. EBUs should develop projects involving people from the various technological areas and are definitely output-oriented.

Organisation by Type of Activity

Another form of input-oriented organisation is that by R&D activity type. Scientists and technicians are organised by phase of the R&D process. A typical view of the R&D process is that it is composed of basic research, applied research, development, design and engineering, prototyping and testing.
Good examples can be found in the pharmaceutical industry, where the R&D process is clearly defined by steps and stages (see Figure 5.3).

Figure 5.3. Organisation by type of activity.

The main pros and cons of the activity-based organisation are those identified for the organisation by scientific discipline.

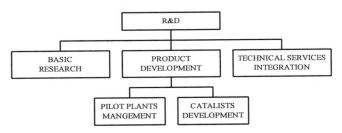

Figure 5.4. The organisation of Montell.

An example of input-oriented structure by activity is that of Montell, the company of the Royal Dutch Shell Group leader in polypropylene and other plastic materials (polymers). Its R&D structure is by activity type (see Figure 5.4). It is structured into three types of activity: basic research, product development (including both development of new products and pilot plants), and technical services (aimed to solve technical problems and assist marketing).

5.1.2 Output-Oriented Organisation

There are two types of output-oriented organisations: by product line and by project.

Organisation by Product Line

The shape of the R&D unit mirrors a typical divisional structure. Within the R&D organisation, people are grouped on the basis of the product line or business unit they are working for. This organisation can be found in multidivisional firm operating various businesses. It can also be used by firms having one business and, within it, different product lines willing to dedicate R&D resources to each product line.

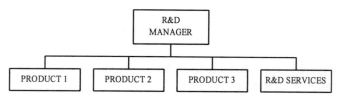

Figure 5.5. Organisation by product line.

The main advantages of this structure are:
(i)   strong orientation to the generation of innovations as people are organised on the basis of the structure of the customer base the firm wants to satisfy;
(ii)   strong customer focus;
(iii) strong integration with the other business activities as the orientation is common;
(iv)   strong managerial and organisational flexibility in the management of the new product development process;
(v)   easy coordination;
(vi)   attention to time and costs of innovation.

Major disadvantages are related to the following factors:
(i)   there is a certain duplication of resources. This occurs because each R&D division is often organised by discipline and this brings a certain duplication of efforts;
(ii)   there may be a low degree of resource flexibility. Resources feel to be related to a specific product line and it may be difficult to move resources from a line

to another; moreover, business managers can raise obstacles to the movement of people;

(iii) the updating by researchers and scientists can be very limited;

(iv) the autonomy of R&D people is low, as there is a strong business orientation.

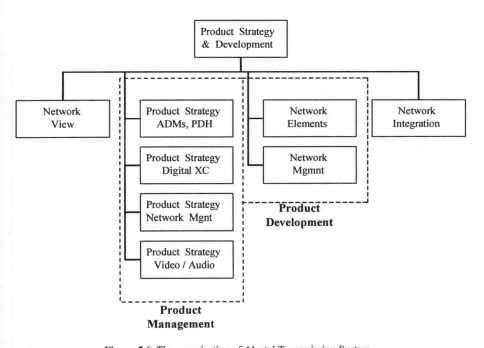

Figure 5.6. The organisation of Alcatel Transmission System.

Organisation by Project

Another form of output-oriented organisation is that by project. In this organisation, technical people are not organised in a stable form by any permanent criteria. When a project starts, people are assigned to it. When not assigned to any project, people spend time to update their competence and are free to carry on personal innovative ideas. This organisation attempts to avoid the strong separation between divisions that may be generated by the organisation by product line, and, in particular, attempts to increase the resource flexibility. It is rather difficult to find units organised in such a way. It may occur that a part of a research unit is organised by project.

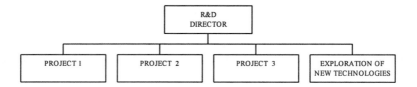

Figure 5.7. Organisation by project.

Box 5.2 - The case of Alcatel Trasmission System

An example of output-oriented structure is found in Alcatel (Figure 5.6). The Transmission System Division R&D unit is structured as follows. There are four product areas: Network View (which concerns the R&D activities on networks), Network Elements (which does research in the area of hardware), Network Management (which is the lab researching on software), Network Integration (which works on the integration of different apparatus in a network). They correspond to four different products. In fact, products (network itself, hardware and software) can be sold either stand alone or integrated as one product. To ensure that there is coordination among the R&D activities of the different labs, product managers look after the design of the integrated offer for a certain type of application and are responsible for their commercialisation. There is a product manager for each type of application (for example, audio/video products, data management systems, etc.). Therefore, the R&D organisation is basically by product or, to better say, by network component (hw, sw, etc.); however, the horizontal coordination is provided by product managers who take care of the customer perspective and the use for application of networks and/or single components rather than their technological composition.

Trade-offs between Input – and Output - Orientation

The traditional choice between input and output oriented organisations presents several trade-offs. In particular, the main factors influencing the decision towards a type of structure or the other are the following.

(i)   Rate of change. If the rate of change in technical disciplines is greater than the rate at which project can be completed, the input-oriented organisation by scientific discipline (or skill-based) is preferred. Vice versa if the rate of change is faster in the project than in the technical discipline the output structure is preferred.

(ii)   Diversification. The higher rate of diversification, the higher preference given to the output oriented structure.

(iii) Newness of a technology. The higher sophistication and youth of a technology, the higher need for acquiring knowledge, accumulating experience and creating good specialists, the higher preference for a discipline-based structure.

(iv) Interdependence between units. The higher interdependencies between technologies in a certain product category, the higher preference for an output oriented structure.

(v)   Scale economies. When large equipment have to be used and their intensive use helps achieve lower unit costs, the discipline based structure is preferred.

As argued from the above cases, organisations are often shaped to catch the benefits of both structures. In fact, although the structure is designed on the basis of a certain orientation, there are in place mechanisms which counterbalance them and give weight to another. This process towards the combination of the two structure has its clear implementation in the matrix structure.

5.1.3 Matrix Organisation

In the matrix organisation, two of the above dimensions are combined. Usually a dimension is by project. As seen above, the organisation by project is introduced in order to put emphasis on the individual project of innovation, each with clearly defined objectives, costs, time schedule. The project-based organisation helps achieve the necessary coordination of the resources involved in the project and the required control over time and costs of an innovation project. This view of a project-based organisation has been largely prevailing and most R&D organisation have chosen to introduce such project orientation in their R&D organisation.

Often, the typical result is the matrix organisation in which the project-based view is combined with another criteria, either input (discipline, activity) or output (product line) oriented. The typical matrix structure is scientific disciplines-projects.

Matrix organisation can assume different forms according to the role assigned to and played by the project or program manager:
-   weak;
-   strong;
-   mixed.

The strength / weakness refers to the authority and power of the project manager. The stronger power of project managers, the greater impact on the organisation due to the introduction of the horizontal dimension by project.

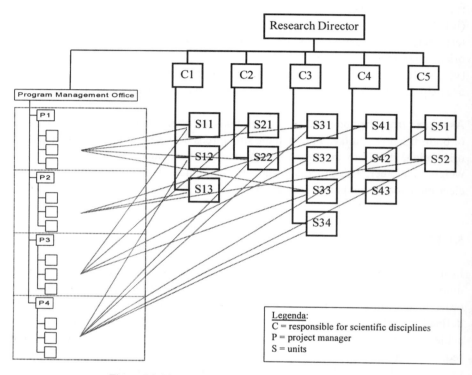

Figure 5.8. The matrix organisation (Source: Allen, 1988).

Weak project management structure. In the weak project management structure, roles and authority of the permanent structure are slightly modified by the project management organisation. The decision to launch a project is taken by top or R&D management and its plan is defined by the R&D director and/or jointly by those responsible for the scientific disciplines (the lines of the R&D). Usually, the steps in which the project is subdivided mirror the functional organisation. Each step tends to coincide with the work of one lab. Therefore, responsibilities, coordination mechanisms and methods used to carry out the project work are in each step those used by the lab fulfilling the task. Also the management of resources (quality, quantity, time) are fixed by line managers. The project manager has no responsibilities over project results. His role is to facilitate relationships among functions, to maintain the project file, keep record of the project progress and provide project report to line managers and R&D managers. This organisation is effective when the project work is easily divided into functional steps which weakly interact. Feedbacks and recycle of activities are rare and the responsibility can be easily transferred from one unit to another in a rally-like mode. This organisation aims to achieve strong resource efficiency.

Strong project management structure. In the strong structure, the project manager is assigned the hierarchical power over resources. The project team is completely assigned the project definition, planning, and control. Usually the project manager is established before the project start and often before the decision whether to launch or not the project is taken. This ensures that the project manager is responsible from the very beginning of the project and completely shares the project objectives and plans. Units/labs have to ensure that resources are appropriately trained and updated, identify and suggest the most appropriate resources to be allocated to a certain project, and make methods and tools available for the project work. Units are seen as reservoir of resources and have to look after their qualitative and quantitative profile and its evolution over time. The project manager is responsible for the project planning, defines the coordination mechanisms to be used during the project, manages and controls the resources. The assignments of resources to a certain project is the result of negotiations between labs managers and project managers. The project manager plays a key role and the appointment of the project manager is the most critical decision. This organisation is adopted when the project to be managed is strategic for the firm. A major disadvantage is that this structure is often not efficient as resources assigned to the project are not used at their maximum capacity during the whole project.

This structure can assume two different characteristics according to the project manager profile. There are organisations in which project managers are permanent which means that at any time they manage projects and usually they are assigned the most relevant projects within the current portfolio. In other cases, project managers are selected and appointed to each specific project and change over time. However, project managers are usually chosen among people well acknowledged within the organisation and with strong charisma.

Therefore the strong project management structure can assume two distinct configurations, one with permanent project managers and the other with temporary project managers.

Mixed structure. This structure is a mix of the characteristics of the previous two. This essentially means two major things:

-    the project manager has to negotiate with the line managers to a larger extent than in the strong structure. Often units appoint a member of their R&D staff to act as the functional interface to the project. The project manager has to negotiate resource assignment with him/her at each stage of the project;

-    the degree of authority of a project manager may change during the project itself. In other words, different forms of relationships can be established between line and project managers at different stages of the project. These variations are related to the different importance and criticality of the work to the final result;

-    the authority of the project managers varies from project to project.

This mixed structure is designed to apply the style of project management (strong vs. weak) on the basis of the importance of the project and of the activities within a project.

The main advantage of the matrix structures (whatever form is taken) is that there is a clear distinction between managerial and professional responsibilities. Within the organisation, R&D managers take care of the professional standards, the competence development and the career development of R&D staff, whereas project managers are responsible for the progress of the project work. The main disadvantage is that there may be ambiguity, as R&D people may be subject to two contemporary and potentially conflicting leads (by R&D managers and project managers).

Pros and cons slightly vary from form to form of matrix organisation. The weak form is the closest to the input oriented organisation, therefore it catches the benefits of that structure and also bear the disadvantages. The strong form grasps the benefits of the matrix organisation to a deeper extent but also shows the disadvantages mentioned above (ambiguity, conflicts, etc.).

It is commonly shared that the matrix organisation is the prevailing structure. This is also confirmed by the empirical base on which this book relies. A case of typical discipline-project matrix organisation is that of Marelli (the largest automotive component manufacturer in Italy) (Figure 5.9). Lines mirror professionals involved in the R&D activities (hardware design, software design, testing, layout, engineering, process technologies). Horizontal lines represent project managers. People from the line units may be involved contemporary in different projects.

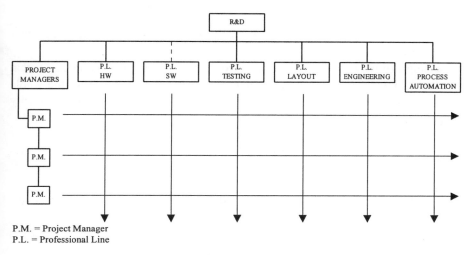

Figure 5.9. The organisation of Marelli.

Often the way how the structure is conceived and implemented dramatically changes from firm to firm. HP is an example of adapted matrix organisation (Figure 5.10). This matrix organisation has both program managers (responsible for the development of new products) and project managers (responsible for the development of new technologies). There are small groups of people (experts of the various technologies) who are permanently assigned to program managers, other professionals remain with the project managers and are involved in the program of new product development when necessary and from time to time. This is defined on the basis of negotiations between program and project managers. This form attempts to achieve a balance between strong and weak forms of matrix organisation.

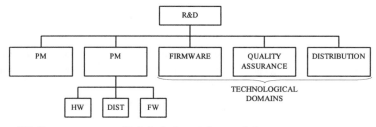

(PM = Program manager responsible for the development of a new product)

Figure 5.10. The organisation of Hewlett-Packard.

The matrix approach has been then extended to the whole innovation process, i.e. the project approach is used throughout the process of innovation including other firm's functions.

An example of matrix organisation extended to the whole innovation process is that of Marelli (Figure 5.11), where the program manager is responsible for the whole product development process which involves sales, production engineers, quality people, people of the purchasing function.

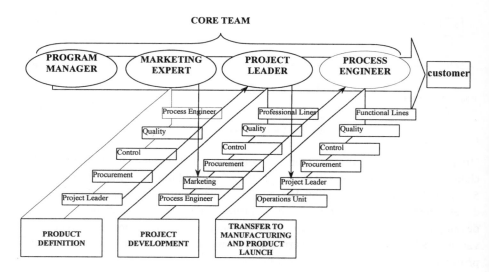

Figure 5.11. The product development process in Marelli.

5.2   THE BALANCE BETWEEN CENTRALISATION AND DECENTRALISATION

A key issue in the design of the organisational structure of R&D in large firms is the balance between centralisation and decentralisation, i.e. where to locate R&D units in the firm's hierarchy and therefore to whom (corporate vs. divisions) to assign the funding and control of the R&D activity.

In a company, where the R&D is concentrated in one organisational unit, the problem relates to the funding and control of that unit. In large (multidivisional) firms, the structure is much more complex. There is usually a corporate R&D and a divisional R&D. The choice between centralisation and decentralisation is, first, mirrored by the division of labour between corporate and divisional R&D, second, by the amount of R&D investment assigned to corporate and to business units, respectively.

The balance between centralisation and decentralisation has recently become a key issue in the structural choice related to R&D. To this end, it seems appropriate to review major contributions to the understanding of this point.

(i)   Recent approaches to R&D management (see Chapter 1) suggest that a central issue is the balance between inner-orientation and outer-orientation of R&D, which can also be traced back to the problem of balancing technology push and market pull factors. In Roussel et al. (1991), the first R&D management generation corresponds to a view of R&D strongly centralised, inner-oriented and technology push minded. The second generation corresponds to a significant decentralisation of R&D, a strong integration with business activities, a prevailing market pull mind set and outer orientation (towards customers and business). The third generation focuses on the interrelationships among projects within a business, across business, and for the corporation as a whole. It introduces the portfolio concept. The result of the strategic management of R&D is a strategically balanced portfolio of R&D projects jointly formulated by general managers and R&D managers. "R&D seeks to respond to the needs of existing businesses and to the additional needs of the corporation while at the same time contributing to the identification and exploitation of technological opportunities in existing and new businesses". R&D strategy formulation needs to be paid attention by top management at both business and corporate level in order to achieve a balanced portfolio of R&D projects in terms of risk and temporal horizon of investments. This calls for a balanced distribution of R&D resources between corporate and businesses, which means increased weight of corporate issues in defining a technology strategy and larger amount of R&D resources at corporate level than in the second generation.

(ii)   The competence- or resource-based view of firms and competition (discussed in Chapter 2) has several implications on a firm's R&D organisation and management:

-    a business unit oriented mind set may imprison the development of resources and technological competencies. Technological competencies cross businesses and grow as they are applied and shared. A business-unit-led process of technology strategy could lead to underinvest in developing core technological competencies and bound innovation;

- a firm's critical capability is often to synthesise and integrate knowledge from different sources. Given that this process is often cross-functional and cross-business, this capability needs to be developed at corporate level;

- given the dynamic aspect of competition, a firm's critical capability is renewing and refreshing the technological competencies over time. However, expanding a firm's capability base in a certain (technological) domain is a function of the firm's level of prior related knowledge. At the initial stage, it is necessary to create an appropriate level of 'absorptive capacity' (Cohen and Levinthal, 1990). This appears mostly to be a corporate rather than divisional task. In other words, when a certain knowledge or technology is promising but, not yet exploited or exploitable at business level, undertaking R&D investments in advance may be critical to take advantage from further developments in that area. Allocating R&D resources on that seems to be typical corporate responsibility.

Therefore, the competence or resource based view emphasises the role of corporate R&D and the need to compensate the dominance of the business-oriented approach (second generation):

(iii) Furthermore, the competence-based approach emphasises that firms have to found their competitiveness on a limited set of competencies where they excel. This means that there is an increasing need to exploit R&D synergies and share a common technology base among different businesses. Corporate R&D plays a critical role if synergies need to be captured across business units (Lewis and Linden, 1990).

All these factors call for a new role of corporate technology. A recent survey on the characteristics of the strategic management of technology in 244 firms (Roberts, 1995a and 1995b) has pointed into evidence that more than 60% of firms are moving upward the control over their R&D activities, in both research and development. This trend is very clear in Japanese firms, significant in European companies. US firms still show a strong preference to decentralise their R&D control (see Figure 5.12). These trends seem to concern both research activities and development.

Therefore, there is an increasing tendency to assign corporate R&D a stronger role than in the past and a key dimension of the R&D organisation is to find the appropriate balance between corporate and divisional R&D.

However, it should be recognised that, historically, there is the habit to go back and forth from a solution to another. The 80s were the years of the decentralisation and companies of which the R&D was highly concentrated tended to allocate a wider amount of resources at divisional or business unit level. In the 90s, most companies have increased the weight of corporate control in R&D.

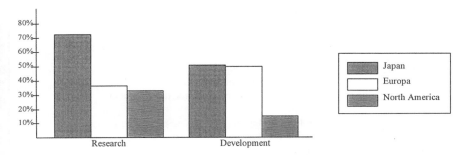

Figure 5.12. Trends in R&D control (% of companies increasing corporate control)
(Source: Roberts, 1995).

5.2.1   The Role of Corporate and Divisional Labs: Types of Structure

A variety of contributions has studied motivations for a firm to have corporate R&D and divisional R&D (among the others: Rieck, 1993; Floyd, 1997; Lewis and Linden, 1990; Eto, 1992). Roles played by corporate and divisional R&D function and their key characteristics are summarised in Table 5.1.

Although the usual tendency and the common knowledge is that corporate is assigned research activities and divisions development activities, it is worth to in depth study such division of labour between corporate and divisions as different solutions are adopted. As a matter of fact, the variety of activities carried out by corporate R&D labs is greater than expected. In his empirical study, Roberts found that corporate labs devote their efforts to research (42%), development (37%), product technical support (11%), process technical support (10%). The IRI annual R&D survey for year 1995 confirms that corporate R&D is more research oriented and that divisions are more development oriented. However, the range of activities looks rather wide. Corporate R&D allocates 39,1% of its funds to basic and applied research, 26,8% to product development, 17,7% to process development, 16,4% to technical service. Divisional labs allocate 21,5% of their funds to research, 35,7% to product development, 21,1% to technical service.

Table 5.1. Roles of corporate and divisional R&D.

Roles and characteristics of corporate R&D
- Monitoring major scientific and technical developments
- Building new technological competencies
- Nurturing the knowledge base of a nascent business
- Identifying potential applications of existing competencies
- Capturing technological synergies across business units
- Integrating different technologies and disciplines
- Developing new technical and human resources
- Establishing the trajectory for knowledge/competence development
- Creating an absorptive capacity
- Long term vision in technology strategy
- Carrying on radical innovation projects
- Avoiding business pressures
Roles and characteristics of divisional R&D
- Increasing market knowledge in innovation
- Searching for incremental innovation and continuous improvement
- Favouring the transfer from R to D
- Favouring the transfer from R&D to manufacturing and marketing
- Decreasing the uncertainty of R&D
- Facilitating the measure of R&D performance
- Putting emphasis on development time, cost and quality

These data show that the distribution of R&D activities between corporate and divisional units strongly varies from firm to firm, that often corporate and divisional R&D co-exist, and, therefore, a key factor is the division of labour between the two. The empirical cases studied showed that there are five main types of structure:
- totally centralised;
- centrally led;
- centrally supported;
- decentralised;
- totally decentralised.

Totally Centralised

The whole R&D activity is done at corporate level. Divisions are receptacle and the commercial arm of what corporate R&D generates. An industry where often R&D is totally centralised is the pharmaceutical. R&D is a major source of advantage. R&D activity is strongly science-based, requires a lot of scientific orientation and critical mass. The integration with the manufacturing function does not represent a critical activity. The only form of integration is with the marketing functions of the divisions which have to provide inputs to the new product development process. However, strategy itself is much more the consequence of what the fuzzy and uncertain R&D work discovers rather than of planned activities of new product development and introduction. For this reason, R&D is often kept in one function at corporate level.

Another typical case is that of recently established corporations from the Far East countries, such as the Korean groups (chaebol) characterised by a strong centralisation culture. Samsung for example does research and development at corporate level. The corporate R&D develops standard products which may then be adapted by technical units located in foreign countries (the internationalisation of R&D is in depth studied in Chapter 7). These foreign units fulfil the task of making the products developed at the central R&D suitable for local commercialisation. Therefore, their activity is usually very peripheral and restricted to few and marginal characteristics of the products.

Box 5.3 - The case of ABB

ABB has a corporate R&D articulated into 8 labs geographically dispersed (Sweden, Switzerland, Germany, Finland, Norway, Italy, 2 in US, Windsor and Raleigh) and 3 proto-research labs which are going to be established (Japan, Poland, Czech Republic). The most significant activity of the corporate R&D is that of the High Impact Projects. These are projects highly risky and of high potential impact on the group. These projects involve various corporate labs and generally are mostly funded by divisions (on the average about 70%, whereas the remaining 30% is funded by corporate). However, there are programs which are entirely funded by corporate. The corporate research is coordinated by 14 Program Managers each responsible for a certain technological area. Their role is to coordinate the research programs of the various labs in their technological area. Another activity of corporate R&D is the technology evaluation and benchmarking which helps divisions to compare their technological capabilities to those of competitors. Divisional labs are responsible for the development of new products, but actually their activities mostly concern the adaptation of existing products and the exploitation of the existing technologies developed at corporate level. They work close to market, attempt to capture customer requirements and adapt products to satisfy their needs. These divisional activities are distributed on an international basis.

Box 5.4 - The cases of Toshiba and Matsushita

Toshiba and Matsushita have the same R&D organisation. They have an R&D structured into three layers: central research at corporate level, product development units at divisional level, and production engineering units at business unit level.

Central research labs at corporate level are funded by both corporate and divisions. Projects funded by corporate usually last more than five years. Their activities concern basic research, advanced research and early applied development. They aim to develop technologies critical to the firm's long term position and applicable across various divisions. Although funded entirely by corporate, the decision whether to undertake such projects is taken by research lab managers, top management, and product division managers. Projects funded by divisions are the result of two processes. On the one hand, product divisions suggest projects they are available to sponsor. On the other hand, the central research labs present projects they are willing to undertake at annual global meetings. The projects are undertaken if division(s) is (are)

willing to fund the project. These projects are therefore specifically developed for the sponsoring division(s).

Divisional units carry out product development and process technology development with projects taking from two to five years. Their project results are product prototypes and pilot plants for production in small volumes. Divisional labs serve a number of different business units. The divisional labs are central in this mechanism and plays a key role in transferring new technological findings into commercial applications.

Production engineering labs are at business unit level and are located close to manufacturing plants. They carry out projects lasting less than two years and cover the engineering phase for mass production.

A similar structure is that of Canon where corporate R&D plays an even stronger role. At corporate level R&D units look after both technologies embodied (or to be embodied) into multiple products and production engineering technologies and techniques for cross-divisional application.

Centrally Led

In this structure there are both corporate and divisional R&D. Corporate R&D plays a key role. It has most R&D resources and manages R&D projects as far as the final stages of engineering and production scale up. Usually, corporate is responsible for exploring and experimenting new technologies and developing projects of high impact leading to the introduction of new technological platforms for different businesses.

Examples of this kind are ABB, the Swiss-Swedish electro-mechanical giant (box 5.3), Toshiba and Matsushita (box 5.4).

Centrally Supported
There are both corporate and divisional R&D. Most R&D is at divisional level. The corporate R&D plays a support role, has not the resources to generate innovations on its own and/or covers a limited part of the R&D process. Three types of support by corporate R&D can be found:
(i)   corporate R&D covers upstream activities of the R&D process, typically basic research;
(ii) corporate R&D covers only one or few stages of the R&D process, where there is the need for central coordination;
(iii) corporate R&D does R&D for businesses different from those served by divisional R&D.

(i)   The first case is the most widely diffused. Corporate R&D is responsible for basic (and applied) research. Often this leads to the creation of corporate centres of excellence. At corporate level there are different labs specialised on the different scientific disciplines and acting as the firm's centre of excellence in that area. Two cases of this kind are Xerox and Alcatel.
Alcatel has centres of excellence for long term basic research. These centres are funded by divisions proportionally to their turnover. New product development is carried out at divisional labs. Centres of excellence work on both long term projects defined by the centres themselves and research themes suggested by divisional labs. However, the result of the activities of these centres of excellence are generally far from the application stage. Centres of excellence are composed of few very bright people searching for new technological solutions and platforms which could be transferred into practice in five to ten years. Most R&D is at divisional level.
(ii) The second case is that of corporate R&D controlling stages or activities of the R&D process where there is a strong need for cross-business coordination and control. An example is NEC, where at corporate level there is an R&D Group for Production Engineering and a Group for Computer&Communication Software Development. Another example is that of Philips who concentrates the product design activities (Design Centre) and the activities for manufacturing technologies (Operations Centre) at corporate level. In Philips the creation of a Design Centre at corporate level was forced by the advent of the multimedia business. It was necessary to ensure that the design of new products of the various divisions

(telecom, consumer electronics, equipment, etc.) is coordinated and integrated each other.

(iii) A third case is that of corporate R&D structure which has units devoted to businesses different from those supplied by divisional labs. The typical example is that of corporate R&D dedicated to the development of new businesses. For example, Xerox generates and controls at corporate level spin-off companies operating into businesses which are too small to become divisions. In other words, spin-offs are generated when new product ideas seem promising to generate a new business; however, the size of the business is still too small. The management and control of the R&D activities of such nascent businesses is at corporate level.

Of course, the three roles of corporate R&D are not mutually exclusive and a mix can be found. For example, in Xerox there are also corporate R&D units doing research related to the current divisions such as the Palo Alto Research Centre (PARC), the Xerox Research Centre (XRCE) in Grenoble, and two other units in Cambridge and Rochester. Therefore the corporate R&D play both the first and the third role mentioned above.

Decentralised
Corporate R&D has very limited resources dedicated to the exploration and scanning of new technologies. Hitachi had traditionally a highly decentralised R&D and left an ancillary role of scanning with its corporate R&D. More recently, there has been a change and corporate R&D has been given a greater amount of resources and responsibilities. Control on R&D has been partially shifted to the corporate. However, most R&D is done at divisional level and therefore is largely decentralised.

Totally Decentralised
This structure has the whole R&D concentrated at divisional level. Everything is done at divisional level to ensure that there is a strong integration with the other business functions and market focus. The characteristics related to divisional R&D listed in table 5.1 are emphasised. There may be a form of corporate R&D constituted by a corporate research management group who has the task to identify technologies which could be critical in the future and suggest where to address the long term R&D activities of the divisions. Of course the power of such group is strongly dependent on the members of the group, their credibility and charisma within the firm. Intel has its R&D totally decentralised, i.e. totally carried out by divisions.

5.2.2 Integrating Corporate and Divisional R&D

The division of the R&D activity between corporate and divisions creates the problem of integrating the two. The need for integration of the corporate and divisional activity strongly depend on the type of structure.

The case of *total decentralisation* does not require any integration. The whole R&D activity is done at divisional level and the integration of R&D with other functions, such as manufacturing and marketing, during the new product development is facilitated as these functions are part of the same division.

In the case of *totally centralised R&D* there are needs for integration. There is no need for integrating R&D units at different levels as the whole R&D is concentrated at corporate level. However, forms of integration are required to ensure that the output of the corporate R&D activity is then accepted by the divisions. As a matter of fact, there may be Not-Invented-Here Syndrome effects. The integration can be managed with a variety of instruments. A first form is the early involvement of marketing and manufacturing people of the divisions during the R&D process. Otherwise, the phase of technology transfer from corporate to divisions at the end of the product development process needs to be carefully managed. Different mechanisms can be adopted: (i) technical people from the corporate labs are transferred temporarily to the divisions, which will commercialise the innovation; (ii) liaison groups are created involving either members of the product development team (the most frequent case) or other personnel appointed to transfer the results to the division; (iii) divisions' technical people are trained at the corporate lab to be able to technically support the product introduction into the market. The former two ways are often used when production process specifications need to be transferred as products are manufactured at divisional level, the latter is more frequent when production takes place at the corporate level.

In the *decentralised* structure, again, the need for integration is limited. Corporate R&D carries out long term projects of exploratory nature with the objective to acquire knowledge on new disciplines and technologies with no focus on potential applications. The corporate R&D mission is to scan the external context and identifies technological opportunities and threats, and to assess and acquire initial knowledge on new technological disciplines (Tidd et al., 1997). These activities are easily separated from those carried out at divisional level.

In the *centrally supported* R&D, the need for integration strongly depends on the role of corporate R&D. If corporate R&D carries out new product development activities related only to the generation of new businesses (the capability to develop new products is used only to incubate new businesses), the need for integration is very limited. Usually, people involved in the R&D activities related to the new business follow the business itself. If a new business unit or division is created they are usually then transferred to the business unit or divisional level, and become the R&D people of that unit. There is a stronger need for integration, if corporate R&D is concentrated on research projects and has to transfer its findings to divisional R&D units. Such need for integration increases when corporate R&D has a role (although limited) in advanced stages of the R&D process.

Finally, there is strong need for integration, when corporate R&D which has the capabilities and is responsible also for advanced stages of innovation, i.e. develops technologies and product prototypes, designs and engineers, even produces the new products, related to the current businesses and therefore to the existing divisions. The transfer of the new finding to the division is critical to the effectiveness of the R&D process. This also occurs in the *centrally led* structure.

Therefore, the centrally led and centrally supported seem to have strong requirements for integration between corporate and divisional labs. To ensure that there is the appropriate integration two major ways can be followed:
-      joint development work;
-      cross-funding.

Joint development work. The R&D work is conducted jointly by groups of researchers and technicians from both corporate and divisional labs. R&D groups are created which follow the project from the beginning (when it is under corporate control) until its end at the factory level. This ensures that there is a strong continuity and the competence developed during the project is totally exploited. This is the case of Matsushita and Toshiba. This mechanism also mirrors the career development of R&D people. Researchers initially spend four to five years at corporate R&D labs, then they move to divisional lab for the design and early engineering phases, finally they move to a business unit and work on the production engineering phase for mass manufacturing. Often they end their career working in that business in the manufacturing or marketing function.

Cross-funding. The most diffused form is that of establishing cross-funding mechanisms. These mechanisms allow divisions to fund research carried out at corporate level and vice versa corporate to fund activities done at divisional level. Tidd et al. (1997) identify the conditions where these mechanisms should be activated:
-      corporate funding of divisional activity are appropriate when potential benefits are corporate-wide and the key interfaces required are with production, suppliers, customers. This may occur in the commercialisation phase of new

technologies or when the new finding can have a cross-divisional impact or technological synergies can be exploited between different divisions;
- divisional funding of corporate activities is appropriate when the potential benefit is division-specific and the key interfaces concern science and technology centres. This occurs in the early development of new technologies and for specific problem-solving activities for established divisions.

Cross-funding often lies upon the use of internal markets. Corporate labs and divisional labs put forward their own project proposals and the counterpart selects those to be funded. In other words, the counterpart buys the result of the project funded.

5.3 THE SEPARATION BETWEEN R AND D

A further aspect of the design of the R&D structure is the decision on whether to separate or not R from D. In a sense, the separation between R and D is often behind the distinction between corporate and divisional activity, as there is a natural attribution of research tasks to corporate and of development tasks to divisions. However, there are signs that the differences between the two are so strong, that even if R and D are carried out at the same level of the hierarchy they are organisationally separated. In the previous section, for example, the pharmaceutical firms have been indicated as typical examples of centralised R&D, i.e. where the whole R&D activity is concentrated at corporate level. Nevertheless, there is an increasing tendency among them to separate their R from their D activities. In other words, both R and D are kept at corporate level and do not belong to different hierarchical levels within firms; however, they are different units, clearly separated, sometimes with different directors. The following box mentions literature contributions which helps identify the differences between R and D. The next section presents the result of a study on the separation of R from D in the pharmaceutical industry carried out by the author. Although limited to the case of a single industry, the separation between R and D seems to be a major trend of future R&D organisations. The reasons behind such organisation are sound for a variety of industries; actually, cases of separation have already been found also in the chemical and tyre industries.

Box 5.5 - Literature works emphasising the difference between R and D

In the literature several contributions have emphasised that within the R&D there are activities which are different by nature. Hedlund (1990) states that strategy can be seen as 'action patterns over time, of which there are two intertwined aspects': there are programmes of experimentation, the primary aim of which is to seek opportunities, and programmes of exploitation seeking the effective use of given resources. Key characteristics of experimentation programmes are a continuous search for new techno-organisational solutions, and a learning process aimed at enhancing the firm's knowledge base. Exploitation programmes aim to create value through current activities, and to innovate by exploiting the skills embedded in a firm's human resources and technical systems. Therefore, whereas exploitation programs seek to identify and use the potential of the current paradigm, experimentation programs aim to identify and define the future paradigm. In turn, technological activities have to fulfil two major tasks: the exploitation of the resources and knowledge base available to compete in the short term (exploitation programmes), and the development of a knowledge base that helps to sustain competition in the long term (experimentation programmes). This distinction is central to the distinction between R and D activities.

Recently Coombs (1996) has stated that R&D has two major articulations: the investment mode, in which activities are concerned with the development of the firm's technological capabilities, and the harvesting mode in which the R&D function participates with the other functions to the market-driven exploitation of specific artefacts and services for customers. He also underlines that the characteristics of technology associated to the two ways of employing R&D activities change. Whereas in the investment mode, the product of the R&D activity is technology seen as knowledge and skills (formal abstract representation of technology in codified form, the capabilities to employ it, the related tacit knowledge), the output of the R&D activity in the harvesting mode is functionality profile and technological recipe (the choice of the particular combination of technologies, design practices, configurations of sub-systems, able to provide a certain range of service and performance).

Another contribution is that of Kodama (1995), who identifies two major stages in an R&D program, the exploratory stage and the development stage. The first includes fundamental research and exploratory development, the second includes advanced development, engineering development and operational system development. The transition from the exploratory to the development state is given by the sharp growth of the expenditure for an R&D program, and, in certain R&D processes, by a strong difference in terms of risk (which is high up-

(follows)

ward in research and lower or may be zero downward).

Similarly, product development literature has talked about two major phases: concept development (where activities focus on customer need identification and technological feasibility), and implementation. The separation between the two is the concept of freeze milestone. Once the concept is approved, it is frozen and, therefore, can not be changed. Iansiti (1997) has identified that flexible models of the product development process make the two stages overlap, implementation starts before the concept is frozen, to allow changes be brought later in the process. However, he recognises that such activities require different skills, organisation and management.

In conclusion, it seems that there is a wide accordance on the fact that there are activities of different nature within the R&D process, one related to exploration and experimentation and therefore to the development of technological capabilities, the other related to the exploitation of such technological capabilities to generate and provide products and services.

5.3.1 The Case of the Pharmaceutical Industry

This section presents the result of a study on the organisation of R&D in the pharmaceutical industry. To a better understanding of the organisational problems, it is worth to briefly describe the R&D process in the pharmaceutical industry (to this end, see Box 5.6).

Box 5.6 - The R&D process in the pharmaceutical industry

The process is composed of two major phases: the drug discovery aimed to discover a new compound, and the development, which is aimed to evaluate the effectiveness of the new compound.

Drug discovery usually includes preclinical activities conducted until a selected compound is identified that possesses a desirable profile of biological activity and a decision is made to start additional animal studies to insure the safety profile of the compound. Safety testing in animals includes both toxicological and pharmacological studies. The amount of pharmacology, chemical studies (including stability) and formulation conducted during the discovery period is highly variable and depends on the amount of research necessary to determine which particular compound is the lead one. It is not always possible to determine the precise point at which the drug discovery phase ends and the drug development phase begins. In general that point occurs when preclinical

(follows)

activities change from a search for an agent with a desired biological profile to the focused evaluation of a specific molecule. Drug discovery may also occur in the clinical phase when a new use for a known drug is found.

Drug development includes the clinical evaluation of drug candidates in humans. It is conventionally divided into four progressive categories or phases denoting the stage of development of the compound. The boundaries between phases are not sharply delineated, and there is generally some overlap between the completion of one phase and the initiation of the next. Clinical trials are broken down into four distinct categories:

Phase 1: Clinical pharmacology and toxicity. Evaluation of drug safety in human volunteers using drug-escalation paradigms. Drug metabolism and bioavailability are also studied at this stage. Phase 1 is generally considered to have been completed after the principal side effects have been elucidated in volunteers, and the maximally tolerated dose has been estimated. Some 20-100 subjects and patients are required for these determinations.

Phase 2: Initial clinical investigation for treatment effect. Early trials generally consist of open-label, single- and multiple-dose studies in patients. Effectiveness and safety of the drug are evaluated. Later, phase 2 trials are usually placebo- or active-drug controlled and designed to obtain more convincing evidence of efficacy. Critical goals of these studies are the definition of a therapeutic dosage range and an appropriate dosage regimen to be used in future large-scale trials.

Phase 3: Full scale evaluation of treatment. Drug candidates that enter phase 3 have usually been administered to several hundred patients and normal subjects. Preliminary evidence of efficacy, a profile of commonly occurring side effects, and the therapeutic dosage range should be tentatively established. Trials are normally controlled; multi-clinic studies, enrolling a total of several hundred to more than a thousand patients, are designed to establish the efficacy of the drug and to define its adverse effect profile as precisely as possible. The program should be designed to produce sufficient efficacy and safety data for registration of the drug.

Phase 4: Post-marketing surveillance to elucidate uncommon side effects. To achieve this goal, long-term surveillance in the form of controlled or, more usually, uncontrolled data collection (i.e. monitoring of clinical experience) is undertaken.

Such clinical studies can take between 6 and 10 years, depending on the therapeutic area and the social environment. For example, the average period required from discovery to approval in US for an antineoplastic drug before the 60s ranged from 2.8 years to 4.5 years. Because of the approval of more and more restrictive drug amendments (to assure the safety, effectiveness and reliability of drugs), the average development span increased from

(follows)

6.5 years to 13.9 years (in the 70s), and recently to 14.8-16 years (in the 80s/90s).

As arguable from the above description, the intrinsic nature of research and development activities strongly differs. Although R&D in total is concerned with discovery and exploitation of promising candidate drugs, increasingly it is recognised that the objectives and the characteristics of discovery (=R) are quite significantly different from those of development (=D).

The *critical mass per se* has a different meaning in research and development. While critical mass for drug discovery could be measured as the 'weight of the average human brain' involved in research, development is strongly dependant on the number of people composing the development team and on the extent to which the project team is focused and structured. In development, a large increase in personnel and funds would have a significant impact on the speed at which the project would proceed. On the contrary, additional resources in R would not speed up the percentage of new ideas or the discovery of a new mechanism of action.

The *investment costs* are much higher in development (on the average, R&D costs in research are one fourth / one fifth of the costs of the development phase).

The *completion time* of an activity can be foreseen with reasonable reliability in development, whereas it is completely unpredictable in research.

The degree to which an activity can be *formalised* in development is very high, whereas it is very low in research.

R&D Organisations in the Pharmaceutical Industry

Traditional R&D organisations in the pharmaceutical industry can be grouped into two categories: functional and therapeutic area-based. In the functional organisation each unit carries out one activity of the R&D process (Figure 5.13). Divisions mirror the flow of activities from research to development, registration and launch. The main problem is the lack of business orientation and the lack of focus of the units in terms of therapeutic area. To overcome this, the therapeutic area based organisation is conceived (Figure 5.14). Each department is concerned with a therapeutic area and conducts the whole R&D process in that area. The advantage is that of concentrating the activities concerning the same therapeutic area in the same department and thus enhancing the integration among the various stages of the R&D process. Major disadvantage is the duplication of activities and specialists in the various departments.

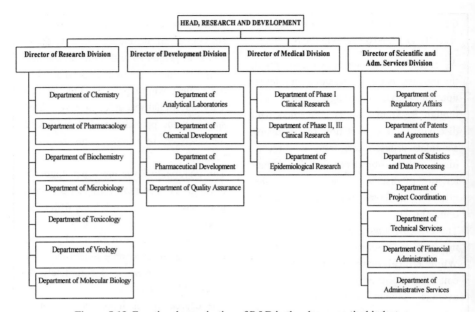

Figure 5.13. Functional organisation of R&D in the pharmaceutical industry.

More recently, companies seem to be oriented to adopt organisational structures different from the traditional ones. A survey has been conducted to understand how and why companies are modifying their organisational structure and the major motivations behind the re-organisation of R&D. The survey has concerned nine companies of which four are European (Glaxo, Hoechst, ICI, Sandoz), two Japanese (Suntory, Takeda) and three American (Schering, Lilly, Merck). The analysis has concerned whether and how the surveyed firms have re-organised their R&D in the last ten years.

Five firms (out of nine) have undertaken changes in order to split their R&D into an R and a D division. Some examples of firms which have recently re-organised their R&D in this direction are here given.

Sandoz (Swiss) has separated R from D to concentrate it solely on the innovative discovery process, the early screening stages, early toxicology, preclinical pharmacology, initial chemistry and pharmacy and the most essential data on safety, kinetic and pharmacodynamics (Phase 1). The team responsible for D should drive the rest of clinical pharmacology, clinical trials, expanded toxicology, regulatory affairs, global drug safety etc.

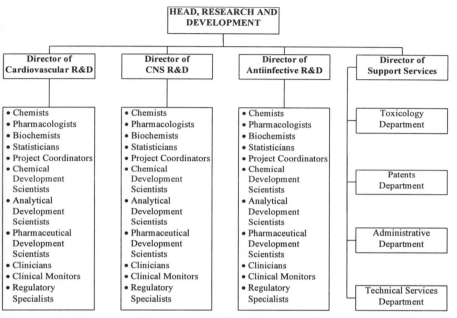

Figure 5.14. Therapeutic area based organisation of R&D in the pharmaceutical industry.

Suntory (Japan) research staff is organisationally and physically separated from those in development. Researchers are working near Kyoto, while developers were integrated with production at the new Bio-Pharma Tech Centre at Gunma.

Hoechst (Germany) has concentrated at corporate level both exploratory and late clinical development activities (to be carried out for each therapeutic area), whereas product group units (divided by therapeutic area) have been created which include activities such as late research phases and clinical development (early phases). Three of the product group units are located in Frankfurt, one at nearby Wiesbaden and one at Somerville, New Jersey. Corporate activities are located in Frankfurt.

Takeda (Japan) has split its R&D organisation into eight divisions: seven research labs operating in different fields and one clinical development unit. The basic research lab is located at Tsukuba and the toxicology lab at Takatsuki, all the other activities are located at Osaka.

Glaxo has five major research bases: Greenford and Stevenage (UK) responsible for gastrointestinal and cardiovascular system, Geneva (Switzerland) responsible for molecular biology, Verona (Italy) where it is conducted research on anti-infectives, Research Triangle Park (North Carolina, US) which concentrates on cancer, inflammation and metabolic deseases. When a drug enters full development (stages 3 and 4), international trials (restricted to Europe and US) are coordinated by the development lab in UK.

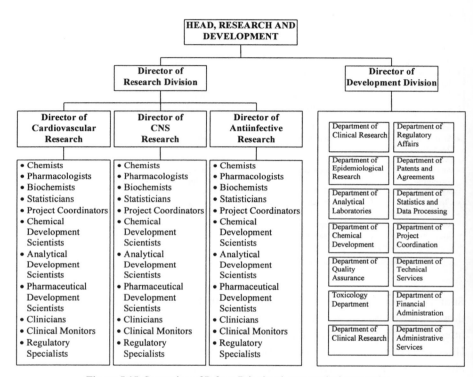

Figure 5.15. Separation of R from D in the pharmaceutical companies.

The key findings can be synthesised as follows:

(i)   Many firms have recently re-thought their organisation and have adopted a solution which can not be classified into one of the traditional (functional, therapeutic area-based). Figure 5.15 shows an example of the structure adopted by most companies. It is based on the separation between 'research' activities and 'development' activities. Research activities include the activities usually defined as research and the early phases of the development process, whereas there is one organisation defined as development carrying out the phases 3 and 4.

(ii) The research department is usually divided into several units, each carrying out research in a certain therapeutic area. The development department is managed as one division articulated into the various units, each dedicated to a certain type of clinical tests.

(iii) In some cases the separation between R and D takes place not only in organisational terms, i.e. splitting the R&D department into two divisions responsible for research and development respectively. There are cases of physical separation. Research activities are often carried out in different locations, each specialised in a certain therapeutic area; development is usually carried out in one centre (when there are multiple centres, they are strongly controlled by the headquarters lab).

However, this approach is not shared by all pharmaceutical companies surveyed. The major elements of debate are the following.

(a) There is not an unanimous consensus on the separation between R and D. The idea of separating R from D represents one of the major differences of opinion (and therefore management style) between US companies and those in Europe or Japan. In US the consensus is that much more would be lost than gained by separating R from D (the three American firms analysed have not separated R from D).

(b) Those firms which have separated R from D have chosen different points where to break the organisation. Actually to define where discovery ends and development begins is a complex and contentious issue. Some companies included in research only the typical phases which have been usually considered as such (chemistry, pharmacology, microbiology, molecular biology).

Other firms have included tasks, previously labelled as part of the *development,* as an integral part of the selection process of a candidate drug. For example, a trend is to make the research team control the means to undertake initial scale up, early toxicity and pharmacokynetic studies. In some companies (Glaxo), R encompasses up to phase 2, thus viewing clinical pharmacology and, where appropriate, early tests in patients legitimately as part of the discovery process. Research staff are sometimes responsible for continued scientific support in late-stage clinical development and after launch. D includes late development (phase 3 and 4) which is seen as an activity which has to be strongly integrated with marketing.

Factors Behind the Separation Between R and D

The survey has explored the reasons forcing firms to design a separation between R and D. Major motivations seem to be the following:

- the adoption of new approaches in research activities;

- the access to external sources of technology;
- the increasing importance of time as a competitive factor;
- the internationalisation of science, technology and markets.

Research approaches. The characteristics of the research activities have been deeply changing since the last decade. The advent of information technology and automated systems has sharply decreased the time required to test new findings. This has emphasised the differences between the R side and the D side of R&D.

A first factor of change has been the advent of biotechnology and the availability of simulation instruments. "The growth of scientific understanding in molecular biology and genetic engineering has clarified important aspects of human metabolism and the chemical and biological action of drugs. At the same time, powerful new instruments make it possible to examine the behaviour of proteins and molecules. This narrows laboratory research and clinical tests to families of molecules whose characteristics are consistent with the 'ideal' molecules" (Arora and Gambardella, 1994). This has consequences on both the content and the process of R activities. On the one hand, the progress in a certain therapeutic area becomes faster and the R activities more and more specialised; on the other, key knowledge concerns the procedures by which the research is done and the ideal molecule designed.

Another approach which has changed the way to do research is the high throughput screening. Once defined the medical target, automated systems can systematically screen a number of molecules to check whether they meet the required objectives. Their use allows to dramatically reduce the time needed to search for potential new drugs (from years to months), and reduces the number of researchers needed. However, there become key decisions to define the medical targets to meet (which means to define the direction where to orient the research) and to select the molecules to develop among those fulfilling the target and checked by the automated system.

As a consequence of these factors:

- research groups tend to be smaller than in the past;
- the degree of specialisation of the knowledge required increases;
- the effectiveness of the process increasingly depends on few key decisions;
- advances are produced more quickly and therefore it is much more difficult than in the past to keep in-house activities up to speed on all fronts. This implies that research management has to do with knowing what is happening in basic research around the world, where to find leads for new compounds, to decide quickly which co-operation to enter and which co-operation to keep.

On the contrary, development comprises highly standardised large scale activities, involves hundreds of developers and generates highly codifiable knowledge. Decisions on whether to carry them in-house or outside (at contract research organisations) are based on factors such as the process efficiency (costs), timeliness, the degree of control on the activities in terms of time and costs.

Therefore, the type of knowledge produced and the knowledge production process in research and development tend to differ even more and this has stressed the differences in terms of the unit size, the skills and, consequently, the organisation required.

Accessing external sources of knowledge. Motivations to access external sources of knowledge and the types of external sources searched for and accessed are radically different. In Research, firms go external to monitor technical progress in a certain area and to pick up good ideas for new products. Partners are usually Universities and research institutions, or small research firms. This in turn means that increasingly R organisations need to have key people, acknowledged internationally within the scientific community, able to facilitate the access to external sources. In Development, the reason to go external is to increase the capacity to do clinical trials and the typical partners are contract research organisations.

Time as competitive factor. A factor which has stressed the differences between R and D is the increasing importance of time as a basis for competition. Generally speaking, R&D expenses tend to grow very rapidly. Being first on the market becomes crucial as it ensures that there is a rapid return on R&D investments. Imitation products, although quickly introduced onto the market, do not allow to make money any more, as the window of opportunity becomes narrower and narrower. But, R activities can not be time compressed, as research relies on creativity, idea creation, and can not be 'managed' to be shortened. On the contrary, in development a certain organisational choice can lead to productivity increase, higher efficiency and time saving. Thus, most corporations paid attention to the organisation of the development process and introduced several changes. The most diffused are:

- organising development by activity type so to increase the efficiency. On the contrary, this can not be done in research where the specialisation of the knowledge requires that units are dedicated to individual disciplines. This means that R and D are designed on the basis of different criteria: the development department by activity type with the appropriate overlapping procedures to avoid the typical errors from the use of sequential approaches; the research department by discipline, as the technical specialisation is still the critical factor. Most pharmaceutical companies actually organise development by therapeutic area to exploit scale economies, efficiently use the equipment and reduce costs, whereas the research department is organised by scientific area;

-    creating integration mechanisms between development and marketing departments. Product managers are responsible for the development and the marketing of a certain product throughout the process. This ensures that there is integration between development and marketing, and that the development process has market orientation;

-    stressing the importance of the phase in which research (knowledge) is turned into development (products). The selection of the candidates for new product is a key decision of the R&D process. This requires that the interface between research and development is fostered and that there is integration between research and development activities in this phase. Paradoxically, this is obtained more easily separating research from development than keeping them in the same organisation. Separation generates higher emphasis on the decision. The separation between R and D makes that a project approved has to be passed from an organisation to another; therefore, the approval is clearly stated with the change of the responsible for the project.

The internationalisation of science, technology and markets. The globalisation of markets, on the one hand, and of science and technology, on the other, forces firms to re-localise their activities. However, the driving forces in research and development are different.

In research, the increasing specialisation of the knowledge means that around the world there tends to create pockets of excellence where specific knowledge is produced. Thus, units are decentralised to access peculiar knowledge and easier recruit technical talents.

In development, units are decentralised to increase proximity to key customers, to quicker gain market knowledge, to be close to governmental institutions which regulate the market, and ultimately to expand the new drug market. In other words, whereas research is affected by the process of internationalisation of scientific and technological sources, development is much more linked to and affected by the process of market internationalisation and the need to exploit a firm's innovations across a larger number of markets.

Therefore, the criteria to locate a research centre abroad (availability of high calibre scientists, supporting university infrastructure, etc.) are rather different from those for development facilities (supporting hospital infrastructure, government incentives, proximity to the production site, large markets etc.).

The different missions of international units also force firms to adopt different managerial approaches (Chiesa, 1996). Research units tend to be given freedom and to be managed locally. Development units are strongly coordinated from the centre. Dispersed development units are part of a process of data collection, registration and launch which needs to be strongly controlled from the centre to avoid duplications and capture synergies.

To summarise, the nature of R and D differs, and now that R&D is under pressure, investments in R&D increases and returns are even more difficult to achieve, these differences are strongly emphasised. Improving returns from R&D is linked, on the one hand, to the ability to discover new findings, on the other hand, to increase the efficiency and timeliness of the process. The areas of improvements and how to get these improvements strongly differentiate research from development.

The basic differences can be summarised as follows:

- the objective in research is effectiveness; the objective in development is to bring a new product onto the market efficiently and timely;
- the key factor in research is creativity, which in turn depends on the human resources available. Therefore, advantages in research with respect to competitors are based on the scientific/technical knowledge of individuals. The key factor in development is the organisation. A better organisation can provide time and cost advantages;
- profiles of human resources involved in R and D differ. Initial stages of the R&D process are conducted by scientists who are specialists of a certain discipline, later stages are carried out by developers who have more general skills;
- locational criteria differ: whereas the geographical dispersion of research facilities is driven by the internationalisation of scientific knowledge sources, the driving force for locating development units abroad is the need for exploiting new products across different markets.

5.3.2 Managerial Implications of the Separation Between R and D

The choice to separate R from D shows both advantages and disadvantages with respect to the traditional organisations. It has been recognised that there are two main advantages from separation: the opportunity to adopt different management styles, the clear definition of an organisational break when potential new products have to be chosen. A major disadvantage is that integration mechanisms are needed between the two.

Managerial differences. Different cultures and managerial principles underlie research and development respectively. Best results in basic research come from small groups. The human factor is vitally important and the importance of individuality is central to research effectiveness. This does not mean that researchers should be kept separated from the other functions of the company but to recognise that they feel themselves part of both the business community and the scientific community. Researchers need to be given the opportunity to take an occasional break such as a sabbatical, to be involved in a variety of projects, to keep strong links with the outside scientific community.

Research management must provide support and constructive criticism, reward achievement, and display flexibility in accommodating individual work styles. Research needs to be very open and sometimes borders on chaos.

Development is a process, which needs planning, fixing milestones and putting up structure and organisation. For each project it is needed to define who is the manager responsible for, who is in the team. The development plan and the individual tasks assigned within it need to be identified in a detailed manner. Once defined and agreed the plan should be followed closely; any significant deviation should become the subject of formal discussion.

Different organisational cultures, organisational mechanisms and people skills are therefore required for the two activities. Table 5.2 summarises the most important differences between R and D. Separating R from D helps manage these two as different organisations and apply the appropriate managerial styles.

Decision-making break. As already mentioned, separation helps give emphasis on the decisional break which takes place when a potential new product has to be evaluated for future developments. The selection process is so important that some companies (for example Glaxo) state that they undertook the re-organisation mostly to create *a clear organisational break* between research and development. Given that development costs are very high and continuously grows, killing projects at early stages is increasingly critical. As said above, creating this break helps to this end.

Integration. The integration between R and D is a major disadvantage of the separation. To make the R&D process work it is needed that integration mechanisms are implemented. In Glaxo, different committees have been established at the different life stages of a new drug R&D process to ensure that there is integration among activities (Research Management Committee, Exploratory Development Committee, Development Group). They involve people from both R and D, and other functions too.

Table 5.2. Main differences between research and development management.

Managerial principles of R organisations	Managerial principles of D organisations
Culture - Creation of a positive environment (freedom to express scientific opinions and flexibility in reviewing projects) - 'Open door' policy - Accept mistakes - Direct communication - Right for initiative for everyone	Culture - Clear cut priority setting - Identify and solve areas of weakness - Play for speed - Formal communication
Organisation - Creation of highly specialised core teams - Sharing information among different scientific disciplines and fields of research - Minimum hierarchical levels - Sound patent strategy (the company cares the results of the research dept.) - Placing pressure not as a deadline but with a sense of urgency ('other groups are in a better position than us...') - Long term commitment - Identification of the external technical centres of excellence with whom to co-operate	Organisation - Teamwork among different technical specialists - Involvement of a number of highly specialised scientific areas - Hundreds of compounds handed area by area simultaneously - Creation of a structure that integrates business and science perspectives - Definition of hierarchy, and fixing of project milestones - Formal planning - Pressures on deadlines - Strong integration with marketing - Coordination of many outside investigators and clinics in several nations (different regulatory and marketing issues)
People - Research is the right place for a 'prima donna' - Reward on qualitative and quantitative output - Company scientists must be integrated and connected to the outside world of science - Opportunities to present their work to peer review committees - The most creative people should not become managers. - Look for public recognition, tangible benefits, support scientific efforts (staff increase)	People - Teamwork - Avoidance of people spending much of their time moving process along - Avoidance of people with pure science credentials - Recruitment of people who can manage across corporate functions (marketing, clinical science etc) - People with broad perspective (business implications of scientific results). - People with long term strategic view plus day-to-day activities - People with an entrepreneurial spirit (winning attitude)

US companies raises the point of the R&D communication as the key motivation for keeping R&D as a whole. They believe that face-to-face communication should be favoured as much as possible: This extends the physical lay-out of facilities which are designed to include areas for scientists to mix during breaks with developers and to minimise delays caused by separating the two.

REFERENCES AND FURTHER READINGS

AA. VV., Industrial Research Institute's Annual R&D Trends Forecast, *Research Technology Management*, 2 (1995).

Allen, J., *Managing the Flow of Technology*, MIT Press, Cambridge (1976).

Amidon Rogers, D.M., The Challenge of Fifth Generation R&D, *Research Technology Management*, July-August (1996), 33.

Arora, A. and Gambarella, A., The Changing Technology of Technological Change: General and Abstract Knowledge and the Division of Innovative Labour, *Resaerch Policy*, 23, 523-532

Bogner, W. and Thomas, H., From skill to technological competencies; the play out of resource boundless across firm, in Sanchez, R., Heene, A. and Thomas, H., *Dynamics of competence based competition: theory and practice in the new strategic management* (Elsevier, London, 1996).

Chiesa, V., Separating Research from Development: Evidence from the Pharmaceutical Industry, *European Management Journal*, 14, 6 (1996).

Clark, K.B. and Fujimoto, T., *Product Development Performance* (HBS Press, Boston, 1991).

Cohen, W.M. and Levinthal, D.A., Absorptive Capacity: a New Perspective on Learning and Innovation, *Administrative Science Quarterly*, 35 (1990), 128.

Collis, D., A resource-based analysis of global competition: the case of bearings industry, *Strategic Management Journal*, 12 (1991), 49.

Coombs, R., Core Competencies and the Strategic Management of R&D, *R&D Management*, 26, 4 (1996), 345.

De Maio, A., Bellucci, A., Corso, M. and Verganti, R., *Gestire l'innovazione e innovare la gestione* (Etaslibri, Milano, 1994).

Eto, H., Classification of R&D Organisational Structures in Relation to Strategies, *IEEE Transactions on Engineering Management*, 38, 2 (1992).

Floyd, C., *Managing technology for corporate success* (Gower, Aldershot, 1997).

Gupta, A.K. and Wilemon, D. (1996), Changing Patterns in Industrial R&D Management, *Journal of Product Innovation Management*, 13 (1997), 497.

Hall, R., The strategic analysis of intangible resources, *Strategic Management Journal*, 13 (1992), 135.

Hamel, G. and Heene, A., *Competence Based Competition* (John Wiley & Sons, Chichester, 1994).

Hamel, G. and Prahalad, C.K., *Competing for the Future* (Harvard Business School Press, Harvard, 1994).

Hedlund, G., The Hypermodern MNC - A Heterarchy?, *Human Resource Management*, 25, Spring (1990).

Heene, A. and Sanchez, R., *Competence-based Strategic Management* (J. Wiley, Chichetser, 1997).

Iansiti, M. et al., Technology integration: turning great research into great products, *Harvard Business Review* (1997).

Kay, N., The R&D function: Corporate Strategy and Structure, in Dosi et al. (Eds.), *Technical Change and Economic Theory* (Pinter Publishers, London, 1988).

Kodama, F., Technology Fusion and the new R&D, *Harvard Business Review*, 70, 4 (1992), 70-78.

Kodama, F., *Emerging Patterns of Innovation* (Harvard Business School Press, Boston, 1995).

Lewis, W.W. and Linden, L.H., A New Mission for Corporate Technology, *Sloan Management Review*, Summer (1990), 57.

Prahalad, C.K. and Hamel, G., The Core Competence of the Corporation, *Harvard Business Review*, 68, 3 (1990), 79.

Rieck, R. et al., A model of technology strategy, *Technology analysis and strategic management*, 3 (1993).

Roberts, E.B., Benchmarking the Strategic Management of Technology - I, *Research Technology Management*, January-February (1995a), 44.

Roberts, E.B., Benchmarking the Strategic Management of Technology - II, *Research Technology Management*, March-April (1995b), 18.

Rothwell, R., Successful Industrial Innovation: Critical Factors for the 1990s, *R&D Management*, 22, 3 (1992), 221.

Rothwell, R., Successful Industrial Innovation: Critical Factors for the 1990s, *R&D Management*, 22, 3 (1992), 221-239.

Roussel, P., Saad, K. and Erickson, T., *Third Generation R&D* (HBS Press, Boston, 1991).

Rubenstein, A.H., *Managing Technology in the Decentralised Firms* (J. Wiley, Chichester, 1989).

Sanchez, R., Heene, A. and Thomas, H., Towards the theory and practice of competence based competition in Sanchez, R., Heene, A. and Thomas, H., *Dynamics of competence based competition: theory and practice in the new strategic management* (Elsevier, London, 1996).

CHAPTER 6

THE GEOGRAPHICAL DISPERSION
OF R&D ACTIVITIES

A variety of contributions puts emphasis on the increasing internationalisation of R&D activities. The geographic distribution of labs has become another structural dimension of the organisation of R&D activities in large firms. Moreover, this aspect is increasingly attracting the attention of managers and practicioners. In a survey, Japanese and American executives ranked the internationalisation of R&D as one of the top priorities in modern competition (Granstrand et al., 1992). Internationalisation, especially of technological activities, is a key factor in accelerating a firm's ability to accumulate knowledge, capitalise learning processes and embed unique forms of competence in the organisation (Prahalad and Hamel, 1990; De Meyer, 1993; Hamel and Prahalad, 1993). The successful model of technology management consists in being able to create 'a network of technology groups in each major market - the US, Japan and Europe - managed in a coordinated way for maximum impact' (Perrino and Tipping, 1989).

Statistics show the growing relevance of R&D internationalisation. The amount of R&D budget firms spend abroad is increasing and in several countries has become a significant percentage of the total R&D expenses (data refer to the late 80s): 17% in German industrial firms (Brockhoff and von Boehmer, 1992), 23% in Swedish multinationals (Hakanson and Nobel, 1989). This figure is lower for US companies (about 10%), according to a National Science Foundation survey[a], and still lower in the case of Japanese companies (less than 5%). Nevertheless, in each country, foreign R&D expenses are growing more rapidly than domestic expenditure. R&D investments abroad by US companies increased by 33% in 1988 and 1987, while in the same period the domestic grew by 6%. A study of the first Fortune 500 companies has shown that between 1970 and 1990, 65% of the new laboratories established were located abroad. Japanese firms (traditionally highly centralised) also showed a greater propensity to decentralise their R&D: only 3 of the 26 new

---

a   As reported in the International Herald Tribune, February 27, 1989, Exporting R&D Operations Could Hurt U.S. Economy.

labs established in the 80s were located in the home country. The table 6.1 lists the largest R&D facilities of non-US firms in the US in the early 90s. It highlights that foreign R&D facilities have a remarkable size.

This trend seems to be confirmed in the 90s. A survey on the strategic management of technology in 244 firms showed that the average percentage of R&D investments abroad is about 30% in European firms, more than 10% in US firms and over 5% in Japanese companies.

Table 6.1. Largest foreign facilities in the U.S.

Company	Location	No. of Employees*
Glaxo (UK)	Research Triangle Park, NC	800
Honda (JA)	Marysville, OH (2); Torrance, CA; Denver, CO	720
Hoechst (GER)	Charlotte, NC	580
Siemens (GER)	Siemens Communications, Boca Raton, FL	500
Hoechst (GER)	Summit, NJ	450
Hoffman LaRouche (Swiss)	Nutley, NJ	350
Toyota (JA)	California (4), Ann Arbor, MI	350
Nissan (JA)	Farmington, Ann Arbor, MI; L. Angeles, CA	320
Philips (NE)	Laboratories Division, Briarcliff, NY	285
Mazda (JA)	Flat Rock, Ann Arbor, MI; Irvine, CA; OH	213
SmithKline Beecham (UK)	West Chester, PA	200
Sandoz (Swiss)	Palo Alto, CA	200
Goldstar (KO)	Englewood Cliffs, New Jersey	200
Robert Bosch (GER)	Farmington Hills, MI	180
Bayer (GER)	New Haven, CT	150
Fujitsu (JA)	Raleigh, NC	150
Toshiba (JA)	Irvine, CA	150
Siemens (GER)	Princeton, NJ	135
ICI (UK)	Slater, IA	130
Affymax Technologies (NE)	Palo Alto, CA	111
Ciba-Geigy (Swiss)	Research Triangle Park, NC	110
Isuzu (JA)	Cerritos, CA; Detroit, MI	100
Ishihara Sangyo Kaisha (JA)	Mountain View, CA	100
BASF (GER)	Cambridge, MA	92
NEC (JA)	NEC Rersearch Institute, Princewton, NJ	85

* Includes technical and administrative employees.
Source: Adapted from Donald Dalton and Manuel G. Serapio, Jr., *U.S. Research Facilities of Foreign Companies*, U.S. Department of Commerce, NTIS, February 1993.

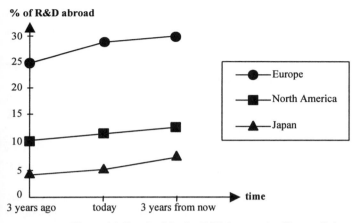

Figure 6.1. Trends of foreign R&D investments (Source: Roberts, 1995a).

In this chapter, the following aspects of the internationalisation of R&D are dealt with:
- determinants of internationalisation and non internationalisation (why and why not);
- types of foreign R&D units (what);
- modes of establishing R&D units abroad (how);
- locational factors (where);
- types of international R&D structures (organisation).

6.1 DETERMINANTS OF GEOGRAPHICAL CENTRALISATION AND DECENTRALISATION

The R&D internationalisation can be seen as a trade-off between factors determining centralisation of R&D at the headquarters and reasons for decentralising R&D (Table 6.2).

Major centralisation determinants (which explain both the tendency to concentrate R&D in a limited number of units and to localise such activities in the home country) are:
- the need to keep technical information and knowledge secret (Rugman, 1981; Terpstra, 1977);

- the increase in the *costs of coordination and control* associated with internationalisation, due to greater difficulties in communication (De Meyer and Mizushima, 1989);
- the presence of *economies of scale in R&D* and the difficulties in achieving the needed critical mass in decentralised units;
- the need to exploit firm-specific technological advantages, emerging from home market conditions, on other markets (as the *international product life cycle* model suggests) (Vernon, 1966).

On the other hand, the main factors which have traditionally been identified as reasons for decentralising R&D activities, can be grouped into two broad categories: demand factors and supply factors (Granstrand et al., 1992).

On the *demand* side, technology transfer between headquarters and subsidiaries, the need to access foreign markets, the need to improve a firm's ability to respond to specific requirements of local markets, and the need to increase the proximity of product development activities to key customers have usually been indicated as relevant factors behind decentralisation decisions (Hirschey and Caves, 1981; Granstrand et al. 1992).

Technology supply factors are related to the fact that the increasing acceleration of technological progress, the increasing costs of technology development and the international specialisation of knowledge sources require firms to access a wider range of scientific and technological skills and knowledge than that available in the home country (Perrino and Tipping, 1989; Howells, 1990; Sakakibara and Westney, 1992; De Meyer, 1992). The access to new or emerging technologies, the recruitment of qualified technical personnel, the exploitation of entrepreneurial and/or technical talents concentrated in geographical pockets of scientific and technological knowledge force firms to decentralise their R&D units to tap into foreign scientific infrastructures (Hewitt, 1980; Pearce, 1989; Hamel and Prahalad, 1993).

Other factors indicated political motivations and image as reasons for decentralising R&D. *Political factors* include local government pressures to increase the local technological content of productions and the need to facilitate interactions with governmental bodies in businesses such as telecommunications and pharmaceuticals (Hakanson, 1992). In other cases, internationalising R&D helps enhance a firm's *competitive image* (Granstrand et al. 1992).

Therefore, the motivation to go abroad and the scope of activities vary substantially from unit to unit. Some activities are decentralised purely to facilitate competition in a certain country and do not take part to the firm's R&D process, and/or are involved in the actual R&D process only in the final stage (product adaptation) and have a local geographical scope. In contrast, other labs play a central role in the firm's R&D process and are the key to access resources and knowledge (either market or technology) not available elsewhere. Their R&D activity has a global impact and is strategic to the firm's process of innovation.

Table 6.2. R&D centralisation and decentralisation determinants.

R&D centralisation determinants	*R&D decentralisation determinants*
Secrecy of technological knowledge	*Technology supply factors*
	Accessing technological centres of
Lowering costs of coordination and control	excellence
	Recruiting qualified technical personnel
Facilitating communication	
	Demand factors
Achieving economies of scale	Responding to local demand needs
	Increasing proximity to key customers
Achieving critical mass	
	Political factors
Exploiting firm-specific technological	Increasing the local technological content
advantages from home market conditions	of production
	Interacting with governmental institutions
	Image
	Enhancing the firm's image on
	international markets

In the past, centralisation forces have prevailed and the propensity to decentralise R&D has traditionally been low. Moreover, most foreign units played a peripheral role. More recently, there is an increasing dispersion of R&D units playing a central role in the firms' innovation processes, i.e. having a global impact. This can be traced back to several reasons. On the one hand, the nature of the technological innovation process changed, affecting the organisational and locational factors within research operations. Especially:
- technological innovations are often the result of the integration of technologies from different disciplines (an example is the convergence of electronic, telecommunication and information technologies). Research operations within a firm embrace a larger range of technological fields than in the past. Access to external sources becomes critical in order to acquire knowledge not available internally and to decrease technology development costs. Decentralising R&D

units is a way of facilitating access to external sources of knowledge (Perrino and Tipping, 1989; Bailetti and Callahan, 1992; Hamel and Prahalad, 1993);

- the increase of inter- and intra-organisational linkages during the technological innovation process means that R&D must interact with other firm functions that are subject to the process of internationalisation[b] and with key customers and lead users who may be dispersed (Prahalad and Doz, 1987; Pavitt, 1990; Pavitt, 1991). In particular, interaction with customers and users has been recognised as a key source of market knowledge: locating R&D units close to these clients increases the market orientation and customer focus of the innovation process (Westney, 1992);

- a sort of division of labour has taken place in knowledge production on a worldwide basis. 'New technologies and the specialised talent that produces them will continue to develop locally in "pockets of innovation" around the world. Nurturing those technologies, uprooting them, and cross-fertilising them for commercialisation and global distribution will continue to be major challenges in technology management' (Perrino and Tipping, 1989). In other words, the increasing specialisation of skills and capabilities required to innovate in certain technological fields has meant that these specialised resources are increasingly concentrated in only certain regions of the world. If a firm needs to access these resources, it has to be there (Sakakibara and Westney, 1992).

On the other hand, time is a critical competitive factor in a number of industries. De Meyer in a study on international R&D in fourteen multinationals has made the point that decentralisation of R&D activities is undertaken to enhance and accelerate the process of technical learning, and this explains why 'companies go through the pain of creating an international [R&D] network ... Learning about customer needs, monitoring the hot spots of the field to quickly learn about most recent developments and having access to resources (engineers, scientists) which can process this information quickly is the objective of the internationalisation process' (De Meyer, 1993).

---

b A strong emphasis has been recently posed on the importance of the combined development of product and production process and on the involvement of customers into the innovation process (methodologies such as concurrent engineering and quality function deployment are well known examples). Of course, these approaches imply the co-location of R&D, manufacturing and marketing activities. This also suggests that the internationalisation of manufacturing and marketing activities (which have a stronger tradition than that of R&D) can 'pull' the internationalisation of R&D.

Furthermore, technological advance in communications reduces the disadvantages of decentralisation. The growth of network and information exchange systems facilitates long distance communication so lowering the increase in control and coordination costs associated with the decentralisation of a firm's activities.

6.2   TYPES OF FOREIGN R&D UNITS

Foreign R&D units can be classified on the basis of two dimensions:
- type of activity, which is the traditional classification into research, development and minor technical activity at later stages of the innovation process;
- geographical scope of the activity, whether the unit's activity concerns innovations to be exploited on a local, regional, global basis.

The types of foreign R&D units are the following (Ronstadt, 1977; Behrman and Fischer, 1980; Hewitt, 1980; Pearce, 1989).

Scanning units. They monitor the technological progress and/or market evolution[c] in foreign countries. They do not carry out actual technical activities; however, they increasingly play a role in the process of innovation of multinational firms. In fact, these units which monitor the technological evolution are located in highly advanced technological contexts. For example, typical areas where electronic and telecommunication companies concentrate their scanning units are California, the Research Triangle Park in North Carolina, and New Jersey. For example, Ericsson has its scanning units at Menlo Park (California) and Raleigh (North Carolina). Japanese electronics firms have also located small scanning units in the UK and Germany near major centres of technological excellence (Oxford, Cambridge, Aachen). Scanning units can also be decentralised to monitor consumers' tastes and habits. This is typical of consumer electronics Japanese firms. Units composed of a few designers are located near key customers. They provide information on market demand for the product development process which take place elsewhere;

Technical support units. They usually fulfil the task of providing technical support and assistance to other firm functions located abroad (typically manufacturing and marketing).

---

c   Monitoring market evolution means that the technical implications of the evolution of market characteristics are captured and studied.

Adaptive units. They adapt products developed elsewhere to local market requirements. This task is often combined in a unit with the previous one. Their geographical scope is by definition local or at most regional. However, they may also play a role as an integrated part of the global R&D structure. Their range of activities encompasses technical support to manufacturing and marketing activities, support in technology transfer to production facilities overseas, product adaptation to local market needs, technical cooperation with suppliers and customer technical service. These activities concern the final stage of the innovation process or, even, the after-sale phase of an innovation. As such, their geographical scope is local. On the other hand, they often act as market scanners and play a role integrated within the global innovation process.

Local original units. They develop new products (production processes) suitable to local markets, i.e. to the country where they are located.

Regional original units. They develop new products (processes) suitable to a region, i.e. a set of adjacent countries.

Global original units. They develop new products suitable for commercialisation on the global market.

Table 6.3. Evolutionary trends of international R&D units.

		UNIT ROLE IN 1993					
		Technology scanning	Adaptive unit	Local original unit	Global original unit	Closed	Total
UNIT ROLE IN 1980	Technology scanning	4	4	-	-		8
	Adaptive unit	11	31	2	-	9	53
	Local original unit	4	8	18	10	1	41
	Global original unit				11		11
	Non existent	19	8	2	14		43
	Total	38	51	22	35	10	156

Box 6.1 - Evolutionary patterns of international R&D

In the last decade, there has been an increase of units playing a role which crosses the national boundaries and impacts on the global performance of innovation. A survey on twelve multinational companies (the description of the empirical basis is later in this chapter) shows that there are in place evolutionary patterns of foreign R&D units. Table 6.3 provides a synthesis of the findings of this study. Columns show the role of the foreign R&D unit in 1993 and the rows in 1980. The matrix is five by five. The four rows and columns corresponding to four unit types (scanning, adaptive, local original, global original) are complemented by a row representing units nonexistent in 1980 but established later; and a column representing units existing in 1980 and subsequently closed.

It emerges that foreign R&D is subject to important changes and evolutionary processes. Major patterns of evolution are the following (Figure 6.2).

Companies tend to concentrate their foreign R&D efforts at the ends of the unit range. At one end, there are technology scanning units which seem to fulfil key tasks, such as gaining information quickly, monitoring key sources of knowledge, and scanning the orientation of technology development centres to understand the directions of technical progress in a certain field.

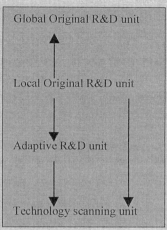

Figure 6.2. Evolutionary trajectories of foreign R&D units.

Adaptive units increasingly combine their traditional role of adapting products to local needs with that of scanning. Small units are therefore dispersed to identify opportunities and catch in advance how markets and technologies will evolve in a certain environment. Technology scanning seems to be the initial stage of a foreign R&D unit. Subsequently, it may become an adaptive unit if local demand is recognised to have specific requirements.

The evolution of a unit from scanning to adaptive seems to be a possible trend in the future. At the moment, there are more adaptive units which become scanning units than the reverse. This means that the rationalisation process to which adaptive units are subject is still in progress. At the other end, there are global

(follows)

original units of which the R&D activities are exploited to global benefits. They are the result of two processes: first, the direct placement of new units in a foreign environment to attract and leverage key people able to process the knowledge produced locally and to exploit this knowledge to global results; second, the assignment of a global mandate to an already existing unit, where peculiar and unique resources have progressively grown and accumulated. As people able to quickly process knowledge in a certain field are increasingly found only in limited regions of the world, companies are forced to locate their resources there, then to disperse their centres of excellence on a world-wide basis, and finally to allow decisions concerning that technological area to be taken locally.

Finally, units which are typically in the middle of the range, such as the local original, seem to become lesser and lesser important. They are linked to a view of international competition as a portfolio of local strategies which aim to optimize R&D activities locally, while companies recognise that taking a global view of their operations increases both the efficiency and effectiveness of their R&D. This does not mean that local original units will disappear but that they tend to be kept where local demand has unique and uncommon characteristics. Moreover, they increasingly tend to be integrated in the global structure in such a way that the innovations performed at these sites (for the local market) which have the potential to be introduced on other markets are exploited across different countries.

6.3   ESTABLISHMENT OF FOREIGN R&D UNITS

Acquisition and direct placement are the two most common methods of setting up technical activities in foreign countries (Steele, 1975; Ronstadt, 1976; Ronstadt, 1977, Behrman and Fischer, 1980; Hakanson, 1992).

Acquisition is a very common means of international expansion. Acquisitions are commonly distinguished between horizontal acquisitions and product diversification. In the first case, the acquired R&D activity is a duplication of already existing facilities; the acquisition of R&D is not the actual objective of the acquisition. However, political reasons - both internal and external (pressures from local governments) to the company - may influence decisions on the acquired unit and lead to keep R&D in that country, so resulting in a duplication. In the case of product diversification, R&D is part of the actual objective of the acquisition: technical resources, knowledge, competence are among the reasons for the acquisition. The acquired R&D usually remains as an R&D centre with global responsibility in a specific field.

The *direct placement* of a lab in a foreign country follows a strategic decision to set up a foreign R&D unit in a specific location. Findings from field surveys have shown that direct placement is rare and usually limited to units performing generic and long range research (Behrman and Fischer, 1980).

Finally, there should be taken into account that an *evolutionary process* may take place in foreign R&D units (as seen in the previous section). For example, small technical activities (such as technical support units) are initially decentralised as a consequence of the internationalisation of other firm functions (manufacturing and marketing) that require local technical support. Once established, foreign technical activities are subject to an evolutionary process (Ronstadt, 1977). They may subsequently evolve to assume new product research responsibility. Studies on this topic seem to agree that research units are often located abroad through direct placement, because they are set up to attract key people in a certain technical area and need to be in certain locations. On the other hand, foreign product development activities are more likely to be the result of an evolutionary path, from trivial technical support to manufacturing and marketing, to adaptation of products developed elsewhere, to development of products suitable for local markets, to the responsibility for developing new products or technologies for simultaneous application across a number of markets.

Arguments to explain why this evolutionary process may take place are the following:

- the willingness of subsidiaries to develop their own R&D resource to become more independent of the centre;
- the strategic intention of the centre to improve a firm's local responsiveness;
- an increasing autonomy allowed to subsidiaries to develop products suitable for the local market;
- spontaneous growth due to the presence in a technologically advanced context or in an evolved market, or merely accidental evolution[d] (Prahalad and Doz, 1987).

This evolutionary process of international R&D may therefore be the result of either accidental development or planned actions, and of actions undertaken at both central and subsidiary levels, even not coordinated each other. This would also explain why R&D activities in different countries may duplicate each other.

---

[d] As Steele (1975) notes: 'Once some technical capability has been established, domestic scientists and engineers are certain to see additional opportunities for improvement'.

However, in the past, the evolutionary process of foreign R&D units has mostly been due to local rather than global factors. Recently, companies tend to take a global view of their research operations and to make efforts to coordinate their dispersed R&D. Therefore, there is a greater central planning and control of the evolutionary processes of international R&D activities than in the past.

6.4   LOCALISATION OF FOREIGN R&D UNITS

A key decision in the geographical distribution of R&D units is the locational choice. There are two major categories of locational factors:
-       a set of R&D related factors, i.e. factors strictly associated with the nature and the content of the R&D activity;
-       a set of non R&D-related factors.

The R&D-related factors include:
-       input factor costs;
-       transfer costs;
-       organisational costs;
-       input resource quality.

Input factor costs include the cost of technical personnel, equipment and facilities.
Transfer costs include:
-       internal costs of transferring information and technological knowledge among R&D labs, between R&D and manufacturing, between R&D and marketing;
-       external costs of getting both market and technical information from outside sources (suppliers, customers, research institutions).

Organisational costs include the costs of building up a new R&D organisation (recruiting local people; mobilising human and technical resources; establishing international reward systems for researchers and scientists; developing the planning and control systems and the communication system).

Input resource quality includes various factors:
-       breadth/depth of the skills accessed;
-       the quality of technical people available;
-       the configuration of the foreign lab: the possibility to achieve the required critical mass and economies of scale (which vary according to the scientific discipline).

The balance among these factors leads to decisions on whether or not to locate a unit abroad and to define the optimal (preferred) locations.

They have to be matched with non R&D-related factors such as:

- existing business locations: the company already has a marketing and/or manufacturing facility at the location and this provides access to existing services;
- local infrastructure: a certain location allows easy access to services, infrastructures or networks that facilitate communication;
- company managerial culture: the culture influences the attitude to centralisation and decentralisation and therefore decisions about R&D locations; for example, companies with centralisation oriented culture may prefer already existing foreign locations rather than ventures in unknown countries.

Figure 6.3 summarises the process of deploying R&D facility abroad.

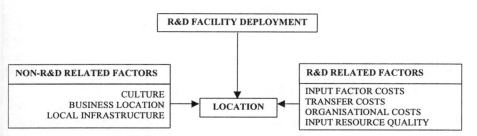

Figure 6.3. R&D facility deployment : locational factors.

6.5   INTERNATIONAL R&D STRUCTURES

The previous sections show that companies, on the one hand, need to manage dispersed R&D that has been located abroad for a variety of reasons, whereas, on the other, the need to improve the performance of innovation processes forces companies to geographically disperse their R&D to a larger extent than in the past, to leverage their foreign R&D and to strongly coordinate all the R&D activities. A major challenge is how to coordinate dispersed R&D, i.e. how international R&D structures are shaped, how research of different units is linked, and what kind of interdependencies exist among units.

An empirical study has been conducted to identify the shape of international R&D structures. The empirical basis is described in Box 6.2.

Box 6.2 – The empirical basis

The field research has been conducted on a sample of twelve multinational companies operating in technology-intensive industries. Four companies are North American, two are Japanese and six European. Some are widely diversified into unrelated businesses. In these cases, the analysis has concerned only a certain set of related businesses and the respective R&D activity. (The activity studied is indicated in table 6.4 under 'company activity'). The sample activities considered concern electronic, telecommunication, chemical and petrochemical operations.

Data have been collected through direct interviews of research managers at both corporate and divisional level. In each firm, at least three managers have been interviewed. Answers were cross-checked and re-submitted when uncertainties and differences emerged. The number of managers interviewed in each firm and the cross-checking of the answers reduced the risk that data and information might be biased by personal views or interests.

The following data and information have been collected for each R&D unit:

- the profile of the unit, especially the scope of the activities, i.e. the range of technologies or products developed;
- the time scale of the projects carried out by the unit;

- the objective of the projects carried out by the unit (developing new products, developing new technologies, exploring new technologies), so identifying whether or not there is a business focus;
- the organisational position of the unit (corporate or divisional level);
- the reason for decentralisation, i.e. why the R&D unit was located at a given site;
- the geographical scope of the activity, which defines the geographical mandate, i.e. whether the unit is assigned innovation programmes for the global or local markets;
- the interaction with external bodies (Universities, Research Institutes, customers, suppliers), identifying the importance of the external context for the R&D work of the unit;
- the interaction with other R&D units within the firm, identifying whether, how and with whom such relationships are maintained during R&D work.

The sample units encompass a wide range of technical activities from basic research to customer service. To avoid the problems usually arising from a too rigid definition of the various types of R&D activity, a taxonomy has been introduced based on the time scale of the projects performed in a certain unit.

(follows)

Foreign R&D activities were classified into four categories on the basis of the type of activity performed.

Support units usually fulfil the task of providing technical support to other firm functions located abroad and also of adapting products developed elsewhere to local market requirements. As these tasks are often combined in a unit, technical support and adaptation R&D are considered as one category. Their geographical scope is by definition local or at most regional. However, as explained below, they may also play a role as an integrated part of the global R&D structure.

Development units are those managing one-to-three year projects that have a clearly stated objective of leading to an innovation, such as a new product to be marketed or a new process to be used. These are divisional units focused on a single product line or corporate units developing products for a set of related businesses. In any case, they have a strong business focus, while they can be distinguished either global or local according to their geographical mandate. For present purposes, those units which have a global mandate and the local units integrated into a cross-national structure are of interest. However, no cases of purely local labs which develop products for the local market and do not interact with the rest of the structure have been found.

Research units manage projects with a longer time scale (more than three years) and usually have the objective of exploring new technologies, researching for new technical paradigms, or accumulating knowledge in a certain field, but are not directly related to a single innovation. They are at corporate level and define their mission on the basis of the range of technologies developed. Some of these units are highly focused on one technology, others conduct research on a wide range of technologies. Their mandate is by definition global because they do not serve a specific market or business, but develop technologies that will be subsequently exploited in new product development activities.

Technology scanning units monitor the technological progress and/or market evolution[e] in foreign countries. Although these units do not carry out actual technical activities, they are part of a firm's international R&D structure and thus are relevant to the present study.

Table 6.4 shows foreign R&D data of the sample companies. Although internationalised R&D is increasing, it should be noticed that the role of home country labs is still central, and most R&D is concentrated in headquarters' locations. This would suggest that within a global R&D structure home country labs still play a leading role.

---

[e] Monitoring market evolution means that the technical implications of the evolution of market characteristics are captured and studied.

Table 6.4. Description of the sample.

Company activity	Scanning units	Research units	Developm. units	Adaptive/ technical support units	Number of employees	Foreign R&D as percentage of total (personnel)	Number of countries involved
Telecomm.	2	-	-	1	230	1%	1
Telecomm.	3	4	10	10	2,580	30%	18
Telecomm.	4	-	4	5	2,376	33%	6
Telecomm.	3	3	5	9	10,800	60%	14
Petrochem.	-	3	4	1	10,350	30%	6
Petrochem.	-	3	3	-	2,113	30%	5
Chemicals	-	3	2	7	7,450	35%	2
Chemicals	-	4	2	-	3,200	15%	5
Chemicals	-	3	4	3	2,630	12%	2
Electronics	6	4	3	2	4,950	28%	4
Electronics	11	2	-	9	150	1%	3
Electronics	9	5	-	12	288	1%	4
Total	38	34	37	59	47,117	-	70

In the following sections, major types of international R&D structures are described in both development and research activities. The distinction is necessary as research and development units have different characteristics and are usually part of different structures. Research structures are concerned with a generic technology or range of technologies, whereas development structures refer to a single product line or set of related products. Furthermore, the two structures usually hold different positions within the organisation: research activities are often managed at corporate level; development activities are managed at divisional level (as seen in chapter 6, in the case of corporate units responsible for advanced stages of the R&D activities, the weight of the divisional managers in the decision taking process of the units is strong).

6.5.1 Development Structures

Four major international structures in development activities have been found (Figure 6.4):
(i) *isolated specialisation structure*, that assigns one foreign unit the full responsibility for developing a new product/process on the basis of a global mandate;

(ii) *supported specialisation structure,* in which one centre (abroad or in the home country) is assigned the global responsibility of the R&D work and a number of scanning units (or adaptive units also acting as scanners) in foreign countries provide innovation stimuli, new product ideas and the technical problems to be solved in relation to the needs and the requirements of the local environment;

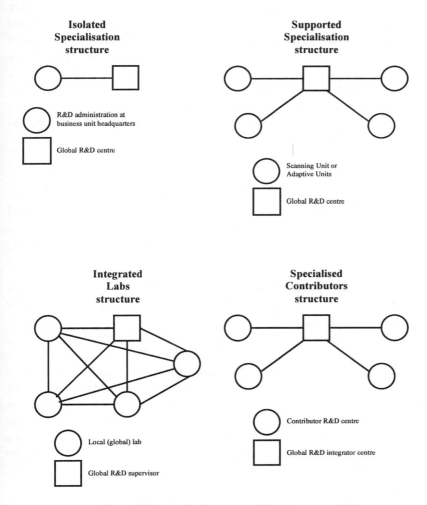

Figure 6.4. International structures in development activities.

(iii) *integrated labs structure* composed of several units, each with a local scope and freedom to undertake R&D works on innovations to be exploited in the local markets. The work and initiatives are, however, centrally monitored and supervised, in order to avoid duplications and coordinate dispersed efforts. Global coordination can take place in two main ways: (a) a weak form, whereby innovations performed at one site are exploited across different markets, but without an effective coordination of the technical activities among units in different countries (*integrated local units*); (b) a strong form with labs working on similar problems forced to establish collaboration and define joint R&D programmes, the results of which are exploited across the different markets (*integrated global units*);

(iv) *specialised contributors structure* where each (contributor) unit is specialised in one or few technology/component and contributes developing a piece of the R&D work which is managed and controlled from an (integrator) R&D centre. The structure has the shape of a star.

Isolated Specialisation

This structure assigns one unit a global mandate in a certain (set of) product(s)/process(es). The objective is to increase the R&D efficiency at global level, concentrating the resources needed for the product or production process in one location. Such concentration allows achieve economies of scale and greatly facilitates coordination[f].

This structure is usually adopted when there is, concurrently, a low dispersion of external sources of market knowledge, and the firm's R&D resources are or can be concentrated in one location.

There are two cases in which external sources of knowledge are not dispersed:

a. one market is the only relevant source of market knowledge.

   If in terms of size and customer importance, there is a leading market for a certain product category, a firm is likely to prefer to locate its development unit in that country to get market knowledge as quickly as possible and develop new products near the most significant customers. For example, when Alcatel acquired Rockwell, it concentrated the R&D of the transmission systems division in that US unit. The presence in the most innovative and sophisticated market has forced the group's R&D for those products to be concentrated there;

---

f   The word 'isolated' refers to the fact that the lab does not interact with other R&D units within the firm. Obviously, a link is maintained with the headquarters, especially in the phase of strategic planning and budget negotiation.

b. sources of market knowledge are not relevant to the innovation process. This happens when markets are undifferentiated worldwide and there is not a specific location that ensures that the necessary market knowledge is acquired quicker. This is the case in commodity chemical and petrochemical products.

The other condition which allows firms to choose the isolated specialisation structure is when the firm's key resources are already found or can be concentrated in one location; in other words, the degree of dispersion of the firms' resources is very low. Indeed, there may already be an R&D centre which clearly has the most qualified competencies in a field.

Another case is when the firm's key resources *can* be concentrated in one location. A firm may recognise that although its R&D resources in a certain field are dispersed, it would be possible to concentrate these in one location. In this case, the implementation of the isolated specialisation structure means a process of rationalisation of technical efforts on a worldwide basis, aimed at concentrating development activities on a certain product in the location where there are the most relevant skills or the key sources of market knowledge exist[g]. The empirical study has shown that firms are willing to undertake a rationalisation process in R&D in two major cases:

a. The rationalisation of technical activities allows duplications, which arise accidentally or as a result of a lack of central control of the evolution of foreign labs and/or acquisitions, to be eliminated. As seen above, firms may find themselves having to manage an uncoordinated dispersion of technical activities. Rationalisation can increase R&D efficiency without loosing technological resources. An example is Shell's rationalisation of its R&D. Fully responsible global units have been created to develop a specific product line. Assignment of a global mandate to a particular unit was decided on the basis of the historical specialisation and the competencies that have traditionally developed at the various sites.

b. The rationalisation process in R&D is the consequence of strategic decisions in other related activities of the firm. For example R&D rationalisation follows a rationalisation of manufacturing facilities: a foreign plant becomes a global supply point and its technical development unit is given responsibility for new product development for the global market. This structure has been chosen by

---

g   The implementation of this process may be hindered as it can imply the closure of labs and the movement of people from one site to another, which often raises organisational resistance.

European chemical companies, which have traditionally remained strongly centralised (Bayer, for example). They have started to establish abroad specialised manufacturing units with groupwide supply responsibility abroad to achieve production scale economies and reduce transportation costs (dyes and pigments in China and Indonesia, organic chemicals and polymers in US, plasma in US). In some cases, they have also assigned global development responsibility for that product to the annexed technical units. The origin of the internationalisation process in R&D has thus been the rationalisation that has taken place in manufacturing activities. As innovation is mostly based on production process improvements, the proximity of R&D units to plants has been considered critical to the effectiveness of the innovation process. This forces to co-locate manufacturing plants and product development units.

In summary, the isolated specialisation structure is chosen when the degree of dispersion of external sources of knowledge is very low *and* the firm's key R&D resources in that technical area are concentrated or can be concentrated.

As stated in a previous note, there may be obstacles to the implementation of this structure because it may imply the closure of units or the movement of people from one site to another. The choice of an appealing location can facilitate this process. Moreover, a unit's credibility within the organisation must be taken into account when assigning global responsibilities: it must be recognised within the organisation as highly skilled and effective in producing innovations.

Supported Specialisation

As in the case of isolated specialisation, resources in each product area are concentrated in one location and a global R&D centre is created. A number of scanning units (or adaptive units also acting as scanning units) are dispersed worldwide to supply market and technical information to the development centre. This structure attempts to reap the benefits of specialisation and concentration (efficiency, economies of scale, low coordination costs) without missing innovation opportunities. The task of the scanning units is to provide information on the particular adaptations to existing products required by the local market. These units play a key role in the development phase, as they represent a major source of innovation stimuli and ideas for new products. A good example is that of Japanese electronics companies which have kept their development resources in the home country but have dispersed a number of scanning units to their foreign markets. Another example is the case of Hoechst in the business areas of functional materials. Centres for superconductive materials, liquid cristal displays and ceramic materials are in Frankfurt (home country), centres for photoresistent and separation materials are in North America. Support labs are dispersed in each major foreign market (North America, Europe and Japan). This structure has been the result of the integration of the technical activities after the merger of Celanese and Hoechst.

This structure is usually chosen when external sources of knowledge are dispersed (key customers or different markets providing ideas for new product development) while a firm's resources are geographically concentrated. A distributed structure is crucial to be able to 'listen' and take the opportunities which may emerge in multiple locations. On the other hand, keeping R&D activity concentrated allows cost reductions through economies of scale, economies of specialisation and the reduction of coordination costs.

Integrated Labs

This structure consists of different units operating in the same product area, and is chosen when a firm's resources are dispersed and concentration in one location would lead to eliminate pockets of technological excellence within the organisation. In other words, as the consequence of a firm's organisational history and administrative heritage, technical capabilities related to a certain (set of) product(s) have been dispersed and have progressively grown. Various units have developed deep, specific and unique competencies. Concentrating resources in one location would mean loosing these resources[h].

Two different structures can be adopted in this case:

a. Each unit is assigned local or regional scope and performs innovations suitable for the local market. There is central supervision which leverages local innovations to global benefits and favours the exploitation of innovations (performed by a unit for the local market) across different countries. The objective of this structure is to combine local responsiveness with global exploitation of the innovations performed by each R&D unit. This structure is that of *integrated local units*.

b. The other structure is that of *integrated global units*. Each lab mostly fulfils a regional or local task. In order to avoid duplications and exploit the R&D taking place at the different locations to global results, forms of collaboration are

---

[h] Concentration would imply a rationalisation process: closure of several centres, movement of people from one site to another and integration among different groups who may have different ideas and approaches to the problems and may also use different practices. This usually means that key people and embodied unique competencies are lost.

established among the different units and integrated and coordinated R&D programmes are defined. Cooperation occurs through the exchange of people, the creation of temporary international teams, the use of common technical systems, and the exchange of data and information through telematic systems during joint development projects.

The question is when one structure is more efficient than another. There seem to be two relevant factors:
-    the degree of product/market differentiation;
-    the role of home country R&D units.

Degree of product/market differentiation. The integrated local labs structure seems to be efficient in those sectors where there is a high degree of market differentiation, key customers are highly dispersed, innovative ideas are likely to be location-specific, and specific technological solutions should be conceived to meet local market demand.

The integrated global labs structure, on the other hand, appears to be more efficient in those cases in which markets show a low degree of differentiation. However, as the firm's R&D resources are dispersed and the concentration would mean loosing key innovative groups and relevant competencies, companies prefer a structure with a number of dispersed inter-linked labs.

The point is that the degree of product differentiation cannot be defined in absolute terms. In other words, it depends, to a certain extent, on two firm-specific variables: strategy and technology. Within the same industry, some firms may base their global strategy on local responsiveness and the ability to cover market niches and customise their products to local users, while others will pursue a more global strategy and develop products to be marketed across different markets, exploiting cost advantages from wider production volumes. The second variable is the available technology. Technology may reduce the complexity of the market, allowing development of product platforms to be embodied into a wide variety of products. Firms possessing these technologies may prefer an integrated global lab structure to a local structure. Coordinating product development at global level allows to exploit scale advantages.

Role and technological capabilities of central R&D units with respect to foreign units. If home country labs have most R&D resources, the integrated local units structure seems preferable. Most product technology is transferred from the centre to local labs, which develop new products. In turn, the result of local development activities can subsequently be exploited worldwide. If foreign labs have technological capabilities as strong as home country units, it is more likely that they will be inter-linked each other in an integrated global units structure.

In the switching equipment industry, there are, at present, examples of both structures, integrated local units and integrated global units. Northern Telecom adopts an *integrated local units* structure. It has traditionally concentrated most R&D in North America. Local labs were initially dispersed to facilitate entries into foreign markets, but the firm later realised that each geographical area can identify peculiar innovation opportunities as communication infrastructures are country-specific and users are accustomed to certain features that are not used or diffused elsewhere. Foreign units have progressively developed specific technological skills, especially in the area of software development providing specific features to meet local market demands. As a result, an integrated local units structure has been created, with the technology base of new switching equipment being provided by the central units. Foreign units perform local innovations by developing and adding specific features to this technology base, while the solutions to particular technical problems developed by a foreign lab are sometimes exploited at global level.

The case of Nissan

Nissan, the Japanese car manufacturer, developed a minivan to be commercialised initially in US and then globally. The product was conceived first for the US market as it was the most interesting for minivans in terms of size and the richest provider of market knowledge. The product was produced and commercialised in US jointly with Ford. However, the product development was entirely carried out by Nissan. This was the result of a transnational project involving the Technical Centre at the headquarters and the three technical centres of Nissan in US, the Nissan Design International in California, the Nissan Research and Development in Michigan, and the Nissan Motor Manufacturing Centre in Tennessee. The US subsidiary was responsible for the styling (Nissan Design), stamping (Nissan Motor Manufacturing), and engineering (Nissan R&D), whereas engines and transmission systems were developed in the home country R&D units. The product concept was defined in US, and Nissan accessed market information collected on the minivan market by Ford. Nissan also did surveys in Japan and on a smaller sample of car drivers in Europe. The product development process took over 4 years. A strong effort of standardisation was done in advance to ensure that there was coordination among units. Quality and design standards were fixed, a standardised project task was defined, common procedures were used to transfer technologies and especially design works. The centres shared one de-
(follows)

sign system and one CAD-CAM system. The development phase involved also about 200 US suppliers, operating in a simultaneous engineering approach. Nissan succeeded in establishing Japanese-style relationships with part suppliers. To this end, it was fundamental the approach taken in the establishment of R&D facilities in US which is explained below.

A project committee was established to coordinate works, take key decisions and solve conflicts. The initial part of the work was carried out in the various locations, although there were frequent reciprocal visits (on the average, two in a month). In the second half, mostly the engineering phase, a group involving people from the various centres established in the US R&D lab.

This project was the first project carried out by the US subsidiary and the home country jointly. The opportunity of doing it was actually the result of long term actions which prepared the ground for a strong collaboration among the units and the creation of an integrated global units structure. When the American technical centres were established, Nissan sent few Japanese researchers and mostly recruited people locally. The (few) Japanese researchers sent to the U.S. lab were very well known and had a very good reputation at the home country centre. This gave the foreign unit credibility within the corporation. They spent time at local Universities and research institutes. This favoured the establishment of first forms of collaborative research with local institutions. In the meanwhile, many U.S. technicians and researchers were recruited and employed at this unit. This facilitated the establishment of good relationships with local actors, such as, in particular, part suppliers that play a key role in product development (as mentioned above, this allowed to establish Japanese-style customer-supplier relationships in the product development, involving suppliers in a simultaneous or black box engineering approach). As part of the training period, US technicians were sent to the Technical Centre in Japan. On the one hand, this allowed to make them familiar with development systems and procedures used at the headquarters; on the other hand, it enabled the firm to bring in creativity from the interchange of different approaches. The long term objective was that of establishing an R&D unit well interfaced with the home country centres able to bring in the creativity and the effectiveness of the US research and technology system.

Good examples of *integrated global units* are those of Alcatel and Ericsson. As the result of its expansion through acquisitions, Alcatel has found itself managing acquired units with a technical background as strong as that in the home country (it has acquired Telettra in Italy, Telefonica in Spain and the European activities of ITT). Given the limited size of its home country, Ericsson has a strong tradition of decentralisation and from its beginnings has dispersed its technical capabilities throughout the world. Whereas, in the past, foreign labs were assigned local tasks and were kept relatively independent and isolated from the rest of the structure, in recent years, Ericsson has strongly favoured a worldwide integration of technological efforts. The structural choice is consistent with the firm's technology policy followed in new switching equipment development, which is based on the modular design approach, allowing the reduction of the development cost of new equipment through the use of the modules, developed at the different R&D sites. To make this structure work, it is necessary that the development activities which take place at the various sites are the result of common technology development programmes. Each foreign unit can thus perform local innovations using modules developed elsewhere, or customising them to local market needs.

As stated above, this strong form of integration means that R&D programmes are so conceived and planned that each unit makes a distinctive contribution in a coordinated manner with the other units. However, integration does not concern only the planning phase. As in development activity, communication is critical and interactions need to be very frequent and two-way: it is not feasible to carry out joint R&D programmes where resources stay in their usual location and communicate through communication systems and networking. The concentration in the same physical location is still necessary to ensure that information is exchanged and communication is frequent. International teams are created, gathering people from the different units involved into one of the existing sites.

The case of a white goods manufacturer

Another example of integrated global units structure is the case of a white goods manufacturer, who recently decided to increase the coordination of its R&D activities in the areas of production process technologies. In the past, each plant and the annexed technical development activities were allowed to carry out their own technical projects. This brought to duplication of efforts and resources. The decision was to establish a body to coordinate R&D activities in production process technologies. This coordinating body (Technology Committee) provides leadership and clear directions for the projects of global interests. The Technical Committee is composed of headquarters top managers, representatives of each region and CTOs of the units around the world developing new process technologies. At the moment, its scope encompasses the (five) key production process technologies used at the firm's plants. Every year, projects of global interests and with great potential (which means that they aim at im-

(follows)

proving key parameters of the concerned process) are proposed by the various subsidiaries and few are selected. These are carried out jointly by different labs and usually the proposing lab has the leadership and hosts the project. People from the other labs are moved to the leading lab. The process technology developed during the project, if successful, is then implemented at global level in each plant using that technology. The first global project concerned the casting technology and was assigned to the Brazilian subsidiary.

The projects are selected and directly supported by the Technical Committee which is chaired by a top manager of the home country. Subsidiaries are motivated to have global projects assigned as this brings credibility and importance within the corporation and higher amount of resources to manage. Non-leading subsidiaries are willing to involve their own people to affect the project and to ensure that results can be of use for them. Given that the responsibility varies from project to project, subsidiaries are forced to collaborate to ensure that when they lead projects, they can rely on the collaboration of technical people from other subsidiaries. Moreover, the involvement of technical people of the various labs and subsidiaries in the projects facilitates the transfer of the project results to the various plants for their implementation.

The next step (not implemented yet) is that of assigning the responsibility for the progress in each technology to one lab favouring a process of specialisation of the labs. In other words, the objective is that of moving to a specialisation based structure.

This can also mean temporary assignment of responsibility for a certain R&D programme to a particular country. The critical decision (taken by the central supervision unit in the home country) is which lab is assigned this task. The main factors influencing this decision are: location of the critical competencies for the specific programme; the international credibility of the R&D manager who is assigned the responsibility for the programme; the transaction costs implied by the assignment as a result of necessary external interactions (with customers and suppliers), internal transactions (with manufacturing plants) and the movement of people to the chosen site.

Specialised Contributors

Each (contributor) unit is specialised in one or few product technology/component and contributes developing a piece of the R&D work which is managed and controlled from an (integrator) R&D centre. The knowledge developed in each unit is transferred to the centre of the structure. Therefore, the centre coordinates the various contributions and integrates these as one R&D project, whereas the contributor units carry out very narrow and specific R&D works which constitute part of a chain of activity planned and managed by the centre itself. This structure attempts to combine the benefits of the specialisation with the superior creativity and innovation potential of the integrated labs structure.

In the initial phases of a development project, there is often a strong flow of information from the units to the centre and among the various units. The phase of project definition is often carried out by international teams where people from the various units are involved: project definition establishes how the R&D work is carried out and divided among the different units. During the real development phase, although each unit works on modules or subsystems, there needs to be a strong coordination. There is a wide use of electronic linkages (technology development tools, design tools, CAD/CAM systems). International meetings are held at project milestones. Steps of the projects may also require co-location. People from the various units gather in one place, not necessarily the centre. They have been found no cases of division of labour in development activities with no co-location in all the project phases.

Therefore, although there is a structural division of labour among labs, which reduces coordination efforts, the managerial and organisational implications of the structure are similar to those of the integrated labs one. Units contribute to joint processes of innovation. Therefore, there need to be the appropriate cultural background and managerial mechanisms as described in the network based structure.

The case of Ford

An example of specialised contributor structure is the development of Mondeo, the global car of Ford. The idea of a global car came in mid '80ies as the company recognised that requirements in the various areas of the world were converging and there were the opportunities to exploit new products globally. Moreover, there were opportunities from the exploitation of the knowledge, experience and specialisation of both the European and the US R&D centres. Therefore a project was launched with the objective to generate a model which had to substitute both the Sierra model in Europe and the Tempo in US with one car to be commercialised on both markets. The project started with the assessment of the requirements and a benchmarking exercise with other car models to identify key parameters and degree of customer satisfaction. Then, a survey on thousands of car drivers in triadic countries was done to identify the areas where to stretch car

(follows)

performance. A project was defined and the 'global car' project started its development phase.

Ford Europe had the leadership of the project, as the car concept was more similar to that of an European car. Gand, the largest assembly centre of Ford in Europe, where the Mondeo had to be produced, was selected as the location of the project leadership and coordination centre. The project was transnational. The project coordination was achieved through project committees at various levels: working groups operating on specific technical problems, Program Control Group composed of the chairmen of the working groups and the Product Committee chaired by the President of the Ford Europe. There was a coordination group (50 people), responsible for keeping communication and relationships among the groups, which ensured that the works were consistent each other. Also suppliers were selected on a global basis: 47 were European and 20 American.

The work among units was divided on the basis of the specialisation of the units.

In the product design phase, they were involved groups in Dearborn, US (6V engine and transmission), Merkenich, Germany (aesthetic design and 4 cylinders engines), Dunton, UK (interiors package). However, technical people were mixed (35 American technicians worked in European labs).

In the prototyping phase, they were involved plants responsible for developing the production processes for new products and pilot plants. Again the responsibilities were assigned on the basis of the specialisation of the units: Bridgend (Wales) for 4 cylinders 1.6 and 1.8 engines, Dagenham (UK) for diesel engines, Cleveland (Ohio) for 6 cylinders engines, Chihuahua (Mexico) for 4 cylinders 2.0 engines. The development of processes was supported by the use of CAD-CAM systems which were shared with the product designers.

In both design and prototyping phases, the coordination of the works took place through a wide use the use of teleconferencing and telecommunication systems. The coordination of the R&D work changed during the engineering phase. The engineering phase was conducted in Gand by engineers coming from the various units involved in previous stages: the co-location was necessary. The Gand team was then partially transferred to Kansas City to take care of the engineering pre-production phase in US.

The Mondeo was presented at the Geneve exhibition in 1993, in US it was introduced 15 months later. In Japan it was commercialised through a joint venture with Mazda.

This structure reveals feasible when there is the opportunity to create a division of labour among units. This strongly depends on the intrinsic nature of the technological innovation process. When a new product or production process can be divided into modules or subsystems, the development work can be divided into different tasks clearly defined and different units can be given responsibilities for the different tasks. There is a coordination effort and technical data and information need to continuously flow among units; however, there is a certain degree of autonomy allowed given that each task concerns a well defined part of the innovation.

6.5.2   Research Structures

Research activities are undertaken in order to identify and learn about future technical paradigms. They are aimed to create and improve the firm's technological capabilities critical for sustaining long term competition. Activities such as basic and applied research on new or emerging product and process technologies, or development of new techniques to use in new product development are typical research activities.

Three main international R&D structures (Figure 6.5) have been found:

(i)   *isolated specialisation*, that creates a single centre of excellence for a certain technology;

(ii)   *specialised contributors*, where different units contribute by experimenting in a certain technical area and transfer the knowledge developed to the centre. There is an integrator centre that coordinates the various contributions and integrates these within its own research;

(iii)   *integration-based*, that leads to the creation of a network of laboratories. Each unit of the network is allowed to undertake its own research initiatives.

Isolated Specialisation

In the isolated specialisation structure, the firm creates a single centre of excellence for a certain (set of) generic technology (ies). This approach is aimed at achieving economies of scale, by concentrating resources in one location.

This structure is chosen when there is a world leading centre of excellence or a geographical area of excellence and a firm needs to be present there to take part to the process of knowledge production and to attract key researchers. A firm can therefore be forced to concentrate its R&D activity for that technological field in that region. The pre-requisite for choosing this structure is a low dispersion of the firm's technical activities in that particular field.

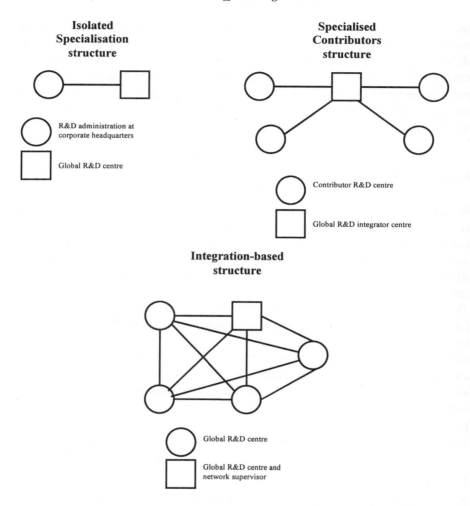

Figure 6.5. International structures in research activities.

Examples of regions where there has been a concentrated and accumulated knowledge in a certain field are the famous Silicon Valley, Route 128 and New Jersey for semiconductors and computers, Massachussets and Berkeley for biotechnologies, the Boston area for genetic engineering (for example, Bayer and Sandoz have concentrated their research on biotechnologies in Berkeley and Palo Alto, California, respectively).

In other cases, this structure has been the result of the historical specialisation of research units. A certain unit has developed competencies in a certain technological field and consequently it has been assigned the role of global research lab for that area.

Specialised Contributors

Each unit contributes by experimenting in a certain technical area and transferring the knowledge developed to the centre. The integrator centre coordinates the various contributions and integrates these within its own research. The contributor units carry out very narrow and specific research which constitutes part of a chain of activity planned and managed by the integrator centre. Technology scanning units can also be part of this structure. They are located near foreign centres of excellence to monitor the technological progress which takes place there.

Three main forms of task interdependencies among the different units have been found:

- sequential (the research output of a unit is the input of another unit and there is a temporal chain of research activities);
- overlapping (the same research activity is carried out by two or more units which approach the same problem in different ways, as a means of enhancing creativity);
- complementary (the research output is the result of the integration of pieces of research carried out in different units where the areas of research are complementary to one another).

This structure is chosen when there are multiple external sources of knowledge and/or there are several units within the organisation with a strong technical background. In the first case, firms need to be present with their technological capacities in various locations; in the second, they tend to leverage the pockets of excellence that have grown locally within the organisation. Such cases have been found in the telecommunications and electronics industries where developments are increasingly the result of the integration of different technological fields. In Siemens, the home country unit for electronics acts as an integrator centre, globally responsible for the research programs and coordinating the research carried out at the other locations. In some specific research fields, world competence centres have been created at foreign locations (Princeton, New Jersey; Zurich; Vienna). In Philips the adoption of this structure has been the result of a profound restructuring of the firm's international R&D in electronics aimed at eliminating duplications and specialising foreign labs in narrow fields of research. Central units in Eindhoven act as the integrator centre and a number of foreign labs contribute in specific fields of study (Briarcliff Manor, New York, in new materials and micro-electronics; Redhill, UK, in semiconductors; Limeil-Brevannes, France, in integrated circuit technologies; Silicon Valley in design methods).

Integration-Based

The integration-based structure leads to the creation of a network of laboratories. Each unit in the network is allowed to undertake its own research initiatives. Within the network, units continuously communicate, interact with each other and exchange results. There is a reciprocal interdependence among research units, although they are physically separated. There is a network supervisor lab which acts as a coordinator within the network (to limit duplications and favour integration among units). Technology scanning units located near foreign technology centres of excellence can also be integrated into this structure.

Ericsson has established networks of labs in several technological fields. It has specialised its R&D units on the basis of their historical background (R&D activities on silicon technology and chip design are carried out in Australia, Finland and Italy; on mobile phone systems in Germany, France, Spain and Greece). Labs working in the same area are integrated in a network supervised by the home country lab.

A network structure is chosen when there are multiple external sources of knowledge and/or there are several units with a strong and wide technical background within the organisation (the same conditions as the specialised contributor structure). The integration-based solution is preferred to the specialised contributors structure in three cases:

a. The intrinsic nature of the innovation process does not allow division of the research work among different units. In other words, work can not be fragmented in chain-linked segments (examples are the chemicals and pharmaceuticals industries).

b. Time saving is the strategic objective. Through the involvement of different units in integrated research plans, firms aim to accelerate their knowledge accumulation and technical learning processes. The continuous inter-unit exchange of knowledge generates accelerated and improved learning processes. The technical learning that takes place in a unit is distributed throughout the rest of the structure and becomes part of a common knowledge base. So, although there may be some duplications, the global learning process is accelerated. Examples have been found in the electronics and telecommunications industries for research in semiconductors and software engineering, respectively. It is especially the case of Japanese companies working in these industries (NEC, Sony, Toshiba, Hitachi). They have recently established small research units near centres of excellence in the US and Europe (especially the UK) which work in a network usually supervised by the home country lab. This approach has been undertaken to cover the gap in basic research from European and American competitors.

c. The process of specialisation in existing units which accompanies the implementation of a specialised contributor structure would lead to a loss of key resources. Ericsson has been forced to a network approach for this reason.

The drawback of this structure is that it is highly costly because of the duplications of R&D activities and of the coordination costs.

Coordination is critical to the effectiveness of the network approach, and information and communication technology are widely used to this end. These systems cannot substitute face-to-face communication, but they help the continuous interaction and exchange of research results. Reciprocal visits and personal meetings are still used when research plans and future research directions have to be discussed and decided.

The success of this structure heavily depends on the organisational system. Discussing how to manage an R&D network would go beyond the scope of this study, but some indications from what has been found will be given below. To create an effective network, a global managerial infrastructure has to be built. De Meyer (1993) identifies three areas that are relevant to this problem: the planning and control system, the communication system, the definition of practices to diffuse and transfer knowledge. He adds that the credibility of laboratories taking part to the network is central to network effectiveness. Another key managerial area is human resource policy, that has to establish how to manage the international mobility of technical staff, define their international career paths and set up an international reward system. To sum up, the analysis suggests that the success of integration based structures heavily depends on a firm's organisational and managerial capabilities and on the creation of organisational systems which facilitate communication.

6.6   AN INTERPRETATION OF THE INTERNATIONALISATION OF R&D

The previous section described the international R&D structures in research and development activities. The table 6.5 shows the type of research and development structure in each sample firm. Referring to it, several remarks can be done:

(i)   in the same firm, different structures can be implemented for research and development activities;

(ii)   in the same firm and type of R&D activity, different structures can operate for different product lines (as far as development activities are concerned) or different generic technologies (for research activities);

(iii) intra-sectoral differences emerge, i.e. firms operating in the same business or set of businesses can adopt different structures.

(iv)   inter-sectoral differences emerge, i.e. there seems to be a tendency for firms operating in telecommunications and electronics businesses to adopt more complex structures composed of dispersed labs where the R&D is integrated and coordinated on a global basis. Chemical and petrochemical firms adopt simpler structures, privileging the concentration of resources in one location (such as the isolated or supported specialisation).

An interpretation of these points and of the overall process of R&D internationalisation is here suggested. Two major factors seem to affect the choice of the international structure.

First, the need to access external sources of knowledge relevant to a firm's innovation process and the related need to shorten the time spent to acquire, internalise and utilise this knowledge to perform innovations. Therefore, a first key factor is the degree of dispersion of external sources of key knowledge.

Second, given that a firm's internationalised R&D is often the result of a number of uncoordinated processes taking place at both local and global level, the historical heritage, i.e. the degree of dispersion of a firm's R&D resources, is the other key factor which affects the structural outcome.

Table 6.5. Type of structure by company and R&D activity.

Company activity	Research structure	Development structure
Telecommunications	-	-
Telecommunications (a)	Specialised contributor (4) Integration based (4) Integration based (3)	Integrated global labs (10)
Telecommunications	-	Integrated local labs (4)
Telecommunications	Integration based (3)	Isolated specialisation (1) Integrated global labs (4)
Petrochemicals	Isolated specialisation (3)	Isolated specialisation (4)
Petrochemicals	Isolated specialisation (3)	Isolated specialisation (3)
Chemicals	Isolated specialisation (3)	Supported specialisation (2)
Chemicals	Isolated specialisation (2) Integration-based (2)	Isolated specialisation (2)
Chemicals	Isolated specialisation (3)	Isolated specialisation (2) Supported specialisation (2)
Electronics	Specialised contributor (4)	Isolated specialisation (3)
Electronics (b)	Integration-based (2)	Supported specialisation
Electronics (b)	Integration-based (5)	Supported specialisation

Notes:

In brackets: in the case of an integrated structure (i.e. integrated local and global labs among development structures, specialised contributor and integration-based structures among the research structure) the number is the number of foreign labs which take part to the structure; in the case of specialisation structures (i.e the isolated specialisation and the supported specialisation among the development structures, the isolated specialisation among the research structures) the number tells how many labs are specialised, in other words, how many specialised structures there are.

(a) Several foreign units carry out both research and development activities. (As they mostly do development activities, they have been classified as development labs in table 2).

(b) R&D centre for development activities in the home country.

6.6.1 External Sources of Knowledge

The need to access multiple sources of knowledge utilised for innovation is a major driver of R&D internationalisation. The knowledge relevant to the technological innovation process concerns both technology and the market. Whereas, as seen above (section 1), the access to technology sources has traditionally been indicated as a major reason to decentralise R&D, it has to be underlined that the process of innovation requires interactions with a number of sources that are not only technological. In development activities, it is becoming more and more important to be able to access key market knowledge sources (lead users, key customers), which provide innovation stimuli and new product ideas and raise technical problems that are often at the origin of the innovation processes.

Accessing knowledge sources (both market and technology) has been recognised as a way of reducing a firm's time-to-market (in short term competition) and of accelerating the process of knowledge accumulation (in the long term). Therefore, the dispersion of the external sources of knowledge affects the international R&D structure in both research and development activities. Structures are shaped to ensure that the relevant external sources of knowledge are accessed. The more dispersed external knowledge sources, the more dispersed a firm's R&D structures tend to be.

The analysis has also highlighted that the degree of dispersion of external sources of knowledge seems to be influenced by two factors (which affect the dispersion of technological knowledge sources and the dispersion of market knowledge sources, respectively):

(a)   *the nature of the innovation process.* The need to access multiple sources of technical knowledge grows with the increase in the number of technologies involved in a given technological innovation. If innovating in a certain field relies on the ability to integrate different technologies, it is likely that not all the technologies are available within the firm, and that external sources need to be accessed. This would provide a first explanation for inter-sectoral differences (for example, between telecommunication technologies on the one hand and chemical technologies, on the other). Innovation in telecommunication technologies depends more and more on integrating different technologies (electronic, communication and information technologies); in contrast, chemical research is highly specialised and based on deepening very narrow fields of study[i].

(b)   *the degree of market differentiation.* The need to access external sources of market knowledge grows with the increase in the degree of differentiation among country or regional markets.

---

i   As Kodama (1992) has pointed out, innovations can be the result of the horizontal integration of different technologies (what he calls technology fusion) or of vertical research.

It should be noticed that although both these factors are industry-specific, their effect on a firm's international R&D structure is also dependent on firm-specific variables. The need to access external sources is a function of the available internally knowledge. If a firm has state-of-the-art knowledge in a certain field available internally, it is not forced to go abroad to access external sources (there are industrial labs recognised as a leading centre of excellence in certain fields). Again, as stated above, the extent to which market differentiation affects international R&D depends on the firm's strategy, whether this is based on local responsiveness or a global approach.

6.6.2 Internal R&D Resources

Companies tend to leverage their internal sources of innovation wherever they are located and to involve these into R&D processes which may lead to innovations to be exploited at global level. Pockets of excellence which may have developed abroad need to be exploited on a worldwide basis. Designing an international R&D structure means identifying these units, and leveraging their capabilities to global benefit, and assigning them responsibilities at global level. A second critical variable affecting the R&D structure (in both research and development activities) seems to be the degree of dispersion of the firm's key technical resources. The more dispersed internal R&D resources, the more dispersed international R&D structure tend to be.

The extent to which a firm disperses its R&D resources seems to be strongly dependent on two factors (which concern both research and development activities):

(a) *the divisibility of labour in R&D*. In fact, the possibility of creating a division of labour in R&D is strongly affected by the intrinsic nature of the technological innovation process. For example, if we compare the electronics and telecommunications industries with the chemicals and petrochemicals industries, we find that, in the first case, products can be divided into modules and sub-systems which can be developed autonomously (provided compatibility is defined in advance) and, then, put together. This allows a division of labour among different units and specialisation of units in different fields. In the chemical industry, the nature of products and production processes often reduces the probability of establishing forms of labour division in R&D, so the technological innovation process needs to be carried out in one physical location. This influences the structural outcome, preventing, for example, chemical firms from implementing dispersed R&D structures, in which research and development activity is divided among different units. Again, this helps explain why firm behaviour may vary from industry to industry[j].

(b)   *the firm's managerial culture.* The other factor which affects the dispersion of a firm's R&D resources is its managerial culture. This variable mirrors the propensity of the firm to decentralise its activities. Therefore, this variable influences the degree of dispersion of a firm's resources, thus also the starting point of the process of building an international structure and, finally, influences the structural outcome. As this factor is firm-specific, it also helps to explain why firm behaviour may vary within the same industry. Companies with a strong propensity to decentralisation are forced to establish more integration among pre-existing units and tend to choose complex structures composed of various units managed in a coordinated way. Companies with a strong centralisation culture tend to implement less dispersed structures.

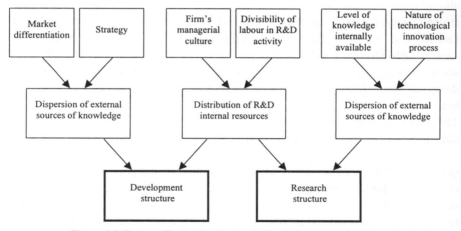

Figure 6.6. Factors affecting the choice of a firm's international structure.

---

[j]   This explains why chemical firms have traditionally kept their R&D concentrated (in the home country or in one foreign location). Later, when challenged to face the increasing dispersion of knowledge sources in development activities, they tend to set up a supported specialisation structure. In their research activities, when forced to go abroad to access external sources, they cannot establish forms of labour division and so adopt the integration based structure allowing activities to overlap.

An example of the co-existence of different structures in the same sector is the case of development activities in the electronics industry. There are firms with a strong centralisation tradition and culture (Japanese competitors) which only recently have started to go abroad with their R&D (to face the dispersion of external knowledge sources), and have implemented simple structures, such as supported specialisation units. In the same industry, European firms (mostly with a strong decentralisation culture) have strongly dispersed their R&D for the last two decades. They tend to set up structures of the integrated labs type.

The framework presented in Figure 6.6 shows the factors which influence the R&D structure. It helps explain the points at the beginning of Section 6.6.

(i)   Firms tend to create certain structures devoted to long term R&D and others devoted to the support of short term competition. Figure 6.7 and Figure 6.8 provide a synoptical view relating each structure type to the two variables described above (the degree of dispersion of external sources and the degree of dispersion of the firm's resources). Matrixes have been built for both research and development activities. The proposed framework has, of course, to be treated with caution. The four areas in each matrix actually overlap each other, as separations among areas are not clear cut.

The framework presented in Figure 6.6 suggests that motivations to go abroad vary from research to development (dispersion of market knowledge sources vs. dispersion of technological knowledge sources). Moreover the firm's history (the dispersion of internal R&D resources) may have been different for research and development.

(ii)   The framework also helps to explain why in the same firm there may be different structures in the same type of R&D activity. The firm's history may have meant that the dispersion and the level of the technical resources in foreign countries varies from product to product (as far as development activities are concerned) and from technology to technology (research). Moreover, the level of knowledge available internally may vary in different technical fields. In a telecommunication company, the traditional specialisation of foreign R&D units has forced to separate research activities for basic electronic technologies, for new switching technologies and for mobile phoning.

(iii) and (iv) The framework shows that there are both firm-specific factors (such as strategy, managerial culture, level of technical knowledge available internally) and industry-specific factors (market differentiation, divisibility of R&D work, the nature of the technological innovation process) which influence both the dispersion of external sources of knowledge and the dispersion of internal resources which, in turn, affect a firm's R&D structural outcome. The firm-specific factors help explain why there may be intra-sectoral differences, while the industry-specific elements are linked to inter-sectoral differences (examples and comments about these points have been given above).

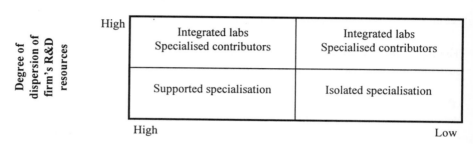

Figure 6.7. The choice of the international structure in development activities.

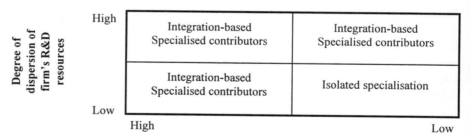

Figure 6.8. The choice of the international structure in research activities.

REFERENCES AND FURTHER READINGS

Bailetti, A.J. and Callahan, J.R., The Coordination Structure of International Collaborative Technology Arrangements, *Proceedings of the R&D Management Conference 'Managing R&D Internationally'* (Manchester, U.K., 6-8 July 1992).

Bartlett, C.A. and Ghoshal, S., *Managing Across Borders. The Transnational Solution*, (Harvard Business School Press, Boston, 1989).

Behrman, J.N. and Fischer, W.A., *Overseas Activities of Transnational Companies*, Oelgeschlager (Gunn & Hain, Cambridge, 1980).

Brockhoff, K. and von Boehmer, A., *Global R&D Activities of German Industrial Firms*, Working Paper, Institute for Research in Innovation Management (Kiel, 1992).

Brockhoff, K.K.L. and Schmaul, B., Organization, Autonomy, and Success of Internationally Dispersed R&D Facilities, *IEEE Transactions on Engineering Management*, 43, 1 (1996), 33-40.

Casson, M., *Global Research Strategy and International Competitiveness* (Basil Blackwell, Cambridge, 1991).

Chiesa, V., Managing the Internationalisation of R&D Activities. *IEEE Transactions on Engineering Management*, 43, 1 (1996), 7-23.

De Meyer, A., Management of International R&D Operations, in Granstrand, O., Hakanson, L., Sjolander, S. (Eds.), *Technology Management and International Business - Internationalization of R&D and Technology* (John Wiley & Sons, Chichester, 1992).

De Meyer, A., Management of an International Network of Industrial R&D Laboratories, *R&D Management*, 23, 2 (1993).

De Meyer, A. and Mizushima, A., Global R&D Management, *R&D Management*, 19, 2 (1989).

Granstrand, O., Hakanson, A. and Sjolander, S. (Eds.), *Technology Management and International Business - Internationalization of R&D and Technology* (John Wiley and Sons, Chichester, 1992).

Hakanson, L., Locational Determinants of Foreign R&D in Swedish Multinationals, in Granstrand, O., Hakanson, A. and Sjolander, S. (Eds.), *Technology Management and International Business - Internationalization of R&D and Technology* (John Wiley and Sons, Chichester, 1992).

Hakanson, L. and Nobel, R., Overseas Research and Development in Swedish Multinationals, *Academy of International Business Meeting*, Singapore, December (1989).

Hakanson, L. and Zander, U., International Management of R&D: The Swedish Experience, *R&D Management*, 18, 3 (1988).

Hamel, G. and Prahalad, C.K., Strategy as Stretch and Leverage, *Harvard Business Review*, 71, 2 (1993).

Hax, A.C. and Majluf, N.S., *The Strategy Concept and Process: a pragmatic approach* (Prentice-Hall International Ed. 1991).

Hedlund, G., The Hypermodern MNC - A Heterarchy?, *Human Resource Management*, 25, Spring (1986).

Hewitt, G., Research and Development Performed Abroad by U.S. Manufacturing Multinationals, *Kyklos*, 33 (1980).

Hirschey, R.C. and Caves, R.E., Research and Transfer of Technology by Multinational Enterprises, *Oxford Bulletin of Economics and Statistics*, 43 (1981).

Howells, J., The Location and Organisation of Research and Development: New Horizons, *Research Policy*, 19 (1990).

Kodama, F., Technology Fusion and the new R&D, *Harvard Business Review*, 70, 4 (1992), 70-78.

Kuemmerle, W., Building Effective R&D Capabilities Abroad, *Harvard Business Review*, 75, 2 (1997), 61-70.

Medcof, J.W., Strategic Contingencies and Power in Networks of Internationally Dispersed R&D Facilities, *Academy of Management Annual Meeting Proceedings*, Boston (1997).

Papanastassiou, M. and Pearce, R.D, The globalisation of innovation and the role of research and development in multinational enterprises, *R&D Management*, 24, 2 (1994).

Pavitt, K., What we Know about Strategic Management of Technology, *California Management Review*, 32, 3 (1990).

Pavitt, K., Key Characteristics of the Large Innovating Firm, *British Journal of Management*, 2 (1991).

Pearce, R.D., *The Internationalization of Research of Development by Multinational Enterprises*, University of Reading of European and International Studies (The MacMillan Press, London, 1989).

Pearce, R.D. and Singh, S., *Globalising Research and Development* (The MacMillan Press, London, 1992).

Perrino, A.C. and Tipping, J.W., Global Management of Technology, *Research and Technology Management*, 32, 3 (1989).

Prahalad, C.K. and Doz, Y.L., *The Multinational Mission: Balancing Local Demand and Global Vision* (The Free Press, New York, 1987).

Roberts, E.B., Benchmarking the Strategic Management of Technology – I, *Research Technology Management*, January-February (1995a), 44.

Prahalad, C.K. and Hamel, G., The Core Competence of the Corporation, *Harvard Business Review*, 68, 3 (1990).

Ronstadt, R., International R&D: The Establishment and Evolution of R&D Abroad by Seven U.S. Multinationals, *Journal of International Business Studies*, 9, 1 (1976).

Ronstadt, R., *Research and Development Abroad by U.S. Multinationals* (Praeger Publishers, New York, 1977).

Rugman, A.M., Research and Development by Multinational and Domestic Firms in Canada, *Canadian Public Policy*, 7, 4 (1981).

Sakakibara, K., *IBM ThinkPad 700C Notebook Computer*, London Business School (1993).

Sakakibara, K. and Westney, E., Japan's Management of Global Innovation: Technology Management Crossing Borders, in Rosenberg, N., Landau, R. and Mowery, D. (Eds.), *Technology and the Wealth of Nations* (Stanford University Press, Stanford, 1992).

Steele, L.W., *Innovation in Big Business* (Elsevier, New York, 1975).

Taggart, J.H., Determinants of the Foreign R&D Location Decision in the Pharmaceutical Industry, *R&D Management*, 21, 3 (1991).

Terpstra V., International Product Policy: the Role of Foreign R&D, *Columbia Journal of World Business*, 12, 4 (1977).

Vernon, R., International Investment and International Trade in the Product Cycle, *Quarterly Journal of Economics*, 80 (1966).

Westney, D.E., Internal and External Linkages in the MNC: The Case of R&D Subsidiaries in Japan, in Bartlett, C.A., Doz, Y. and Hedlund, G. (Eds.), *Managing the Global Firm* (Routledge, New York, U.S.A, 1992).

CHAPTER 7

THE ORGANISATION OF THE EXTERNAL ACQUISITION OF TECHNOLOGY

7.1   INTRODUCTION

As seen above, a key strategic decision is whether to acquire a technology externally or develop a technology internally. The external acquisition requires that the form of such acquisition is defined. In other words, the decision-maker, once decided that a certain technology is to be acquired externally, has to identify the most appropriate mode for such acquisition.

% of companies with high reliance on external sources for technology

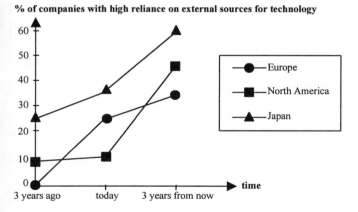

Figure 7.1. Reliance on external sources of technology (Source: Roberts, 1995).

Resorting on external sources of technology is a major trend of the last decade. Roberts (1995), in his survey on the world's largest R&D performers, revealed that the reliance on external sources sharply increased and was expected to increase, and that Japanese firms depend on outsiders far greater than other firms (Fig. 7.1). After the rapid increase in early and mid eighties, the reliance on external sources of technology has become part of the firms' technology strategy. Both the IRI R&D trends forecast for 1998 and 1999 have shown that nearly 40 percent of the US firms and 50 percent of the European firms expect increased participation in alliances and joint ventures, and that only 10% sees a decrease in the participation to such initiatives.

There are several ways to acquire technology from external sources. Table 7.1 reports the most common forms and the related definitions.

Table 7.1. Organisational modes for external technology acquisition.

acquisition	a company acquires another company in order to access a technology (or technological competence) of interest
educational acquisition	a company recruits experts in a certain technological discipline or acquires a smaller company, in order to obtain people familiar with a certain technological or managerial competence
merger	a company merges with another one that possesses a technology (or technological competence) of interest, and a new company emerges from the two existing companies
licensing	a company acquires a license for a specific technology
minority equity	a company buys an equity in the source organisation in which a technology (or technological competence) of interest is embedded, but does not have management control
joint venture	a company establishes a formal joint venture with equity involvement and a third corporation is created, with a definite objective of technological innovation
joint R&D	a company agrees with others to jointly carry out research and development on a definite technology (or technological discipline), with no equity involvement
R&D contract	a company agrees to fund cost of R&D at a research institute or university or small innovative firm, for a definite technology
research funding	a company funds exploratory research at a research institute or university or small innovative firm to pursue opportunities and idea for innovation
alliance	a company shares technological resources with other companies in order to achieve a common objective of technological innovation (without equity involvement)
consortium	several companies and public institutions join their efforts in order to achieve a common objective of technological innovation (without equity involvement)
networking	a company establishes a network of relationships, in order to keep the pace in a technological discipline and to capture technological opportunities and evolutionary trends
outsourcing	a company externalises technological activities and, then, simply acquires the relative output

---

Box 7.1 - Motivations for technological collaborations

In the phase of the *context foresight*:
- monitoring customers' needs;
- monitoring suppliers;
- monitoring competitors;
- grasping market opportunities and new product ideas;
- monitoring the R&D/technological context.

In the phase of *technology development*, the technological partnering can contribute to the firm's learning process and to improve the firm's innovative capabilities. Factors stimulating to cooperate are:
- increasing the technological innovation potential and the firm's creativity;
- integrating scientific and technological disciplines;
- increasing the firm's flexibility;
- broaden the technology range;
- increasing the continuity of innovation.

On the other hand, technological collaborations can help improve the technological innovation process performance and therefore:
- reducing, sharing, minimising technical risk;
- reducing, sharing, minimising costs;
- improving time-to-market.

In the phase of new *technology introduction*, the major motivations to cooperate are:
- accessing to distribution channels;
- accessing to complementary assets to the innovation;
- commercialising the innovation in foreign countries and/or entering foreign markets;
- entering new markets;
- setting standards.

In part I, the topic of the external acquisition of technology has been treated from a strategic point of view. In the technology development activity, the decision is about whether to develop a new technology internally, cooperate or buy. In new technology introduction, the alternatives are to commercialise the new technology, to cooperate or to sell the technology. Cooperative activities can also support the development of the context foresight. Therefore, motivations to technologically cooperate are multiple. A summary is reported in Box 7.1.

7.2   ORGANISATIONAL FORMS FOR EXTERNAL TECHNOLOGY ACQUISITION

Generally speaking, the acquisition of technology from external sources means the establishment of a relationship between two or more actors. The form of acquisition can be described on the basis of the type of relationship which is established between the actors and by the type of tangible and/or intangible resources allocated by the two.

The very general frame is shown in Fig. 7.2. Any action of external technology acquisition can be described by four elements:

-    the type of actor(s) involved, i.e. the actors which allocate the tangible and/or intangible resources needed for the technological activities concerned;
-    the resources allocated by the actors, i.e. their specific contribution;
-    the activities carried out to achieve the objective (the output), and the resources used to this aim;
-    the output, i.e. the results obtained.

The relationship, which is therefore characterised by the actors, the resources, the activities and the output of the collaboration can be formalised within contracts or informally defined by the partners. Therefore, the formalisation of the contract is a fifth element characterising the external technology acquisition.

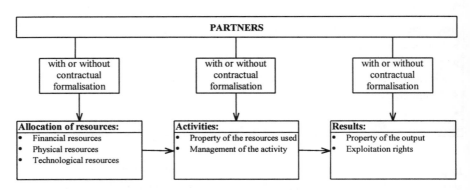

Figure 7.2. A general frame for external technology acquisition.

More in details, the different organisational forms of external technology acquisition can be identified and described through specifying:

-    the type of resources allocated by each partner (financial contribution, physical asset, technology and know-how) and the entity of the contribution;

-    the property of the resources involved in the collaboration: whether the resources become property of a third party or they are owned by the partner who provide them;
-    the management of the collaboration activities: to what extent each partner is involved in the management and the tasks each fulfils;
-    the property of the output of the collaboration and the relative exploitation rights.

Finally, each of the above elements (the allocation of resources, the criteria for managing the activities, the property of the resources used in the collaboration, the property of results and the exploitation rights) can be defined with a certain degree of formalisation.

Four major categories of organisational forms to acquire technology externally can be identified:

-    acquisition;
-    joint venture;
-    outsourcing;
-    alliance.

7.2.1 Acquisition

Acquisitions can be described as in Fig. 7.3.

One partner (P1) allocates financial resources; the other one (P2) gives its tangible and intangible resources. P1 acquires the full property of the resources and the results achieved, as well as of the rights to exploit them. A formalised contract usually rules the acquisition.

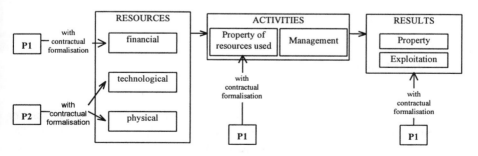

Figure 7.3. Acquisition.

Two cases of acquisition can be identified from a managerial point of view:

-   *managerially integrated acquisition*: in this case, P1 is fully responsible for the management of the activities and defines (sometimes jointly with P2) the managerial principles and mechanisms to be used in the management of the technical activities of the acquired company. This can be either stated in the acquisition contract or defined informally by the partners. Canon, for example, in 1989, acquired a small company, Lepton, in order to acquire technology and competencies on electron beam technologies. Lepton has been fully integrated and put under the direct control of the Micrographics business unit of Canon. The competence of Lepton was of interest to develop new aligners used in the design of circuits on micro-chips. The business unit of Canon involved had the required competencies on large scale manufacturing of such devices and integration was required to ensure there was the exchange of knowledge;
-   *managerially autonomous acquisition*: in this case, P2 keeps the responsibility of the management of the collaboration activities. Therefore, P2 becomes an autonomous unit (division). The managerial autonomy of P2 can be either stated in the acquisition contract or defined informally by the partners. An example of this case is that of Microcontrol, a small innovative Italian company developing systems for the electronic control of mechanical machinery. Microcontrol has been acquired by Finmeccanica, an Italian large electro-mechanical company. In order to maintain its innovative attitude and spirit, Microcontrol was left to act as an autonomous unit within Finmeccanica. The management board was not changed, as well as the R&D personnel. Another case of autonomous acquisition is the acquisition of Rolm by IBM. The expertise of Rolm in telecommunication was very interesting for IBM in mid 80s when the convergence of computer and telecommunication was a clear trend. Rolm was acquired and left as a separated business unit. This prevented from integrating the two competencies which was the main objective behind the acquisition and, in the end, Rolm was sold.

7.2.2   Joint Venture

Joint ventures can be described as in Fig. 7.4.

Two partners (P1 and P2) allocate resources (financial and/or physical and/or technological) for the creation of a third corporation with equity involvement. The property of resources used for the collaboration activities belongs to the third corporation created. A formalised contract usually defines the partners'

corporation created. A formalised contract usually defines the partners' contribution, the property of the results and the exploitation rights. A joint venture may involve more than two partners.

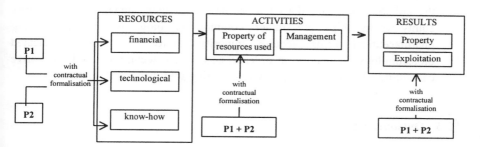

Figure 7.4. Joint venture.

Other forms of collaborations can be considered particular types of joint ventures:
- *mergers*, in which the two partners allocate all their resources (the whole company) to create a new company;
- *minority equity*, in which a company acquires an equity participation in the technology sourcing organisation, to access results of technological activities but does not have management control;
- *equity consortia*, in which several companies and public institutions join their efforts (with equity involvement) to achieve a common technological objective.

From a managerial point of view, joint ventures can be classified into:
- *collectively managed joint venture*, the case in which the two (or more) partners jointly manage the collaborations' activities. This is the most common form of joint venture. An example of this case is the joint venture between Philips and Du Pont to develop a new process for mastering compact disks. Both companies provided human resources and technologies to the joint venture and a joint team has been created to manage the collaboration. Consortia involving an equity participation of partners are part of this category. For example, a consortium with equity involvement has been created by Ratti (an Italian textile company, leader in silk clothing), and some French research centres, textile companies and silk-worms breeders, for the development of a totally innovative system for growing silk-worms "in vitro" (the consortium is called Eurochrysalide). A new company was created, of which the aim, scope, time and management criteria have been defined jointly by the partners;

- *single side managed joint venture*, the case in which a single partner manages the activities, with or without contractual formalisation. Minority equity partnerships are part of this category, since one partner manages the activities and the other(s) acquires (a minority share of) property of resources used for the collaboration, and does not participate to their management. Minority equity partnerships are rather common in biotechnology, where big pharmaceutical firms acquire minority equity into small dedicated biotechnology companies, in order to access their technology and innovative capabilities, but are not involved in managing activities.

7.2.3 Outsourcing

The case of outsourcing is represented in Fig. 7.5.

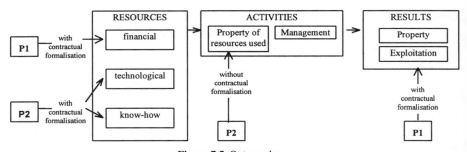

Figure 7.5. Outsourcing.

One partner (P1) provides financial resources and the other (P2) all the other resources needed to perform the technological activities concerned. P1 defines the required characteristics of the final output and acquires the full property of the results obtained and, hence, the right to exploit them. The resources used for the collaboration belong to P2, and P2 keeps the property of its own resources. Actually, P1 buys the results of a certain activity realised by P2.

Particular forms of outsourcing are:

- *licensing*, which is the acquisition of a technology license;
- *research contracts or research funding*, in which a company funds the costs of R&D of another company, a university or a research institute.

The role of the partners is usually formalised in a contract which fixes the required results, the amount of financial resources provided by P1 and the property rights of the results. No contractual formalisation is needed to define the property of the resources used in the collaboration activities, given that P2 simply uses its own resources.

From a managerial point of view, they can be identified:

- *negotiated outsourcing*, the case in which the activities to be conducted are negotiated by P1 with P2, with or without a formalised contract. In this case, P1 influences the management of the collaboration activities, even if the implementation is actually left with P2. This is typical of Contract Research Organisations (CRO) in the pharmaceutical industry. Big pharmaceutical companies assign CROs the task to carry out (pre-)clinical activities. These activities are highly codifiable and this characteristic makes easier outsource. The company defines the characteristics by which the activities have to be done (the scope of the activity, the number of patients to involve, how to make tests, the timing, etc.). Then, the CRO itself brings out activities accordingly;

- *autonomous outsourcing*, the case in which the management of activities is totally left with P2, i.e. P1 does not influence the implementation of the collaboration. The criteria used by P2 to manage the collaboration activities can be either formalised in a contract or informally defined by P2. This is the case of research contract and research funding, where a company simply pays a research institute to have the results of a certain research. Some Italian firms, for example, such as Agip, Edison, Pirelli collaborate with Politecnico di Milano, funding doctoral studentships or definite research projects. They define the type of research they want to fund and, then, acquire property of the results achieved.

7.2.4 Alliance

Alliances can be generally described as in Fig. 7.6.

The alliance is a fourth basic form of collaboration. Two or more partners allocate their physical and technological (know-how) resources and each partner keeps the property of its own resources used for the collaboration activities. Each partner has the property of and the rights of exploiting the results obtained. A formalised contract may or may not be signed to define the resources provided by the partners, the property of results and the relative exploitation rights. The alliance can assume several configurations: the number of partners involved, the type of resources provided by each partner, the use of contracts to define the division of labour among the partners (i.e. to identify the respective tasks) and to share the exploitation rights of results can vary significantly. As a matter of fact, forms of collaboration, such as non-equity consortia, partnership agreements, joint R&D projects etc., can be described as forms of alliances. A critical factor which distinguishes the forms of alliances is the role played by the partners in the management of the collaboration activities. More specifically, we can define:

- *collectively managed alliance*, the case in which the partners collectively manage the collaboration's activities. In this case, a team is created involving people from the various partners, which is assigned the implementation of the collaboration. The role of the various partners in managing activities can be either formalised in a contract or informally defined by the partners. This is probably the most common type of alliance. An example is the case of the partnership between ST Microelectronics and Hewlett-Packard for the joint development of components for peripherals and PCs. People from the R&D departments of the two companies worked together for two months, collectively defining the product specifications and the process characteristics. Then, in the late development phases, weekly meetings were arranged among people of the two companies to monitor the evolution of the projects and daily contacts, by telephone or e-mail, were established;

- *individually managed alliance*, the case in which each partner autonomously manages a definite (set of) activity(ies) and fulfils a specific task(s). In this case, a division of labour among the partners is established, which can be either formalised in a contract or informally defined by the partners. Non-equity R&D consortia, such as those created within the EU programmes (Brite, Esprit, etc.) are shaped as individually managed alliances. As a matter of fact, each partner has a definite task and, usually, autonomously defines how to accomplish the task.

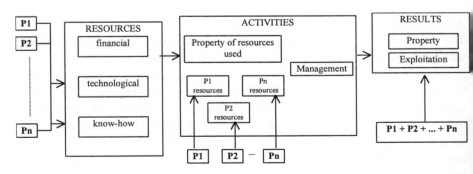

Figure 7.6. Alliance.

7.3   MANAGERIAL AND ORGANISATIONAL IMPLICATIONS OF THE FORMS OF EXTERNAL TECHNOLOGY ACQUISITION

The different organisational forms of collaboration (described in the previous section) have different managerial and organisational implications. Therefore, when the decision maker has to select a definite form for a given collaboration, he/she has to take into account such characteristics and implications. In this section, the key managerial and organisational characteristics associated to each form of collaboration are analysed. Such characteristics are:

- *impact on the firm's resources,*
- *time horizon,*
- *level of control over activities,*
- *level of control over results (output),*
- *start up time and costs,*
- *risk,*
- *level of reversibility.*

Impact on the firm. More precisely, it concerns:

- the organisational structure of the companies. Whereas outsourcing does not significantly impact on the organisation, acquisitions radically modify the firm's organisational structure, since the acquired company is internalised into the acquiring one. For example, a new division and/or function may be created, the acquired resources and activities may be fully integrated and co-ordinated with the existing ones, and the roles and responsibilities of people often need to be re-defined (Roberts and Berry, 1985);
- the firm's assets (the tangible and intangible resources). Mergers and acquisitions mean that assets and liabilities of the acquired firm are internalised in the acquiring (merging) company. In contrast, outsourcing impacts on the firm's assets only when a patent or a license is acquired and, even in this case, the impact is rather limited. Furthermore, acquisitions and mergers generally require availability of a great amount of (financial and non financial) resources (Millson et al., 1996; Chatterji, 1996);
- the human resources. Acquiring a firm means that human resources have to be integrated within the existing organisation. Hence, the problem is to create and diffuse a common corporate culture, to harmonise different languages and behaviours, to share a set of principles and values. In most cases, acquisitions are negatively perceived by people, who are frightened of downsizing and restructuring. In some cases, they loose motivations, their efficiency falls and

skills and competencies embedded in people become difficult to exploit. To a lesser extent, joint ventures present similar problems, particularly with reference to the harmonisation of cultures, languages and values. On the other hand, outsourcing does not present such difficulties (Chatterji, 1996).

Time horizon, i.e. the duration of the work. Outsourcing typically has a definite - usually brief - time horizon. Licensing, research funding and research contracts usually concern a well defined period of time, after which a new contract has to be established if the collaboration is to continue. On the other hand, mergers and acquisitions are not usually given a time horizon, that is a 'deadline' after which the collaboration is broken and the acquired firm is dismissed. Hence, these are intrinsically long-term oriented (Hagedoorn, 1993; Chatterji, 1996).

Control (over people, activities, organisation, information flows etc.). When a firm outsources an activity, it has no control over it. At most, an *ex ante* assessment of the partners' resources and an *ex post* evaluation of the output produced can be made. In contrast, acquiring a firm involves taking control over its activities and resources (Chesbrough and Teece, 1996; Millson et al., 1996; Chatterji, 1996).

Control (over results). Whereas strongly integrated forms of collaboration such as acquisitions, mergers, joint ventures allow a stronger control over collaboration results, alliance and outsourcing may mean weaker control and reduced opportunities (rights) to exploit the collaboration output.

Start up time/costs. Equity modes of collaboration and, in particular, acquisitions need a deep and well formalised analysis. For example, the use of DCF (Discounted Cash Flow) techniques is necessary to establish the value of the acquired firm and the acquisition price. This analysis requires time and resources. Furthermore, the final decision is usually taken by top management and, hence, the decision process is often long and complex. Even when a deep and formalised analysis is conducted for outsourcing contracts, the limited scope, time and objectives of the contract make the analysis much easier and faster (Roberts and Berry, 1985; Hagedoorn, 1993; Chatterji, 1996).

Risk. Each form intrinsically means a different degree of risk. Acquisitions and joint ventures usually involve higher financial resources and the associated risk is high. Less integrated forms of acquisition, such as alliances or outsourcing, mean lower degree of risk.

Reversibility, i.e. the extent to which the characteristics of the collaboration can be modified. Outsourcing contracts and alliances are rather flexible. Changing their characteristics (objectives, time, partners, organisation etc.) requires (relatively) short time and low costs. For opposite reasons, acquisitions and also joint ventures are not very flexible (Millson et al., 1996).

According to these factors, the four basic modes described above can be evaluated in terms of their organisational and managerial implications.

7.3.1 Acquisition

Acquisitions have a great *impact on the firm's resources*, since they usually require allocation of a large amount of financial resources (the amount may be small in absolute terms but is large relatively to the other possible forms of collaboration). This also means a high level of *risk*, given that all activities and results are fully owned and controlled by the company. Risk is also high because of the large amount of resources allocated. The *time horizon* of acquisitions is intrinsically long term oriented. Actually, it is not usually defined a time horizon, i.e. a 'deadline' after which the relationship is broken and the acquired firm dismissed.

The *level of control over activities* and *over results* is obviously very high, since both - activity's resources and results - become property of the acquiring company. Furthermore, contractual formalisation guarantees and reinforces such control.

Start up time and costs are usually high, given the typology and amount of resources provided by the company. This, indeed, usually stimulates companies to bring out a deep and technically complex analysis. For example, the use of DCF (discounted cash flow) techniques is necessary to establish the value of the acquired firm and, then, the acquisition price. This analysis requires time and adequate resources. Furthermore, the final decision is usually taken by the top management and, hence, the decision process may be quite long and complex. The need to contractually formalise the acquisition further increases such time and costs.

Given the typology and amount of resources provided by the company, and given that the full property is acquired on activities resources and results, acquisitions are characterised by a low *degree of reversibility*.

With respect to *autonomous acquisitions*, in *integrated acquisitions* the impact on the firm is higher, since technology and know how are not only internalised in terms of ownership, but they also have to be directly managed. This also increases the level of control over activities and results and reduces the level of reversibility, since the acquired unit looses its autonomy and becomes steadily part of the whole company's structure. Start up time and costs are higher for integrated acquisitions, given the need to define how to integrate the acquired company within the current structure and how to manage activities.

7.3.2 Joint Venture

Joint ventures have a significant *impact on the firm's resources*; however, it is lower than   acquisitions. As a matter of fact, it requires that the firm allocates technologies, know how, people and financial resources (as in the case of acquisition), but, *ceteris paribus*, the relative amount is usually lower. The risk associated to this form is rather high, given that the company has the property of part of the resources; however, this form brings to share the risk with partners.

As far as the *time horizon* is concerned, considerations are similar to the case of acquisitions, given the typology and amount of resources allocated and integrated by the company. Hence, the time horizon is usually long and joint ventures are generally created for medium-long term activities to be done.

Given that property is shared, *control over activities* and *results* is also shared by the partners.

Start up time and costs are high, as in the case of acquisitions, given the typology and amount of resources allocated and given the level of formalisation required. Joint ventures need a decision making process as complex as for acquisitions. DCF techniques are used again in most cases, in order to determine and evaluate the financial contribution of the partners. The participation of the top management in decision making is needed too. Joint ventures are characterised by a low *degree of reversibility*, as the change of the relative role and contribution of the partners, or even abandonment of the venture, needs time and resources.

With respect to *single side managed joint ventures*, in *collectively managed joint ventures* the start up time and costs are higher, because of the need to collectively define the criteria for managing the collaboration. In single side managed joint ventures, the firm which is assigned the responsibility to manage the collaboration's activities bears greater impact. On the other hand, the company has greater control over activities, since it autonomously decides the way in which resources have to be used and, hence, directly determines and maintains the desired 'direction' of the collaboration activities over time.

7.3.3 Outsourcing

Outsourcing implies for a very low *impact on the firm's resources*: only financial resources are allocated by the company and no external resources (technology, know how or people), used for the collaboration, are integrated within the company. The company acquires property only of the results and there is no direct involvement in the collaboration's activities. As a consequence, outsourcing implies for a very low level of risk, given that activities remain external to the company (in terms of property of the related resources) and only the final results are integrated.

Outsourcing typically has a brief *time horizon*, according to the fact that only financial resources are allocated, that no new resources are integrated, but only results. Funding or research contracts usually concern a well defined (short) period of time, after which a new contract has to be established for the relationship to go on.

The *level of control over activities* is low, since the property of the used resources belongs to the partner. *Control over results* is high, since the company acquires property of them and rights of exploitation.

Start up time and costs are usually limited, as the typology and amount of resources allocated suggest. Furthermore, only two partners are involved and this further limits transaction costs. Even when a deep and formalised analysis is conducted for outsourcing and a contract is drawn up between the partners, the limited resources involved and the low involvement of the company into the activities make the analysis much easier and faster than in the case of acquisitions and joint ventures.

The *level of reversibility* is very high, because of the typology and amount of resources provided and the lack of direct involvement into the activities.

With respect to *autonomous outsourcing*, in *negotiated outsourcing* the level of control over activities is higher, since the company is involved in defining how such activities have to be performed by the partner. In some cases, a formalised contract can reinforce such control. At the same time, start up time and costs may rise, due to the higher transaction costs to define in details the way in which activities should be carried out and the characteristics of the output. This is often the case of pharmaceutical companies and CROs (Contract Research Organisations), which are usually assigned certain specific types of clinical tests on new compounds.

7.3.4 Alliance

The *impact on the firm's resources* is significant, since technology and people are provided by the company and are directly involved into the collaboration's activities. However, the limited amount of resources allocated usually limits such impact. The level of risk is rather low, given that, even if the company is directly involved into the activities, other partners are involved as well and, hence, the related risk is shared among them. Furthermore, the company maintains property of its own resources but does not integrate other resources.

The *time horizon* is usually shorter than more integrated forms of collaborations (acquisitions, joint ventures), as no resources (used for the collaboration's activities) are integrated by the company.

The *level of control over activities* is medium level, since, on the one hand, the company actually maintains property of its own resources (know how, technologies, people), but, on the other, the management of the collaboration activities is shared with other partners. The contractual formalisation of the 'management rules' of the collaboration could reinforce control for the company.

The *level of control over results* is medium, since the company acquires property of results, which are shared with the other partners. Contractual formalisation of the exploitation rights could assure higher level of control.

Start up time and costs may be not very low, given the number of partners involved and the typology of resources allocated. The need for contractual formalisation can further increase time and costs. However, it is not too high, since sophisticated analysis and evaluation of resources are usually not used.

The *level of reversibility* is medium, because the typology of resources allocated and the direct involvement into activities means low reversibility, whilst the low amount of resources allocated and the lack of resources integrated increase reversibility.

With respect to *individually managed alliances*, in *collectively managed alliances* the start up time and costs and the time horizon usually increase, given the need to collectively define the way in which the resources provided by the different partners are exploited. A team usually has to be created, in which people from the different partner companies are involved, which is responsible for the implementation of the collaboration activities. In terms of level of control over activities, both individually and collectively managed alliances are characterised by medium level of control. As a matter of fact, in collectively managed alliances, the company directly participates to the definition of the management criteria, but decisions have to be taken in agreement with the other partners. In individually managed alliances, the company

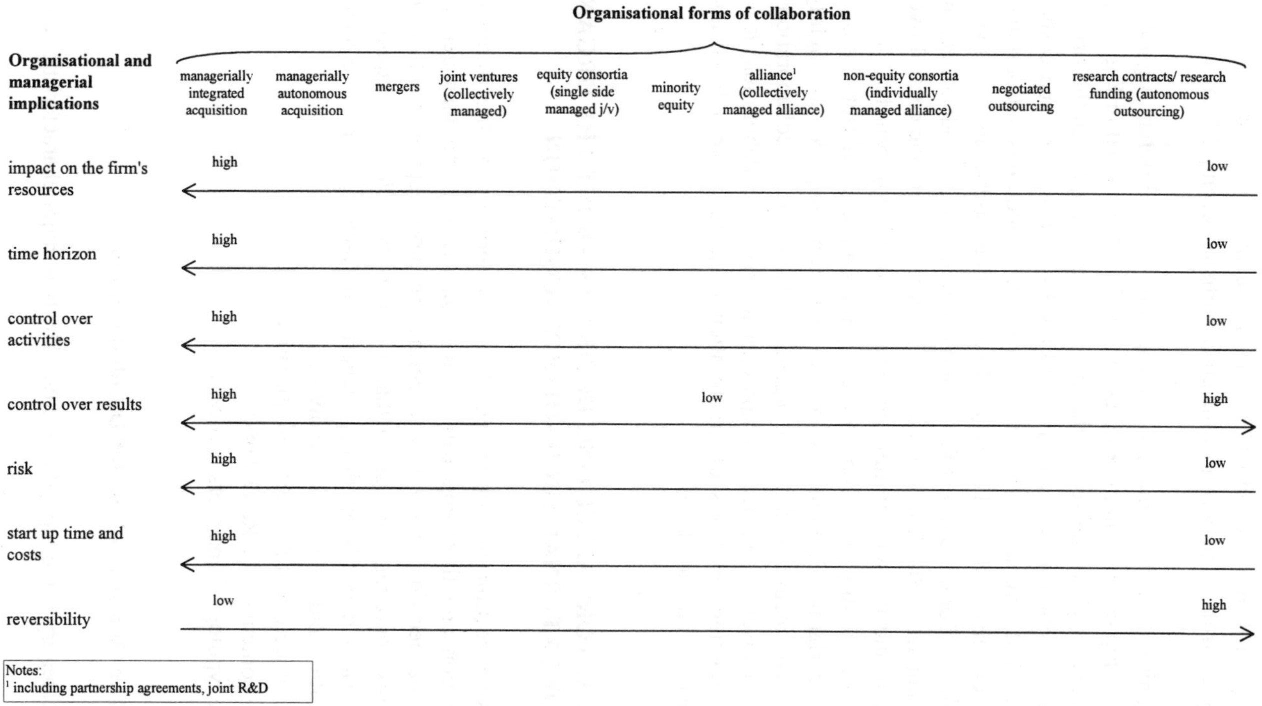

R&D Strategy and Organisation

Organisational forms of collaboration

Organisational and managerial implications	managerially integrated acquisition	managerially autonomous acquisition	mergers	joint ventures (collectively managed)	equity consortia (single side managed j/v)	minority equity	alliance¹ (collectively managed alliance)	non-equity consortia (individually managed alliance)	negotiated outsourcing	research contracts/ research funding (autonomous outsourcing)
impact on the firm's resources	high									low
time horizon	high									low
control over activities	high									low
control over results	high						low			high
risk	high									low
start up time and costs	high									low
reversibility	low									high

Notes:
¹ including partnership agreements, joint R&D

Figure 7.7. Organisational and managerial implications of the different form of relationship.

has full control over the activities done to accomplish its own task, but does not have any control on the way how the other partners accomplish their own tasks.

The organisational and managerial implications of the different organisational form of relationship can be summarised as in Fig. 7.7. As showed in Fig. 7.7, integrated acquisitions are characterised by the highest level of impact on the firm's resources, time horizon, control over activities and results, start up time and costs and by the lowest level of reversibility. On the other hand, autonomous outsourcing has totally opposite organisational and managerial implications. Between these two extremes, a 'continuum' of organisational forms of collaboration can be identified, in which the level of impact on the firm's resources, the time horizon, the control over activities and results and the start up time and costs gradually go from high to low and the level of reversibility goes from low to high. As a matter of fact, the organisational and managerial implications of two contiguous sub-categories are slightly different. Hence, a continuum of different organisational forms of collaboration should be accepted. However, to select the appropriate form of collaboration, it is critical to make distinctions in terms of organisational and managerial implications of the technology acquisition form.

7.4   FACTORS AFFECTING DECISIONS ABOUT THE ORGANISATION OF EXTERNAL TECHNOLOGY ACQUISITION

The above section has described the characteristics of the various forms of collaboration and their implications in organisational and managerial terms. Of course, the decision maker has to define the most appropriate form of external technology sourcing, once given that a certain technology is acquired externally. This decision depends on three categories of factors, which are specific to the collaboration and the partners involved:
-    the objective of the R&D collaboration;
-    the content of the R&D work;
-    the typology of partners involved.

7.4.1   The Objective of the R&D Collaboration

A first category is the type of objective. The two major characteristics are:

- *broadness vs. narrowness of the objective*. When the collaboration is not focused on a specific target, such as a product, or limited to a given and defined project, and the objectives are broad and/or multiple, complex and integrated forms of relationship are preferred, such as joint ventures or acquisitions. In contrast, when a precise and limited objective is defined, alliances and outsourcing are preferred. A broad set of objectives often means a long-term relationship, relevant resources from each partner, involvement of various functions and of several technological competencies. Furthermore, high level of control is required;

- *degree of learning orientation of the firm*. Formal and integrated relationships do not facilitate information flows and know-how diffusion among the partners. This seems to be related to the employees' negative perception of acquisitions and mergers (see section 1). Hence, when the objective is to maximise learning from partners[a], more flexible and less controlled forms of collaboration (such as alliances), which have a low impact on the firm's organisation and human resources, are preferred. An R&D manager at the Philips Italian subsidiary identifies non-equity consortia as the most appropriate form of relationship to share research efforts and to maximise learning and know-how exchange among a great number of partners.

7.4.2 The Content of the R&D Work

The choice of the organisational form also depend on the characteristics of the content of the work to be done during the collaboration. In particular:

- the *definition of the content*. In some cases, the content of the collaboration cannot be clearly defined. This is typical, for example, of research collaborations, where opportunities are sought for new technologies, products or processes, but research results cannot be clearly envisaged *a priori*. In this case, collaborations are characterised by great uncertainty and complexity and, hence, a formalised rigid agreement is not appropriate. On the contrary, a flexible, non formalised relationship is preferred, fundamentally based on trust. Research funding or research contracts are typical forms. Often in this

---

a   In his paper on inter-partner learning during collaboration agreements, Hamel (1991) widely discusses about the different approaches firms may have to partnerships. Some firms are purely oriented to achieve the output of the collaboration (for example, a new product), whereas others regard internalisation of skills and learning from partners as a primary benefit of collaborations.

case, firms do not put up a real collaboration but limit themselves to networking activities, i.e. establishing a network of contacts through, for example, participation at conferences and meetings with competitors and research institutions. Most R&D managers see this as the best way to exchange knowledge on research opportunities and to stimulate ideas for new research areas to explore. Networking is thus a very common form of relationship when a distinct content for collaboration does not exist yet. When the intent is that of monitoring the technological pace in a certain discipline through contacts with customers, suppliers, competitors, research institutions, networking is the preferred form;

-    the firm's *familiarity* with the content of the collaboration. The more familiar firm with technology and market related to the collaboration project (i.e. it possesses the required knowledge and competencies), the more integrated form of collaboration (for example, acquisitions) tends to be chosen. Joint ventures are preferred to acquisitions when the companies involved have limited knowledge of each other's business. When a firm lacks technical *or* market competencies, alliances and joint ventures are preferred, since these allow access to the partners' complementary resources like scientific, technical and managerial capabilities and knowledge. Finally, when a firm completely lacks both technical *and* market competencies (and its relative size and power is adequate), educational acquisitions can be used. Canon, for example, in order to acquire competencies on electron beam technology, identified a small company, Lepton, which possessed the competencies of interest. However, Canon completely lacked both market and technical knowledge on electron beam technology. Hence, it first recruited experts with the appropriate competencies (educational acquisition) and, then, acquired the company;

-    the *relevance for the firm's competitive advantage*. When collaborations concern a firm's 'core' technological competence, it is critical to keep control over such distinctive knowledge. Furthermore, given that competence building is the result of a series of actions within a coherent trajectory, the time horizon of such collaborations is usually rather long. Hence, when core competencies are developed and/or enhanced through collaborations, i.e. when there is a high potential for the firm to create and/or maintain competitive advantage, high integration is needed in the mode of co-operation. When, on the other hand, collaborations concern non-core technologies and competencies, there is no need for strong control. Therefore, firms tend to maximise flexibility, for example through alliances. Finally, when a company completely lacks competence in a non-core technology or discipline, the most viable and useful solution is usually to completely outsource. At Ericsson the "technology sourcing strategy" has been clearly defined: the "core system" of the company has been identified, and only internal R&D is used to carry out the related R&D projects, whereas support systems, applications, standard components, which have been recognised as non-core, are completely externally outsourced;

- the *technology life cycle*. Mature technologies are usually diffused among competitors and do not provide the basis for competitive advantage. Collaborations concerning mature technologies do not need strong control and are usually concerned with minimising costs and time. Furthermore, several qualified suppliers can be found for mature technologies. Hence, outsourcing is a viable option. Usually, when mature technologies are regarded, collaborations are mostly concerned with commercialisation and marketing issues. As explained below (see 'the phase of the innovation process'), this factor also forces firms to choose weakly integrated forms of collaboration such as outsourcing. Most Italian textile companies, such as Ratti, outsource the development and manufacturing of their machinery since several suppliers are available on the market and technological knowledge is widely diffused. In contrast, Ratti is directly involved in an equity consortium with an equity participation, in the research project Eurochrysalide, for the development of a totally innovative system to grow silk-worms "in vitro";

- the *level of risk*. Sharing risk with other partners is one of the most important motivations for technological collaboration. Obviously, the higher level of risk related to the project, the more relevant this factor. Hence, in risky projects, an organisational mode of collaboration has to be chosen which helps sharing risk with partners. As such, joint ventures are preferred to acquisitions and alliances with many partners are preferred to both. In acquisitions one firm faces the whole risk, whereas in joint ventures and alliances the risk is shared with partners. For example, a Virtual Centre of Excellence in Mobile and Personal Communications has been created in November 1996, involving seven U.K. universities and twenty-four companies operating in the electronic and telecommunication industry (among others, Nokia, Philips, Sony, NEC, AT&T and Motorola). This is aimed at developing new knowledge and leading edge technological solutions in mobile and personal communication. A major motivation stimulating companies and universities to join this centre was the need to share the high risk associated with R&D in this field;

- the *appropriability of the innovation*. In technological collaborations a relevant factor in the choice of the organisational form is the appropriability of innovation. In tight appropriability regimes, that is when a firm is 'really' protected by patent or copyright, a firm can collaborate with partners, for example to access complementary assets, or to commercialise the innovation, and does not need strong control. In these cases, weakly integrated modes of co-operation, such as alliances, can be used without undermining the innovator's rents. In weak appropriability regimes, there is the need to strongly control the collaboration, to avoid the flow of critical knowledge to the partners, and to internalise the results to exploit the innovator's rents. Hence, highly integrated modes of co-operation are more appropriate, such as mergers and acquisitions. The Italian R&D centre of Glaxo-Wellcome, for example, continuously monitors the activities of small innovative biotechnology companies. When it finds a small firm researching in an area of interest, its acquisition is considered in order to achieve full property and control;

- the *phase of the innovation process*. In early phases of the innovation process, that is in research and early development, collaborations should favour knowledge exchange. Therefore, flexible forms are preferred, such as alliances and outsourcing. This is also related to the partner typology which usually varies from phase to phase of the innovation process. As stated by an ST manager, research collaborations are usually conducted with competitors, whereas, in development and manufacturing collaboration, suppliers and customers are the usual partners. As explained later, this makes alliances preferable to more integrated forms of relationship in research collaborations. Consortia are rather common in early phases of the innovation process (as in the already mentioned cases of VCE in Mobile and Personal Communication and Eurochrysalide in textiles);

- the *level of assets specialisation*. When the assets sought are highly specialised, and cannot be easily acquired on the market, a highly integrated mode of co-operation is needed, in order to acquire control over such assets and to ensure that they can be exploited by the firm;

- the *divisibility of assets*. When the assets sought are embedded in another company's assets, from which they cannot be divided, but which the firm does not really need, high integration is not desirable. With an acquisition, the non-desired assets are also internalised and therefore need to be managed. Joint ventures are preferred to acquisitions, since they allow access only to the needed assets.

7.4.3   The Typology of Partners Involved

A third category of factors affecting the choice of the collaboration form concerns the typology of partners involved.

-   *vertical vs. horizontal collaborations*. Vertical collaborations, in which the partners are suppliers or customers, are usually aimed to reduce time and costs of a specific project of innovation. Hence, they are usually medium-short term oriented and need a high degree of reversibility (the supplier/customer chosen for the collaboration has to be easily changed, if the co-operation does not seem to be efficient and effective) and can be well formalised in contractual forms of collaboration. The sample firms recognised that most collaborations (about 70%) involve buyers and suppliers and, among them, about 80% are formalised in contracts, with definite time horizons, objectives and game rules. Horizontal collaborations often involve competitors, and are more frequently concerned with early phases of the innovation process (basic and applied research). As a consequence (as argued above), control over information flow, high reversibility and medium-long term orientation are needed. In horizontal collaborations, indeed, long term alliances and consortia are often appropriate solutions;
-   *cultural differences*. When partners are from different countries, cultural, institutional and social barriers and high transaction costs can make collaboration difficult. A weakly integrated mode of collaboration with smaller impact on a firm's organisation and human resources, is preferred. Alliances and outsourcing seem to be more appropriate. Similarly, if partners operate in different industries or do very different activities, cultural differences can make the collaboration difficult. An example is that of collaborations involving companies with universities or research centres. Mostly, such collaborations simply consist of research funding. Some Italian firms, for example Agip, Edison, Pirelli collaborate with Politecnico di Milano, funding doctoral studentships or specific research projects;
-   *the relative bargaining power between partners*. A more powerful partner will tend to choose 'hierarchical' and/or formal modes of collaboration (such as acquisitions or alliances with contractual agreements), in order to impose their desired conditions on the less powerful partner(s). The same is true when partners differ in terms of size. Large companies can impose rigid, controlled and formalised collaborations. Obviously, size and power are frequently inter-related to each other.

The above discussion has analysed how each factor affects the choice of the form of technological collaboration. However, in decision making, all the analysed factors have to be jointly considered: the chosen organisational form needs to be coherent with the objective, content and partners of the collaboration. The various factors may lead to different requirements. For example, collaborations concerned with basic research require high reversibility and low control but if, at the same time, they are related to the production of critical knowledge then the need to protect that knowledge will necessitate strong control and low reversibility. A synoptic view of the requirements associated with the characteristic of each factor is given in Table 7.2. In most cases, it is necessary to balance opposite forces, leading to different organisational solutions (Hendry, 1995). Taking decisions about the organisational form of technological co-operation is thus a complex process and needs a rational analysis in order to understand and balance factors of unequal influence. The process of selection is analysed in the next section.

Table 7.2. Factors affecting the choice of the form of relationship.

FACTOR		PRIORITY REQUIREMENTS
Objective:		
	broad	- long term orientation
		- medium-high control
		- medium-high formalisation
	limited	- short term orientation
		- medium-low control
		- minimise impact on the firm
	learning oriented	- high reversibility
		- low control
		- low formalisation
		- minimise impact on organisation and human resources
Content:		
identificability	good	- no particular requirements
	bad	- low formalisation
		- high reversibility
familiarity	none	- see: learning oriented objective
	with market or technology	- see: learning oriented objective
	with market and technology	- high control
		- high formalisation
relevance for competitive advantage	high	- high control
		- long term orientation
	low	- high reversibility
		- minimise time/cost for establishing relationship
		- minimise impact on the firm

(follows)

technology life cycle	maturity phase	- high reversibility
		- low control
		- minimise time/cost for establishing relationship
	embryonic phase	- long term orientation
		- high control
		- medium-high reversibility
level of risk	high	- high reversibility
		- minimise impact on the firm
		- low formalisation
		- organisation which lowers risk
	low	- no particular requirements
appropriability of innovation	weak	- high control
		- high formalisation
	tight	- no particular requirements
phases of the innovation process	early	- high reversibility
		- low control
		- see: learning oriented objective
	late	- high formalisation
		- minimise time/cost for establishing relationship
assets specialisation	high	- high control
	low	- no particular requirements
assets divisibility	low	- low integration
		- minimise the impact on the firm
	high	- no particular requirements
Partners typology:		
link with the firm	vertical	- medium-short term orientation
		- minimise time/cost for establishing relationship
		- high reversibility
		- medium-high formalisation
	horizontal	- low formalisation
		- high reversibility
		- medium-long term orientation
original country	different	- high reversibility
		- low control
		- minimise impact on the firm
	same	- no particular requirements
sector of activity	different	- high reversibility
		- low control
		- minimise impact on the firm
	same	- no particular requirements
size/power	different	- high control and formalisation
	same	- no particular requirements

7.5   THE PROCESS OF SELECTION OF THE ORGANISATION FOR EXTERNAL TECHNOLOGY ACQUISITION

The above framework can help firms to select the appropriate form of external technology acquisition. In other words, once decided that a certain technology is to be acquired externally, the company should identify an 'optimal' solution, i.e. the specific organisational form it wishes to adopt. The selection process of the optimal form of external technology acquisition is composed of two major steps:

-        the identification of the optimal solution by the firm on an individual basis,
-        the negotiation with partners and the identification of the optimal solution on a collective basis.

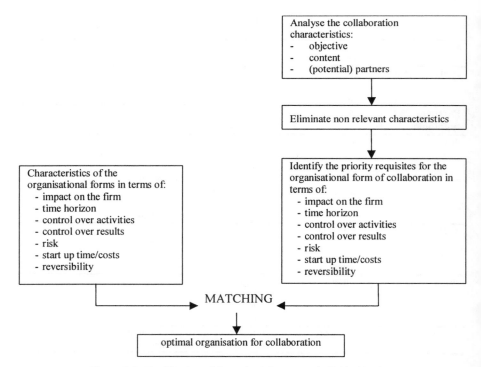

Figure 7.8. Identification of the optimal form on an individual basis.

The identification of the optimal solution on an individual basis involves the following steps (Fig. 7.8):

(i)　to analyse the characteristics of the collaboration, in terms of objective, content, and (potential) partners to be involved in the collaboration;

(ii)　to eliminate the non relevant characteristics, i.e. those which do not provide any requisite for the choice of the organisational form, and, therefore, do not affect the choice. This allows to simplify the problem, reducing the number of characteristics to be considered and focusing the analysis on the relevant ones, i.e. those which bring to specific requisites;

(iii)　to identify the priority requisites for the organisational form. The selected characteristics provide requirements on the organisational form of collaboration. In this phase, a 'map' of the characteristics and of the relative requisites / constraints can be used, such as that reported in Table 7.2. It is important to notice that different characteristics might determine contrasting requisites and/or constraints. Defining the final choice thus requires to solve conflicts among opposite requisites. This phase should lead to define the key or priority requisites. Hence, the decision maker has to identify the priority requirements, which are considered important for the company. This means to assign a weight to each characteristic and, hence, to each requisite;

(iv)　to match the priority requisites with the organisational and managerial characteristics of the different forms of collaboration. Such matching is done comparing the dimensions above identified, i.e. impact on the firm, time horizon, control over activities, control over results, start up time and costs, risk, reversibility. The most appropriate organisational form of collaboration is then identified through matching the priority requisites with the characteristics of the different organisational forms that could be adopted.

Once identified the optimal solution on an individual basis, the organisational form has to be negotiated with partners and therefore, the process of the identification of the optimal solution on a collective basis starts. This involves the following steps (Fig. 7.9):

-　to negotiate the form of collaboration to be adopted with the potential partners. Within the process of technological collaboration, the decision about the form of the relationship is the first collective act (together with the definition of common objectives). Each partner has its own objective and has identified the other(s) as potential partners (Chiesa and Manzini, 1998). The negotiation process is necessary as partners may have different requirements as far as the form of collaboration is concerned;

-    compare the requirements defined on an individual basis with the characteristics of the negotiated organisational forms of co-operation. This phase may have significant feed-back effects. In some cases, the need to agree on a definite organisational solution can lead partners to modify their respective objectives. In other cases, the impossibility to agree on a certain solution may lead to change partner(s) or abandon the collaboration;

-    choose the most appropriate organisational mode for co-operation amongst those identified, if it satisfactorily matches the collaboration requirements identified on an individual basis.

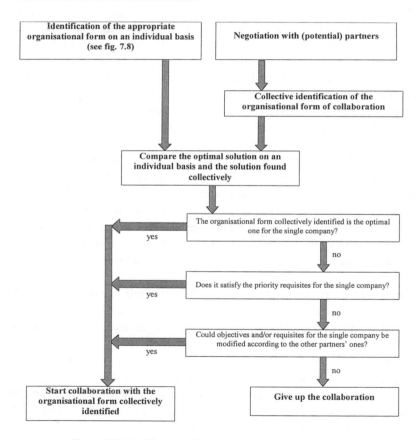

Figure 7.9. Identification of the optimal form on a collective basis.

APPENDIX 1 – CASE STUDIES

Case 1 - The ST - Bosch partnership

Objective of the collaboration	To exploit the BCD technology (developed by ST) for the joint development of new products dedicated to the automotive industry. The objective: - is rather limited; - requires significant knowledge transfer and information flows.
Content of the collaboration	Developing and commercialising a set of new products based upon the BCD technology. The content: - is well defined (a single technology is exploited); - requires competencies on which the partners have complementary knowledge (ST is familiar with the BCD technology, Bosch with the automotive market); - competencies needed are not critical for the competitive advantage of the two partners; - is related to a technology in the growing phase; - is characterised by a medium-low level of risk; - is related to the late phases of the innovation process (development and commercialisation); - the appropriability regime is weak.
Partners	ST (Italy) and Bosch (Germany): - operate in different sectors; - come from different countries, but both are multinationals; - are linked by vertical relationship (ST is a Bosch supplier); - have a different power: Bosch is undoubtedly more powerful.

According to Table 3, the major requirements for the collaboration are:
- medium reversibility;
- medium degree of control;
- high degree of formalisation;
- short term orientation.

Matching the above requirements with the characteristics of the different organisational solutions, it seems that an appropriate mode of collaboration could be an alliance (a cooperation agreement or a joint development project) between the two partners, with a formal definition of procedures for managing and monitoring the relationship, with no equity participation.

The organisational mode actually used by the partners was a joint R&D project with a formal contractual agreement.

Case 2 - The ST - Northern Telecom partnership

Objective of the collaboration	To improve the efficiency of a NT plant for semiconductors production; to exploit that plant and the partners technological competencies for developing, producing and commercialising existing and new products; to improve the partners' core knowledge (ST in silicon and NT in systems). The objective: - is quite broad, since it concerns different activities (applied research, development, production, commercialisation) and multiple new products; - requires some knowledge transfer and information flows.
Content of the collaboration	The content: - is rather broad (a single plant is considered, but several activities, technologies and resources are included in the collaboration); - requires competencies on which the partners have complementary knowledge (ST familiarity with silicon technology and NT familiarity with system technology). However, both partner have some familiarity with the other partners' business; - competencies needed are critical for the competitive advantage of the two partners; - is related to technologies in the early growing phase; - is characterised by a medium-high level of risk; - is related to a broad set of phases of the innovation process (applied research, development, production and commercialisation); - the appropriability regime is weak; - assets involved in the collaboration (the plant, with its technologies) can easily by divided from other NT assets.
Partners	ST (Italy) and Northern Telecom (USA). The partners, indeed: - operate in different sectors; - come from different countries, but both are multinationals; - are linked by vertical relationship (ST is a NT supplier); - have similar power.

According to Table 3, the major requirements for the collaboration are:
-    medium reversibility;
-    high degree of control;
-    medium-high degree of formalisation;
-    long term orientation.

Trying to match these requirements with the characteristics of different organisational solutions, it seems that an appropriate mode of collaboration could be a medium-highly integrated form of relationship, so as to increase control, to maximise the partner commitment and to attain, in the long term, multiple objectives. For example, a joint venture, in which NT provide the plant and ST the competence in semiconductors and the relative managerial capabilities, could be an adequate solution.

In the real case, joint venture has been considered as a compromise, since it fitted with the need of control and formalisation, but it did not fit with the need to fuse complementary knowledge. Hence, the partnership has been splitted into two. First, ST acquired the NT plant. As a consequence, NT transferred ST the production of certain products, which required the NT plant technologies and the ST competencies. Then, an informal agreement was signed, according to which applied research on (potential) new products was conducted independently by the two partners and, then, the results were discussed by NT and ST R&D managers and transferred to the NT managers and employees.

APPENDIX 2 - THE EMPIRICAL BASIS

The empirical study involved 21 firms from different industries (pharmaceuticals, electronics, telecommunications, public utilities, electro-mechanical, textile, domestic electric appliances and automotive) and countries (see Table 7.3).

Table 7.3. The research sample.

Firm	Sector of activity	Country	Number of employees	Sales (million $)	Role of people interviewed[b]
Agip	Extraction, processing and marketing of minerals	Italy	8317	7598	Chief Executive Production Services
Alcatel	Telecommunications	France	190600	31684	Chief Technical Officer
Bosch	Motor and Vehicle parts	Germany	186481	27340	R&D Specialist
Canon	Computer, office equipment	Japan	75628	23516	Chief Designer
Edison	Power generation	Italy	1324	980	Responsible for Strategic Planning
Electrolux - Zanussi	Radio, TV and domestic appliance	Sweden	20176	3463	Chief Executive Production
Enel	Power generation and electricity utility	Italy	93879	23833	Responsible for Strategic Planning
ENI	Energy	Italy	83424	38843	R&D Director
Ericsson	Electronics	Sweden	93949	15300	Telecommunication Department R&D manager
Glaxo - Wellcome	Pharmaceuticals	UK	53460	13025	R&D Director
Magneti Marelli	Mechanical and electric engineering	Italy	25044	3612	R&D Specialist
Nissan	Motor vehicles and parts	Japan	135331	59118	Responsible for Nissan R&D operations in US;

(follows)

---

b   In this table it is reported the role of people interviewed during the first phase of the empirical study.

Nokia	Telecommunications	Finland	31723	8454	Vice President Advanced Development and R&D; Assistant to the Responsible for R&D and marketing;
Pharmacia - Upjohn	Pharmaceuticals	Sweden - US	30.000	5080	R&D manager
Philips	Electronics	Netherlands	262500	41037	Italian subs R&D Director
Pirelli	Rubber and Cables	Italy	36534	5689	Managing Director Pirelli Cables;
Ratti	Textile	Italy	1273	181	Vice President Production; Responsible for Ratti Technology
SGS - Thomson	Electronics	Italy-France	7455	1519	R&D Director; Strategic Marketing Director for DPG;
Smithkline Beecham	Pharmaceuticals	UK	52900	12376	R&D manager; Italian subsidiary R&D Director; Human Resource Director
Telecom Finland	Telecommunications	Finland	32721	2092	Vice President R&D; R&D manager responsible for development
Zambon	Pharmaceuticals	Italy	2597	349	R&D Planning and Control Manager

The field study started with interviews with R&D managers on the organisation and management of technological collaborations in general and the firm's approach to external sourcing of technology. The managers interviewed are all responsible for the firm's technology strategy (at least in a certain technological discipline) and therefore also for the decisions about external technology sourcing. During their career, all of them have been directly involved in the management of technological collaborations. This ensured that information collected comes from people with a deep knowledge of the problem and a significant experience of the related strategic, managerial and organisational implications. In this phase of the study, a non-structured interview guide was used, which is reported in Table 7.4.

Table 7.4. The interview guide.

• Motivations that stimulate the company to search for external sources of technology.
• The degree of importance of external technology sourcing with respect to internal development.
• Kind of activities (research, development, manufacturing etc.) where technological collaborations are mostly used.
• The most common typologies of partners and how they are selected.
• Organisational forms used in practice.
• Organisational implications of different organisational forms for technological collaborations.
• Managerial implications of different organisational forms for technological collaborations.
• The factors to be considered when the organisational form of relationship have to be chosen and at which level the final decision is taken.
• The main success / unsuccess factors in technological collaborations.

This phase allowed to acquire initial knowledge on the problem of external technology sourcing and on how companies actually deal with it. The view of people directly responsible for decision making, and, in most cases, operating in high technology intensive industries and in tenths of collaborations, provided significant insights on both the characteristics and management of different forms of technological collaboration. During these interviews specific cases were identified as significant to the end of this work. These cases, briefly described in Table 7.5, became the subject of a deeper analysis (the second step of the empirical study). The sample of cases was defined in order to cover the whole range of collaboration forms.

In this second phase of the empirical study, people directly involved in the collaborations have been contacted. For each partnership, at least two managers for each partner have been interviewed: usually, one was responsible for the economic and financial issues of the partnering, whereas the other was more involved in scientific and technological aspects.

The in-depth investigation has concerned the following topics:

- the specific motivations/objectives of the collaboration analysed;

- the process of selection of the partner(s);
- the process through which the organisational form and the 'game rules' among partners have been defined;
- the resources (human, technical, financial, ...) allocated by each partner to the collaboration;
- the organisation and management in the implementation phase of the collaboration;
- the criteria for exploiting the achieved results;
- the results actually achieved;
- the success/unsuccess factors.

Table 7.5. The cases studied.

Partners involved	Organisational form	Brief description
Electrolux - Zanussi	acquisition	acquisition of Zanussi competence in compressor technologies for refrigerators
Finmeccanica - Microcontrol	acquisition	Finmeccanica acquired Microcontrol to internalise a highly innovative company developing systems for the electronic control of nechanical machinery
ST - Northern Telecom	acquisition + alliance with contractual formalisation	exploitation of a NT plant and of the partners technological competencies for developing, producing and commercialising existing and new products (semiconductors)
Philips - Du Pont	joint-venture	development of machinery for CD mastering and printing
Ratti + other textile European and Japanese companies + research centres (Project Eurochrysalide)	equity consortium	research and development of an innovative system for growing silk-worms "in vitro"
Pirelli - Dunlop	alliance	improving timing and efficiency of new product introduction in the tire sector
Nissan - Ford	alliance	joint development, production and commercialisation of minivan for the US market
Philips, Toshiba, JVC, Sony, Hitachi	alliance	joint definition of a technological standard for the Digital Video Disk (DVD)

(follows)

Alcatel - Mitsubishi	alliance with contract formalisation	joint development of electro-optical interfaces for transmission on optical fibres
Pirelli Cables and Politecnico di Milano	consortium	research on optical fibre for telecommunications
ST - HP	joint development project with a contractual formalisation	development and manufacturing of a set of new components for PCs and peripherals
Agip - Politecnico di Milano	research contract	development of new materials resistant to corrosion

REFERENCES AND FURTHER READINGS

Bidault, F. and Cummings, T., Innovating through Alliances: Expectations and Limitations, *R&D Management*, vol. 24, n. 1, 33-45.

Brockhoff, K., Research and Development cooperation between firms. A Classification by Structural Variables, *International Journal of Technology Management*, 6, 3-4, May-August (1991), 361-373.

Bruce, M., Leverick, F., Littler, D. and Wilson, D., Success Factors for Collaborative Product Development: A Study of Suppliers of Information and Communication Technology, *R&D Management*, 25, 1 (1995), 33-44.

Chatterje, D., Accessing External Sources of Technology, *Research & Technology Management*, March-April (1996), 48-56.

Chatterji, D. and Manuel, T.A., Benefiting from External Sources of Technology, *Research & Technology Management*, November-December (1993), 21-26.

Chesbrough, H. and Teece, D.J., When Is Virtual Virtuous? Organizing for Innovation, *Harvard Business Review*, January-February (1996), 65-73.

Chesnais, F., Technological Agreements, Networks and Selected Issues in Economic Theory, in Cooms, R., Richards, A., Saviotti, P.P. and Walsh, V. (Eds.), *Technological Collaboration* (Edward Elgar Publishing Limited, Cheltenham, 1996).

Chiesa V. and Manzini R., Organizing for technological collaborations: a managerial perspective, *R&D Management*, vol. 28, n. 3 (1998), 199-212.

Coombs, R., Richards, A., Saviotti, P.P. and Walsh, V. (Eds.), *Technological Collaboration* (Edward Elgar Publishing Limited, Cheltenham, 1996).

Davidow, W.H. and Malone, M.S., *The Virtual Corporation* (HarperBusiness, New York, 1992).

Doz, Y. L., "The Evolution of Cooperation in Strategic Alliances: Initial Conditions or Learning Processes?", *Strategic Management Journal*, vol.17 (1996), 55-83.

Dyer, J.H., Specialized Supplier Networks as a Source of Competitive Advantage: Evidence from the Auto Industry, *Strategic Management Journal*, vol.17 (1996), 271-291.

Farr, C.M. and Fischer, W.A., "Managing International High Technology Cooperative Projects", *R&D Management*, vol. 22, n. 1 (1992), 55-67.

Forey, D., The Secrets of Industry are in the Air: Industrial Co-operation and the Organizational Dynamics of the Innovative Firm, *Research Policy*, 20 (1991), 393.

Forrest, J., Japanese / US Technological Competitiveness and Strategic Alliances in the Biotechnology Industry, *R&D Management*, 26, 2 (1996), 141-154.

Forrest, J.E. and Martin, J.C., Strategic Alliances Between Large and Small Research Intensive Organisations: Experiences in the Biotechnology Industry, *R&D Management*, 22, 1 (1992), 41-53.

Gersony, N., Sectoral Effects on Strategic Alliance Performance for New Technology Firms, *The Journal of High Technology Management Research*, 7, 2 (1996).

Goldman, S.L., Nagel, R.N. and Preiss, K., *Agile Competitors and Virtual Organisations* (Van Nostrand Reinhold, New York, 1995).

Hagedoorn, J., Understanding the Rational of Strategic Technology Partnering: Interorganisational Modes of Cooperation and Sectoral Differences, *Strategic Management Journal*, 14 (1993), 371-385.

Hagedoorn, J. and Schakenraad, J., Inter-firm Partnership and Co-operative Strategies in Core Technologies, in Freeman, C. and Soete, L. (Eds.), *New Explorations in the Economics of Technological Change* (Printer, London, 1990).

Hakansson, H., *Industrial Technological Development: A Network Approach* (Croom Helm, London, 1987).

Hakansson, H., Technological Collaborations in Industrial Networks, *European Management Journal*, 8, 3, September (1990), 371-379.

Hamel G., "Competition for Competence and Interpartner learning within international srategic alliances", *Strategic management Journal*, 12 (1991), 83-103.

Harris, R.C., Insinga, R.C., Morone, J. and Werle, M.J., The Virtual R&D Laboratory, *Research & Technology Management*, March-April (1996), 33-36.

Hauschildt, J., External Acquisitions of Knowledge for Innovation - A Research Agenda, *R&D Management*, 22, 2 (1992), 105-110.

Hendry, J., Culture, Community and Networks: The Hidden Cost of Outsourcing, *European Management Journal*, vol. 13, n. 2 (1995), 193-200.

Hennart, J.F. and Reddy, S., The Choice between Mergers/Acquisitions and Joint Ventures: The Case of Japanese Investors in the United States, *Strategic Management Journal*, 18 (1997), 1-12.

Jolly, D., Co-operation in a Niche Market: The Case of FIAT and PSA in Multi Purpose Vehicles, *European Management Journal*, 15, 1 (1997), 35-44.

Kotabe, M. and Swan, K.S., The Role of Strategic Alliances in High-Technology New Product Development, *Strategic Management Journal*, 16 (1995), 621-636.

Millson, M.R., Raj, S.P. and Wilemon, D., Strategic Partnering for Developing New Products, *Research & Technology Management*, May-June (1996), 41-49.

Mitchell, W. and Singh, K., Survival of Businesses Using Collaborative relationships to Commercialize Complex Goods, *Strategic Management Journal*, 17 (1996), 169-195.

Nakane, J. and Hall, R.W., Holonic Manufacturing: Flexibility - The Competitive Battle in the 1990's, *Production Planning & Control*, 1, 1 (1991).

Nixon, B., Research and Development Alliances and Accounting, *R&D Management*,. 26, 2 (1996), 169-175.

Pearce, R. and Papanastassiou, M., R&D Networks and Innovation: Decentralised Product Development in Multinational Enterprises, *R&D Management*, 26, 4 (1996), 315-334.

Quinn, B. and Hilmer, F.G., "Strategic Outsourcing", *Sloan Management Review*, Summer (1994), 43-55.

Richardson, G.B., The Organisation of Industry, *Economic Journal*, Vol. 82 (1972).

Roberts E. B. and Berry, C.A., Entering New Businesses: Selecting Strategies for Success, *Sloan Management Review*, Spring (1985).

Roberts E. B., Benchmarking the Strategic Management of Technology - I, *Research Technology Management*, January-February (1995).

Rothwell, R., Towards the Fifth-Generation Innovation Process, *International Marketing Review*, 11, 1 (1994).

Teece, D.J., Profiting from Technological Innovation: Implications for Integration, Collaboration, Licensing and Public Policy, *Research Policy*, n. 15 (1986), 285-305.

Turpin, T. and Garret, S., Bricoleurs and Boundary Riders: Managing Basic Research and Innovation Knowledge Networks, *R&D Management*, 26, 3 (1996), 267-282.

Tyler, B.B. and Steensma, H.K., Evaluating Technological Collaborative Opportunities: A Cognitive Modeling Perspective, *Strategic Management Journal*, 16 (1995), 43-70.

Upton, D.M. and McAfee, A., The Real Virtual Factory, *Harvard Business Review*, July-August (1996).

Veugelers, R., Internal R&D Expenditures and External Technology Sourcing, *working paper, Katholieke Universiteit Leuven*, September (1996).

Walsh, V., Design, Innovation and the Boundaries of the Firm, *Research Policy*, 25 (1996), 509-529.

Williamson, O.E., *Markets and Hierarchies: Analysis and Anti-trust Implications* (Free Press, New York, 1975).

Williamson, O.E., *The Economic Institutions of Capitalism* (Free Press, New York, 1985).

INDEX